ZEN AWAKENI

Zen Awakening and Society

CHRISTOPHER IVES

Forewords by Masao Abe
and John Hick

University of Hawaii Press
Honolulu

© Christopher Avery Ives 1992
Foreword © Masao Abe 1992
Foreword © John Hick 1992

Published in North America by
UNIVERSITY OF HAWAII PRESS
2840 Kolowalu Street
Honolulu, Hawaii 96822

Published in the United Kingdom by
THE MACMILLAN PRESS LTD
Houndmills, Basingstoke, Hampshire RG21 2XS

Second printing 1994

Printed in Hong Kong

Library of Congress Cataloging-in-Publication Data
Ives, Christopher, 1954–
Zen awakening and society / Christopher Ives.
p.   cm.
Revision of the author's dissertation (Claremont Graduate School).
Includes bibliographical references and index.
ISBN 0–8248–1452–5 (cloth). — ISBN 0–8248–1453–3 (pbk.)
1. Zen Buddhism—Social aspects.   2. Buddhist ethics.   3. Zen
Buddhism—Doctrines.   I. Title.
BQ9268.I93   1992
294.3'5—dc20   91–35863
                                                              CIP

To Abe-sensei

Contents

Foreword by
Masao Abe

The basic question of Christianity is What is God? or Who is God? By contrast, the basic question of Zen is What is the self? or What am I? Although Christianity does raise this question about the self, it always does so in relation to God. Lacking a notion of God, Zen raises this question in relation to the self, that is, it engages in a self-inquiry into the self. This is why the primary concern of Zen traditionally has been *koji-kyūmei*, 'investigation of self', which is to inquire into and awaken to one's own true self or 'original face'.

This does not indicate, however, that Zen is not concerned with others or is indifferent to human morality and ethics. Along with *koji-kyūmei*, Zen emphasises the Fourfold Great Vow of a Bodhisattva, in which the salvation of others – 'However innumerable sentient beings are, I vow to save them' – is given first priority as the necessary prerequisite for one's own awakening, which is expressed in terms of the extinguishing of passions, mastery of the Dharma-teachings, and the attainment of the Buddhist-Way.[1] Traditionally Zen emphasizes *jikaku-kakuta*, 'self-awakening and awakening others', and *jiririta-enman*, 'the fulfillment of self-benefit and benefitting others'.

It is also undeniable, however, that through its long history Zen did not sufficiently or systematically clarify how to save others in their individual and social life beyond the problem of awakening to each person's true self. Zen has provided a basic framework for the relationship between self and others but almost no definite form of human morality or social ethics except monastic regulations. This is due largely to its overwhelming emphasis on individual self-awakening. This relative lack of concern with individual and social ethics becomes an increasingly serious problem as Zen begins to confront issues in contemporary society and enter Western cultures. This book is an attempt to address this issue by an American Zen Buddhist scholar.

Christopher Ives, the author, is one of my old students. With me he studied Buddhism, particularly Zen and the Kyoto School of Philosophy, for a number of years in Japan and the United States.

In Kyoto he practiced Zen with the FAS Society[2] and came to be deeply impressed by the personality and thought of Hisamatsu Shin'ichi.[3] Through his studies and practice of Zen and his excellent command of Japanese, he has gained a penetrating understanding of Zen and Japanese philosophy. From his student days, the problem of ethics, especially social ethics, has been a persistent concern of his. It was hence quite natural for him to take up 'Zen and Social Ethics' as the theme of his Ph.D. dissertation at the Claremont Graduate School in the 1980s. As a member of his dissertation committee, I approved his dissertation with high distinction, and this book is a revised version of it.

In this book, Ives has engaged in an extensive study of the ethical dimensions of Zen practice and philosophy and the development of Zen in Japanese history. He discusses not only ethical themes and issues in the history of Japanese Zen, but also recent Buddhist movements in Sri Lanka and Vietnam and several twentieth century Japanese Zen thinkers – Hisamatsu Shin'ichi, Ichikawa Hakugen and myself. He also highlights aspects of Zen around which revolve serious doubts about the ethical nature of the tradition: the overwhelming emphasis on Awakening as the basis of a truly ethical way of life; the apparent tension between *śūnyatā* and ethics; the stress on immediacy, non-discrimination and suchness; and the accompanying espousal of 'transcending good and evil'.

Ives recognises that although Zen does have a religiously transformative effect, because of its ethical neutrality it has not led to one specific social ethic. This is a pitfall for Zen. He points out:

Without careful reflection – grounded in self-critical examination of Buddhist texts, principles, and values – Zen may continue to wander through a range of social orientations, some of which may run contrary to the principles and spirit of the tradition.

He adds:

Historically, monastic Zen has not studied, analysed, or responded self-critically to the full range of suffering in the social world. This lack of a critical spirit has contributed to problematical support of the status quo, whether the aristocracy, samurai dictators, militarists, or certain large corporations.

Most importantly, Ives offers constructive thought about possibilities for a Zen social ethic that may be applicable in the world to come. Based on his conviction that the non-dualistic view of selfhood provides Zen with resources for a novel approach to ethics, he argues, for instance, that justice might be understood not in terms of judgmental justice or in terms of a balance of power in society but in terms of participatory justice. And rights may be understood in a trans-anthropocentric dimension common to all beings in the natural world. In this context of a non-dualistic view of selfhood, he discusses from a novel angle such issues as responsibility, power, violence, work and economic systems. In this he never overlooks the aspect of negation in Zen; nor does he overlook the pitfalls into which Zen has fallen, the aspect of which Japanese Zen Buddhists are often not clearly aware. He offers a constructive view of Zen social ethics applicable to both the East and the West and to a future humanity. Thus the book is not only a significant contribution to the understanding of Zen and its social ethics in the West, but it is also a valuable stimulus to Zen Buddhists in Japan.

MASAO ABE
San Francisco

Foreword by
General Editor, John Hick

Buddhism has shown, and continues to show, a remarkable capacity to take varying forms as it enters new cultures and historical epochs. Beginning in India in the mid-first millenium B.C.E., the *dharma* spread some five centuries later into China, and from there into Tibet, Korea and Japan. In this northern expansion it developed different emphases, embodied in the Mahayana, reflecting something of the more world-affirming and optimistic Chinese outlook in distinction from the generally more world-denying and pessimistic Indian cast of mind. These are of course very rough and inadequate characterisations, and the differences should not be exaggerated. The basic concern was the same, whether spoken of as the attainment of *nirvāṇa*, realising one's Buddha nature, achieving *satori*, enlightenment or awakening. Each refers to the same radical change from encounter with the world as centering upon a supposedly enduring self, which is made anxious and unhappy by the ever-threatening inevitabilities of pain, loss, sorrow, decay and death, to an awakening to *nirvāṇa*, or the eternal Buddha nature, as permeating and transcending the ever-changing continuity of consciousness and world. But whereas in Indian Buddhism, and in the continuing Theravada of Sri Lanka, Burma, Thailand and elsewhere in south-east Asia, the emphasis was on *liberation from* the endless round of rebirths in a world of suffering, in the Mahayana it was more on *liberation into* a new way of experiencing and inhabiting that world, devoid now of all that we normally project upon it from the point of view of an anxious self-enclosed ego. But to the 'selfless self' this voidness or emptiness (*śūnyatā*) is also a fullness of 'wondrous being'; for the distinctive insight of the Mahayana is that *saṃsāra*, the wheel of life and death, and the blessed state of *nirvāṇa*, are the same world experienced in radically different ways.

This capacity of Buddhism to unfold in new ways as new aspects come to light within the ethos of different cultures is fully in harmony with the belief that all human formulations of the *dharma* are instances of *upāya*, 'skilful means' to enable different mentalities to attain to liberation. Thus Buddhism has within it a principle of change, adaptation and plurality in its historical forms. So long as the basic reality of the liberative transformation of human life is served, a great variety of meditative practices and philosophical superstructures has proved to be possible; and there is no reason to think that this proliferation of expressions of the *dharma* has come to an end.

The Zen Buddhism which Christopher Ives discusses in this book is part of the Mahayana development, particularly in its Japanese form. But he is himself also part of a further development which is coming about as the *dharma* takes root in the western, and particularly the American, cultural world. As an American who has spent many years in Japan, becoming fluent in Japanese, and who there became a practicing Zen Buddhist, Christopher Ives embodies both the traditional Zen concern for inner liberation and an activist concern for social justice and for human liberation from the economic, political and social structures which make it almost impossible for the majority of people, in both east and west, to attain now to their awakening. Within the new generation of North American Buddhists, exemplified in Ives, a hitherto largely latent aspect of the *dharma* is thus coming to consciousness.

But Ives is not making some brash attempt to create a new American form of Buddhism. He is deeply rooted in Japanese Zen and is exploring its resources, particularly in the work of the influential Kyoto School of philosophy, for a further development which is faithful both to the Buddhist tradition and to characteristic contemporary western insights and concerns. His uncovering of a Zen basis for social ethics may well prove fruitful not only within American Buddhism but also in contemporary Japan, whose younger generation is itself undergoing a rapid cultural 'westernisation'.

This very carefully and responsibly worked investigation by one who has a practical and theoretical knowledge of Zen, as well as a thorough western academic training, is thus to be warmly welcomed as a significant new contribution to East-West interaction.

JOHN HICK
Claremont Graduate School
California

Acknowledgments

This book originated in the 1970s when I was studying and practicing Zen with Abe Masao, Tokiwa Gishin, and other members of the F.A.S. Society at Reiun-in, a subtemple of Myōshinji in Kyoto. My studies with that group led to translation work with Professor Abe and eventually to graduate study under him at Claremont Gradute School. His insight into Zen, commitment to interfaith dialogue, and gentle presence have made an immeasurable contribution to me and to this book over the years.

Translation work with Professor Tokiwa of Hanazono University during my time in Japan promoted my understanding of Hisamatsu Shin'ichi's thought and the significance of the F.A.S. Society. Professor Tokiwa's dedication to Hisamatsu's way of Zen was a significant factor behind my initial interest in Hisamatsu and subsequent writing on Zen and ethics.

I am also highly indebted to Professors John B. Cobb, Jr., John Hick, and John A. Hutchison, who served as my dissertation committee at Claremont Graduate School. Their guidance and feedback during the writing of my dissertation provided a solid foundation for reworking the manuscript into this book. In particular, their expertise in philosophy of religion, Christian theology, and religious ethics assisted me in clarifying issues, and it was their influence that prompted me to move from descriptive work to speculation about how Zen might go about constructing a social ethic. I am especially grateful to John Hick for offering to include this book in his series on religion and philosophy.

As an outside reader of my dissertation, Professor Francis Dojun Cook of the University of California at Riverside offered incisive feedback, especially about Soto Zen and ethics. On several occasions he was quite generous with his time, meeting with me to discuss issues I had raised in the manuscript.

Over the past few years numerous scholars and colleagues have responded to drafts of the manuscript or conference papers based on, or destined to become, material in this book. This group includes Professor Dan Rhodes of the School of Theology at Claremont, Professor Steve Davis of Claremont McKenna College, Professor Rita Brock of Hamline University, Professor John Eusden and his Religion seminar at Williams College, and Professors John Magee, Darrell Reeck, and Del Langbauer of the University of Puget Sound. I also thank Professor Winston King, who obtained my dissertation through University Microfilms and wrote me a long letter full of constructive advice.

During the final stages of this project Professor Steve Smith of Claremont McKenna College and Dr. Peg LeVine of the Morita Therapy Centre of the Pacific Rim spent great amounts of time reading drafts of the book. With his training as an ethicist, Quaker background, and ongoing practice of Zen, Steve provided invaluable feedback about specific points and directed my thinking to a range of issues related to the content of the book. Based on her study and practice of Morita Therapy and Zen, Peg offered discerning responses that shed light on my blindspots and opened up new angles on the material. I am also grateful for her support during the final push to complete the manuscript.

During the last stage of preparation this book benefitted from a typing grant given by the University of Puget Sound. Ms. Carol Avery's outstanding word-processing skills, perseverance, and sense of humour made the creation of a polished final typescript possible.

Introduction

The word 'Zen' may conjure up images of monks sitting quietly in meditation, oblivious to the world around them. Or it may elicit associations to tea ceremony, Noh drama, landscape painting and other fine arts in Japan. To most people, however, it does not suggest the 'moral realm' of decisions, actions and responsibility, for Zen often appears divorced from or perhaps even contrary to ethics. In large part this appearance derives from the inward orientation of the tradition, possible connotations of such Buddhist terms as 'no-self' and 'emptiness', statements that Zen is beyond good and evil, stories about iconoclastic Zen teachers, and accounts of close connections between Zen and the samurai class in Japan. Modern writers on Zen may give mixed messages about Zen and ethics when they proclaim that Zen is 'beyond' morality while also arguing that it transforms human character. In one essay, D. T. Suzuki asserts that 'Zen leaves, as it were, morality where it belongs and as it is . . .';[1] yet in another essay he claims, 'From the ethical point of view . . . Zen may be considered a discipline aiming at the reconstruction of character.'[2]

Although some observers recognise such a 'reconstruction' of an individual Zen practitioner's character, they often harbor doubts about the social impact of Zen and, by extension, about the ability of the tradition to generate a social ethic. These doubts have not been voiced only with regard to Zen, for some writers have contended that estrangement from society pertains to Buddhism as a whole. In a discussion of possible connections between Buddhist religious ideals and society, Max Weber declares, 'No bridge connects them. Nor is there any actively conceptualised "social" contact . . . . The specific asocial character of all genuine mysticism is here carried to its maximum.'[3]

This book examines the relationship between Zen Buddhism and ethics, especially in society.

In effect it asks and offers answers to a set of questions: What is Zen? (Chapter 1); What are the ethical fruits of Zen practice and the ethical ramifications of central Zen concepts? (Chapter 2); What have historical Zen figures in Japan stated about ethics and actually done in their society? (Chapter 3); What have been recent developments

1

in Zen ethical reflection and action? (Chapter 4); How might central Zen concepts be clarified and expanded to provide a foundation for a Zen social ethic? (Chapter 5); and finally, based on available resources, what initial formulation of the social good might Zen offer? (Chapter 6). In terms of the two parts of the book, Part I is a descriptive discussion of the 'given' – ethical resources and pitfalls in Zen up to the present – and Part II is a constructive discussion of what 'might be' – possible lines of development of a Zen social ethic.

The central thesis emerging from Part I is that Zen does contain significant resources for a social ethic, but, judging from the history of Japanese Zen, it does not *necessarily* lead to social engagement; and the engagement that has occurred has assumed varying forms, some of which stand in tension with certain Buddhist principles and ideals, in part due to a historical lack of self-critical, systematic consideration of Zen and social ethics. Proceeding from this finding, Part II indicates how Zen may begin to articulate a social ethic in congruence with Zen principles and ideals. By drawing from the ideas of Buddhist and other thinkers, this book attempts to set a stage – and serve as a catalyst – for further discussion of Zen and social ethics.

As outlined in chapters 1 and 2, the ethical components of Zen find a practical basis in actual Zen religious life and a theoretical basis primarily in the Mahāyāna Buddhist concept of *śūnyatā*. As a logical and metaphysical[4] term, *śūnyatā* indicates both the lack of any independent essence or self in things and the interrelational dynamism that constitutes things. As a soteriological notion, *śūnyatā* signifies the elimination of the suffering (Sanskrit, *duḥkha*) that arises when people posit themselves as independent 'selves' over and against independent 'things' and through this fixation[5] sever themselves from the world and cling to objects or conditions that bolster their sense of security yet inevitably change in a universe characterised by impermanence (Skt., *anitya*).

Given this metaphysical background to Zen, the term 'ethics' must be used carefully in discussions of Zen. 'Ethics' is word with a Greek derivation, *ethikos*, which derives from *ethos*, connoting custom, mores and usage. 'Ethic(s)' has been defined as 'the discipline dealing with what is good and bad and with moral duty and obligation . . . a set of moral principles or values . . . a theory or system of moral values . . . the principles of conduct governing an individual or a group.'[6] In contrast, the ethical facets Zen revolve around a change in the way one experiences rather than a practical reason generating moral principles or an exertion of the will to perform good conduct. More specifically, Zen does not presuppose the ordinary ethical agent as some sort of essentially independent entity and then focus on specific rules of behavior or principles that guide decisions and actions. Zen begins with an inquiry into what the 'self' is, into human being, rather than with an inquiry into what the 'self' does, into human doing. The crux of Zen is an existential and epistemological reorientation on the basis of which one lives life anew. With this approach Zen promotes what might be called a 'foundational' ethic, for it concentrates on fundamental ways of being as opposed to principles of good and evil applied to extreme situations. Rather than start with consideration of possible responses to a violent parent, Apartheid or nuclear weapons, Zen first scrutinises one's way of experiencing the world and its impact on ordinary living, inclusive of one's beliefs, values, fears, and daily interactions with others. This approach aims at uprooting the underlying causes of assault, racial oppression and the arms race, although Zen can also inform responses to problems like these that have already arisen.

Moreover, use of 'ethics' and other terms originally foreign to Zen may prove misleading unless shifts in definition are noted. Western thought – with such terms as 'ethics', 'philosophy', 'religion', 'epistemology', and 'metaphysics' – reached the shores of Japan primarily in the late 19th century.[7] This stimulated the creation of neologisms for the imported concepts. For example, the rendering of 'philosophy' in Japanese, *tetsugaku* (literally, the study or science of wisdom), was coined by Nishi Amane (1829–97), a pioneer in the study of Western thought in the early Meiji Period (1868–1912).[8] Prior to then, reflective thought was referred to either as *gaku*, meaning study, learning, or science, as in *kokugaku*, the school of National Learning founded by Kada Azumamaro (1669–1736), or as *kyō*, teaching, as in *jukyō*, Confucianism, or *bukkyō*, the teachings of the Buddha (Buddhism). The character *kyō* appears in the compound for religion, *shūkyō*,[9] another term coined in the early Meiji Period.

It is also important to note that traditional 'social ethics' in Japan have encompassed both 'ethics' in the more technical sense and 'etiquette' or 'proper manners'. In Japanese, such terms as *dōtoku* (the virtue of the Way), *dōgi* (the duty of the Way), *tokkō* (virtuous conduct) and *shūshin* (self-cultivation) have indicated the former, whereas *reishiki* (forms of propriety) and *reigi-sahō* (propriety and decorum) have expressed the latter.[10] Given the major impact of Confucianism, with its emphasis on propriety, filial piety and duty in the context of the Five Relationships,[11] strict distinctions between 'ethics' and 'etiquette' do not hold here. It is in conjunction with this that Japanese ethics have been largely situational rather than universal, although this point has been overstated by many writers on the Japanese.

Zen and Confucianism are, of course, two different traditions and Zen ethics are not to be conflated with popular Japanese ethics. Yet some of the actual ethical teachings and social stances of Zen in the course of Japanese history reflect the degree to which Zen has functioned in concert with Confucianism and popular Japanese ethics. This interconnection is not surprising given the degree to which central traditions in Japan – including folk religion, Shintō, Confucianism and Buddhism[12] – have influenced and at times overlapped with each other while generally speaking to different issues and fulfilling different needs in Japanese religious life.

Zen and Buddhism in general did not first consider ethical issues in the Japanese cultural milieu. The historical Buddha, Śākyamuni, treated a range of ethical and social issues in teaching a way of overcoming human suffering. As recorded in the *Majjhima Nikāya* and *Saṃyutta Nikāya* of the *Sutta Piṭaka*,[13] he encapsulated his teaching in the 'Four Noble Truths'. Briefly stated, the first 'truth' is suffering and the second truth is its cause, which is the clinging that results from ignorance of the impermanent nature of reality; the third truth is the cessation of suffering (Skt., *nirodha*), and the fourth is the Noble Eightfold Path (Skt., *āryāṣṭāṅgika-mārga*) leading to the cessation of suffering.

The Noble Eightfold Path consists of eight components,[14] which encompass the areas of wisdom, ethical guidelines,[15] and meditation. In Śākyamuni's formulation of the Path, the two wisdom components of right understanding and right intention are followed by three moral components: right speech, right action and right livelihood. Right speech aims at eliminating such negative types of speech as lying, gossip, self-praise and harshness. Right action consists of conduct that does not harm the moral and 'spiritual' condition of oneself and other people; it gains expression in the Five Precepts: no killing, no stealing, no sexual misconduct, no lying and no consumption of intoxicants. Right livelihood indicates occupations consistent with Buddhist values, and hence traditionally has excluded the work of butchers, executioners and manufacturers of (and dealers in) intoxicants and weapons. These ethical facets of the Path support meditation and religious insight. Expressed slightly differently, in early and Theravāda Buddhism, proper ethical behavior serves largely as a *means* to or precondition of the cessation of suffering,[16] and for this reason practice comes to be seen as a gradual process of purification, an approach that reflects Hindu attitudes and finds expression in such Theravāda works as Asvaghosa's *Path of Purification (Viśudhimagga)*. Along these lines the tradition has generated classifications of certain obstacles to a full realisation of *nibbāna*. These obstacles include the Three Poisons (ignorance, greed and hatred) and the Five Hindrances (anger, greed, pride, jealousy and hatred).

This ethical orientation finds support in early Buddhists 'taking refuge' in the Buddha, the Sangha (the community of monks and nuns) and the Dhamma (the Buddha's teachings and the truth conveyed therein). To 'take refuge in the Buddha' usually connotes modelling oneself after him. This Buddha as an idealised religious and ethical role-model finds a vivid expression in the *Jātaka Tales*,[17] which relate how in past lives he performed good deeds and self-sacrificial acts of compassion, followed the precepts fully, and perfected himself in the process of attaining Buddhahood. In actual Buddhist religious life, taking refuge in the Buddha consists largely of practicing the moral components of the Noble Eightfold Path. The laity observe the five precepts while monks and nuns observe these precepts and five more: to eat moderately and only before noon; not to experience such forms of entertainment as dancing, singing and drama; not to use perfume or jewelry; not to sleep on wide, luxurious beds; and not to handle or possess gold or silver. When leading a monastic life in accordance with the *Vinaya Piṭaka*,[18] monks and nuns follow several hundred additional guidelines as well.

The ethical guidance offered by Śākyamuni consists of more than what may appear to be heteronomous rules and negative injunctions. Just prior to his death he exhorted his followers: 'Be ye lamps unto yourselves.' In part this saying calls for the cultivation of positive virtues. Of primary importance here are the four *brahmavihāras* ('sublime abodes'): loving kindness (Pali., *mettā*; Skt., *maitrī*), compassion (P. and Skt., *karuṇā*), sympathetic joy (P. and Skt., *muditā*) and equanimity (P., *upekkhā*; Skt., *upekṣā*). Based on a sense of identity with others, 'loving kindness' here is a concern for the welfare of all beings in the world. This overlaps with compassion, about which one Buddhist writes, 'The realization of "one's" identity with "others," the elimination of distinction between the experience of happiness and sorrow of "others" and the happiness and sorrows of "one's self," is called "karuna."'[19] Working together with compassion is 'sympathetic joy in another's joy or success, forgetful of one's own success or failure, distress or happiness, and totally without any envious or jealous feeling. It is the analogue on the happy side, to compassion on the unhappy side of human life.'[20] Upekkhā connotes a calm, detached impartiality. Though seemingly divorced from ethics, it is the ability to maintain composure in the midst of chaos and struggle, and with this character it provides a basis for effective action without entanglement in narrowly personal desires or rigid attachment to the fruits of actioh.[21]

Perhaps the most important ethical statement in early Buddhism is the Dhammapada,[22] a collection of verses attributed to Śākyamuni and compiled in the second or third century before the common era. It includes the oft-quoted verse:

> The eschewing of all evil,
> the perfecting of good deeds,
> the purifying of one's mind –
> this is the teaching of Buddhas.[23]

In elaborating on this basic maxim, the Dhammapada extols the virtues of self-control, courage, forbearance, nonviolence, peacefulness and compassion. The ethical concern expressed in this text does not stop at the personal level, however. Several verses convey Śākyamuni's criticism of the Hindu caste system. For example, he reportedly said, 'Not by matted hair, not by lineage, not by caste does one become a Brahmin. He is a Brahmin in whom there are truth and righteousness. He is blessed.'[24] All who follow Śākyamuni's teaching can achieve religious liberation, not simply those born into the highest, priestly caste.

Other social teachings find expression in Buddhist scriptures. As pointed out by Ken Jones in his recent work on Buddhism and society, several early texts convey social messages. Sections of the Aṅguttara Nikāya call on Buddhists to 'live for the welfare of the many'; the Cakkavatti Sihanada Sutta (in the Dīgha Nikāya) ascribes violence and other social problems to a failure to provide for the poor; and the *Kutadanta Sutta* advocates the promotion of social welfare over punishment as the most effective response to harmful behaviour in society.[25]

Śākyamuni also taught that religious liberation is possible for women, although scriptural sources indicate that he balked when his aunt and a group of women walked to him and asked to be accepted as disciples, and that it was his disciple Ananda who convinced him to accept them into the Sangha. He declared that if a woman follows the Noble Eightfold Path, she can achieve liberation in this lifetime; she does not have to be reborn as a Brahmin male, as claimed by the Hinduism of his time. Whatever the circumstances, the Sangha did come to include communities of nuns. This provided 'a liberating option beyond marriage and motherhood. It meant a sort of career, a chance for greater independence.'[26]

The pervasive ethical content of Śākyamuni's talks has led some to contend that the ultimate goal of his path, *nibbāna* (Skt., *nirvāṇa*), is primarily ethical. T. W. Rhys-Davids writes, 'Nibbana is purely and solely an *ethical* state, to be reached in this birth by ethical practices, contemplation and insight.'[27] Although this contention is debatable, it reflects the key role of ethics in early and Theravāda Buddhism.

Theravāda Buddhists have expressed their faith at the institutional and social levels. The Sangha has exerted a significant influence on society, with monks and nuns functioning not only as religious leaders but also as ethical role models, counselors, educators and community organisers. In his study of Buddhism and politics in Burma and other parts of Asia, Trevor Ling writes, 'The fact that, until recently, the majority of Burmese received at least some of their schooling in the monasteries, which were also the village schools, indicates another of the close links between the life of the monastery and the life of the people.'[28]

Theravāda Buddhists have articulated models of benevolent kingship based on Buddhist ideals. Certain texts offer guidelines for 'enlightened' kings who, as protectors of the Sangha and Dhamma, guarantee economic and political conditions that satisfy basic needs and, by extension, the ability to practice Buddhist meditation and engage in meritorious almsgiving. About the guidelines set forth in *Aṅguttara Nikāya*, G. S. P. Misra writes, 'This notion that the general righteousness of the people depends on the king's personal righteousness lays a moral pressure on the ruling agent to be good and righteous; it imposes all responsibility of any untoward happening in the country on him.'[29] The most famous example of an actual ruler portrayed as embodying this Buddhist ideal of kingship is Ashoka, third ruler in the Maurya dynasty during the 3rd century BCE in northern India. As expressed in the 'Edicts of Ashoka' carved on rocks and stone pillars around the kingdom, Ashoka's governance featured (1) 'transcendentalism' in the sense of seeking religious goals rather than royal conquest, material possessions or self-aggrandisement; (2) nonviolence with regard to humans *and* animals; (3) religious pluralism and support for education; (4) a compassionate welfare policy providing hospices, support for the practice of medicine, care for the families of convicts, and investigations of judicial corruption; and (5) a combination of central authority and decentralist sharing of power with regional governors.[30] Remarkable in Ashoka's case is both his conversion away from violent conquest to benevolent rule, and the fact that this took place in the third century before the common era, when this type of kingship was rare. In modern times, such rulers as U Nu of Burma and Junius Richard Jayewardene of Sri Lanka have striven to integrate Buddhist ideals into their governance. The word 'striven' is apt here, for U Nu reportedly 'confessed to a friend that his duties as head of state – including that of encouraging his troops to fight the insurgents – were at odds with his personal efforts to achieve enlightenment'.[31]

Theravāda Buddhists have applied Buddhist teachings to several other aspects of the social realm. In the eighteenth century, Burmese Buddhists wrote a new 'Code of Manu', which is 'largely devoid of the hierarchical inequality before the law that characterises its wider known Brahmanic namesake'.[32] In the 1920s, monk U Ottama led Burmese efforts to expel the British.[33] Such contemporary Theravāda Buddhists as Anagarika Dharmapala (*Return to Righteousness*) and D. C. Vijayavardhana (*The Revolt in the Temple*) have called for a 'this-worldly interpretation of *nirvāṇa*',[34] for a '*nibbāna* of this world' (P., *loka nibbāna*). The Thai monk Buddhadasa has wrestled with a range of social issues over the years. The Thai layman Sulak Sivaraksa has served as head of the Asian Forum on Cultural Development, an interreligious, grass-roots community development organisation in Southeast Asia, and has been an inspiring presence in the International Network of Engaged Buddhists. For Thai Buddhists, however, political involvement is not without its hazards. As Ken Jones notes,

In recent years the Thai government has attempted, not altogether successfully, to exploit the traditional popular prestige of the monks by involving them in government community development projects, counterinsurgency, and questionable national and cultural integration schemes for ethnic minorities.[35]

Sri Lankan Buddhists have created the Sarvodaya Movement, drawing from not only Buddhism but also other Sri Lankan religions, including Hinduism, Christianity and Islam. Sarvodaya means the awakening (*udaya*) of everyone (*sarva*), or total awakening. The movement that goes by this name started in 1958, when a young Sri Lankan high-school teacher, A. T. Ariyaratna, helped several students organise a two-week work camp in an isolated outcaste village. The movement grew to the point where in 1984 it was 'active in over four-thousand towns and villages, operating programs for health, education, agriculture and local industry'.[36] The movement aims at satisfying what are referred to as the Ten Basic Needs, several of which are absent or only implied in economic thought about 'development': clean water; food; housing; clothing; health care; communication; fuel; education; a clean, safe, and beautiful environment; and a cultural and spiritual life.

Though ethical concern runs throughout Theravāda Buddhism, several aspects of the tradition can undermine concern for social ethics. These include the view held by some Theravāda Buddhists that *nibbāna* is a transcendent, unconditioned realm divorced from actuality; the derivative split between the world of the Sangha and the world of laypeople and between the systems of morality in each world;[37] deterministic and fatalistic interpretations of *kamma* (Skt., *karma*); possible 'hedonistic' consequentialism in the doctrines of *kamma* and merit;[38] and possible aloofness from the mundane realm on the part of the *arhat*, the ideal religious figure who is seen as having travelled the Noble Eightfold Path to the end and realised *nibbāna*.[39]

The Mahāyāna tradition espouses a set of religious and moral values significant for social ethics. The *bodhisattva* ideal and the accompanying notions of compassion, altruism and group salvation are pivotal in this stream of Buddhism. Early Mahāyāna

Sanskrit writers concentrate on the *bodhisattva's* vows to refrain from 'entering' full nirvana until all other beings enter (see the *Sukhavātī-vyūha* or Pure Land Sūtra), on the transference of merit to others (*Brahmajāla Sūtra* or Brahma Net Sūtra), on skilful means (Skt., *upāya*) of leading others to nirvana (*Saddharma-puṇḍarīka* or Lotus Sūtra), on the insight and compassion attainable by laypeople (*Vimalakīrti-nirdeśa Sūtra*), on the existence of Buddhanature in all people (*Avatamsaka Sūtra*), and on the importance of practicing and embodying the perfections exemplified by a *bodhisattva* (*Prajñāpāramitā Sūtras* or Wisdom Sūtras, including the *Prajñāpāramitā-hṛdaya Sūtra* or Heart Sūtra and the *Vajracchedika Prajñāpāramitā* or Diamond Sūtra).

Though mainly known for laying the groundwork of Mahāyāna philosophy, Nāgārjuna (circa 150–250 C.E. in India) also set forth views on ideal kingship. In his *Jewel Garland of Royal Counsels*, written for King Udayi of the Satavahan Dynasty in southern India, Nāgārjuna articulated values similar to those promulgated in Ashoka's edicts. He stressed what Robert Thurman terms (1) 'individualist transcendentalism' in the sense of a benevolent, enlightened ruler overcoming narrow self-interest; (2) 'self-restraint' in terms of both detachment from the objects of passion and pacifism; (3) 'transformative universalism' in the sense of broad educational efforts with an emphasis on teachers who exemplify the ethical perfection of the Buddha; and (4) 'compassionate socialism' in the form of health care, parks, canals, and provisions for travelers.[40]

Since Nāgārjuna's time Mahāyāna Buddhism has generated a range of sects and ethical stances. In recent years Mahāyāna Buddhists have been giving explicit attention to social issues. In the 1960s Vietnamese Mahāyāna Buddhists joined together to form the Unified Buddhist Church and adopted means of nonviolent protest in an effort to steer a third course between those opposed to and those aligned with the United States. As Ken Jones writes:

> The movement for peace was linked with action for social justice and social revolution. From the two radical Buddhist bases of Van Hanh University and the School of Youth for Social Service young people went into the country to work alongside the peasants on rural development projects, and a number of unions and other organizations were formed which also embraced urban

workers, women, youth and students. An extensive anti-war literature flourished, of poetry, satire, song and prayer.[41]

Out of this movement emerged one of the key Vietnamese Zen activists, Thich Nhat Hanh.

Tibetan Buddhists in Asia and West have lobbied through such organisations as the Foundation for the Preservation of the Mahāyāna Tradition for social justice in Tibet under Chinese rule. For his advocacy of nonviolent efforts toward peace and justice, the Dalai Lama received the Nobel Peace Prize in 1989.

With their faith in the 'other power' of Amida, Pure Land Buddhists here started to address human rights issues in Japan. For example, in response to the continuing problem of discrimination against the *burakumin*,[42] the Higashi Honganji branch of the True Pure Land Sect (*Jōdōshinshū*) has established the Dōwasuishin Honbu, which literally means 'headquarters for advancing equality and harmony'.

Several 'new religions' in Japan that are based in Mahāyāna Buddhism have worked for peace. The Sōka Gakkai, a Nichiren Buddhist lay movement that has been criticised for proselytising and having an apparently materialistic orientation, advocates chanting the Japanese name of the Lotus Sūtra as the key to world peace. Another new religion indebted to Nichiren Buddhism, Risshō Kōseikai, has directed its energies toward such issues as famine relief. Monks and nuns of Nipponzan Myōhōji, a Nichiren movement founded in the twentieth century by Fujii Nichidatsu, have recently played a visible role in peace efforts in Japan and North America. While beating drums and chanting, several marched across the United States in 1976 to protest the creation and stockpiling of nuclear weapons.

It was out of the Mahāyāna strand of Buddhism, with crossfertilisation from Taoism, that the Chan (Zen) tradition emerged in sixth-century China. In recent decades Zen has expanded beyond East Asia and Vietnam, and this expansion has been accompanied by increased reflection on ethical facets of Zen and by increased activity in response to social issues.

Part I
The Zen Tradition
and Ethics

1

The Zen Path

Discussion of Zen and ethics benefits from an answer to the preliminary question, 'What is Zen?' With a focus on elements generally common to the particular forms of the tradition,[1] this chapter outlines four overlapping areas of the Zen path: practice, Awakening, wisdom and compassion.

Traditionally, Zen practice begins when an aspirant arrives at the closed gate of a monastery and, after waiting for several days, is asked, 'Who are you?' or 'Where did you come from?' This is no mere question about someone's name or hometown, for the person is being asked to express his or her deepest self-understanding. This inquiry runs throughout Zen practice. For example, in a classical text, the *Wumen-guan*, Huineng (J., Enō; 638–713) asks a monk, 'What is your Original Face?'

Zen poses such questions with an eye toward revealing a paradox inherent in human existence. Though as infants people originally do not distinguish themselves from the world, over time they begin to make distinctions between themselves and other things, between 'here' and the world 'out there'. In this bifurcation, they come to define or fixate themselves as subjects over and against experienced objects, thinking in terms of 'me' and 'mine'. They progressively bolster this fixation by construing themselves as independent, enduring selves, especially as they acquire distinctive personal memories and characteristics. This process may lead to the supposition of an eternal, unchanging soul beneath observable consciousness.

The ability to make distinctions between self and non-self has crucial practical significance. To survive one must be able to distinguish oneself from an oncoming car. But, to the extent one engages only in this self–other mode of experience and holds on tightly to the accompanying distinctions, certain problems arise. Existentially, one becomes estranged from the world, from the matrix that gave rise to and now sustains oneself. One may also feel cut off from other people, especially when conflicts emerge and one becomes trapped in considering oneself right and the other person wrong, thereby losing the ability to see things clearly and act wisely. In the words of Sengcan, the third 'founding teacher' of Zen,

> Abide not with dualism,
> Carefully avoid pursuing it;
> As soon as you have right and wrong,
> Confusion ensues, and Mind is lost.[2]

Self-centered entrapment in dualism plays itself out at the inter-group level when people succumb to an us-them orientation *vis-à-vis* the 'other' and encase this antagonism in ideology.

When asked 'Who are you?' this 'fixated' or 'dualistic' subjec-tivity[3] also falls into the clutches of an infinite regress: trying to catch itself through reflection, but always being able to reflect one more time on the previous reflector. This can only end in frustra-tion. Francis Cook explains, 'The mind as an object of itself is abstract because the mind as true subject can never catch itself in its own form as vibrant, concrete, lived experience. It can only seize a past image of itself in the form of memory and thus there is a saying in Buddhism to the effect that "a knife cannot cut itself."'[4] Subjectivity comes to stand precariously on a split between itself as objectified and itself as objectifier. The 'self' is now cut off from all things, including itself, and remains forever anxious and restless.[5]

Moreover, through language and conceptual thought humans distinguish, label and analyse the various objectified 'things' in the world. And on the basis of memories of how reality was and images of how they want reality to be, people react emotionally, intellectually and volitionally to each of these 'things' encountered. They come to perceive things in terms of attraction and aversion, valuing that which enhances a sense of security and avoiding whatever is deemed threatening. Sengcan writes:

> To set up what you like against what you dislike –
> This is the disease of the mind;
> When the deep meaning [of the Way] is not understood
> Peace of mind is disturbed to no purpose.[6]

In the words of a contemporary Zen teacher:

> There is 'me' and there is this 'thing' out there that is either hurting me or pleasing me. We tend to run our whole life out of

that condition, trying to avoid everything that hurts or displeases us, and running after the objects, people or situations that we think will give us pleasure. Our whole life is caught up in that pleasure and pain, avoiding one and pursuing the other . . . . We remain always separate from our life, looking at it, analyzing it, judging it, trying to figure for each situation 'What am I going to get out of it? Is it going to give me pleasure or should I run from it?'[7]

Because of this conceptual and valuational overlay on experience, people fail to see themselves and reality clearly in the concrete immediacy of the present. They get trapped in fixed patterns of response to the world. And in objectifying things and constantly being attracted to some and afraid of others, they become bound to them, in the sense of being caught up in conditioned reactions to them.

Moreover, because all things inevitably change, people experience unnecessary pain to the extent they take themselves to be permanent or clutch to things and situations deemed necessary for fulfillment. More specifically, faced with mortality and deep-rooted anxiety concerning death, people consciously or unconsciously attempt to defend themselves from painful transiency. They may try to avoid looking at death and find security by focusing themselves on family life, a career, amusements, sexuality, or drugs. Or they may struggle to attain unending life, goodness and peace at the exclusion of death, evil and anguish. Such one-sided fulfillment, however, forever eludes them. Although they may find temporary, relative satisfaction or security, they soon collide with the negation of that satisfaction. As Hisamatsu Shin'ichi points out, each relative satisfaction or 'synthesis' is only partial – in time, the antithesis arrives and destroys the synthesis. In this ongoing process, no ultimate synthesis is possible. Hisamatsu sketches this predicament with the metaphor of water and waves: to the extent people exist as waves, as the agitated surface of an expanse of water, they are eternally unsettled, for waves continue to rise and fall in endless opposition.

In short, although dualistic subjectivity is a pragmatically significant part of being human, to the extent that it is one's *only* way of experiencing, one becomes cut off from the world, and this alienation is exacerbated to the extent one becomes lost in concepts about and reactions to reality and becomes attached to objects or situations that seem to promote security yet inevitably change. From the Zen perspective, entanglement in this dualistic, judgmental, and attached subjectivity constitutes the fundamental human religious problem,[8] termed *duḥkha* in traditional Buddhism, meaning suffering or dis-ease. And Zen views this entanglement as the primary cause of the situations to which systems of social ethics respond.

Zen practice aims in large part at liberating humans from entanglement in this subjectivity. The tradition attempts to lead the practitioner to an awareness – said to be inexpressible with words – in which the distinction between subject and object drops away. From a slightly different angle, Zen practice cultivates a full awareness of – and *as* – what most concretely exists here and now,[9] and leads to a realisation of immediate experience prior to the swirl of thoughts about how reality is or how it needs to be for one to be fulfilled, the anxious thought process that causes unnecessary and otherwise avoidable pain. In the words of one Zen teacher:

> What I need to know is what sorts of thoughts I persist in entertaining right now, today . . . . In noticing the thoughts . . . my false identification with limited self . . . slowly fades. More and more I can be who I truly am: a no-self, an open and spacious response to life.[10]

One way Zen promotes this shift in experience is through the practice of *zazen*. Sitting with a balanced, erect posture and partially open eyes, the practitioner attends to the breath. Thoughts come and go and they may pull attention away from the breath, but as one continually returns to the breath and attention to it deepens, one gradually breaks free from anxious thought and begins to enter more fully into immediate experience.

This practice is central to daily Zen life, and it is pursued intensively in a *sesshin*, a period of practice usually lasting seven days. Contact with the outside world is severed, most physical labor and administrative duties around the monastery or centre are put on hold to allow for full concentration on formal *zazen* practice, and daily interviews with the *rōshi* (literally, 'old teacher'; often rendered as 'Zen master') are increased. In a *sesshin* at a typical Rinzai Zen monastery, monks or nuns rise at around 3:00 a.m. and during the day practice *zazen*, have up to four or five interviews, hear a 'Dharma talk' (*teishō*) by the *rōshi* on a classical Zen text,[11] eat highly ritualised meals as a continuation of *zazen*, and chant sutras, vows, and other writings. Formal practice in a *sesshin* ends at around 9:30 p.m., although students may engage in 'night sitting' (*yaza*) on their own. Work around the monastery and artistic pursuits function as additional forms of practice. When done with full attention, these activities provide ways of 'giving oneself away' or merging with the task at hand, free from reflection on how one is doing or on possible outcomes. (In Zen parlance, one engages in these activities 'without leaving a trace'.) As one Zen teacher said, 'If you walk, just walk. If you sit, just sit. Don't wobble!' When the person pours[12] herself into the activity, it takes on a new flavour and depth.[13]

In Rinzai monasteries, most monks or nuns proceed on the basis of these facets of practice to work with *kōans*.[14] '*Kōan*' (Ch., *gong-an*) literally means 'public measure' or 'public proposal'. *Kōans* focus on statements and actions connected with enlightenment experiences of, or dialogues between, Zen figures of the past. An example is the question–answer dialogue (*mondō*) in which Zhaozhou (J., Jōshū; 778–897), when asked why Bodhidharma, the founder of Zen, came to China from India, exclaims, 'The cypress tree in the courtyard',[15] or the question formulated by Hakuin (1685–1768), 'What is the sound of one hand [clapping]?'

A student receives a *kōan* from a *rōshi*. Even with its powers of reflection, reason, analysis and judgement, dualistic subjectivity cannot comprehend the *kōan*. Nevertheless, in a traditional monastery the practitioner cannot back off, for he or she must keep going to interviews (*sanzen*) with the *rōshi* to express an understanding of the *kōan*. D. T. Suzuki writes, 'The *koan* is neither a riddle nor a witty remark. It has a most definite objective, the arousing of doubt and pushing it to its furthest limits.'[16] This doubt develops into an existential impasse. Suzuki writes:

When Joshu says 'the cypress-tree in the courtyard,' or when Hakuin puts out his one hand, there is no logical way to get around it. You feel as if your march of thought had been suddenly cut short. You hesitate, you doubt, you are troubled and agitated, not knowing how to break through the wall which seems altogether impassable. When this climax is reached, your whole personality, your inmost will, your deepest nature, determined to bring the situation to an issue, throws itself with no thought of self or no-self, of this or that, directly and un-reservedly against the iron wall of the *koan*.[17]

When this process reaches an extreme point, called the 'Great Doubt Block', the practitioner in effect becomes the *kōan*, embodying it as a fundamental existential problem. Unable to function, the person is, so to speak, locked into the Doubt. Becoming this Doubt, fixated subjectivity is

> functionally and structurally disabled and immobilised. Its being objectless and subjectless is a negativity of an exhaustive bondage and obstruction, in which subject and object in their contradictory, dualistic polarity totally impede and impound each other in an all-comprehensive, helpless clog. Being thus negatively objectless and subjectless, having neither body nor mind, is not sufficient. Without body, without mouth and without mind, there must be expression. The root-contradiction-great-doubt-block remains to be in-divisibly broken up and resolved.[18]

Hakuin provides a metaphorical description of this:

> A person went astray and arrived at a spot never trodden before. Before him there yawned a bottomless abyss. His feet stood on the slippery moss of a rock and no secure foothold appeared around him. He could step neither forward nor backward. Only death awaited him. The vine which he grasped with his left hand and the tendril which he held with his right hand could offer him little help. His life hung by a single thread.[19]

Thwarted in this 'doubt block', fixated subjectivity 'dies' what Zen calls the 'One Great Death'. This is not merely negative, for it is simultaneously *satori*,[20] usually rendered in English as 'Enlightenment' or 'Awakening'. Hakuin expresses this in the following way:

> . . . suddenly it occurs that with the *kōan* both body and mind break. This is the instant when the hands are released over the abyss. In this sudden upsurge it is as if one drinks water and knows for oneself heat and cold. Great joy wells up. This is called rebirth. This is termed seeing into one's own nature.[21]

A traditional characterisation of Rinzai Zen is that, compared with Sōtō Zen and its emphasis on 'just sitting,' it takes a more dynamic approach by using *kōans* to bring about Awakening. Further, while Hakuin and other Rinzai figures give a depiction of Awakening as an abrupt,[22] dramatic event, Sōtō Zen portrays Awakening as a gradual process, or as an event that occurs whenever a one 'exerts' (*gujin*) oneself in the sense of giving total attention to what one is doing or experiencing in the present moment.[23] In a discussion of Dōgen (1200–1253) and his Sōtō writings, Francis Cook comments, 'it is said that enlightenment itself is always enlightenment in a particular situation, and so consequently, rather than enlightenment being a once-and-for-all event, it must be actualised over and over as each new event is experienced'.[24]

In any case, Zen claims that its practice opens up subjectivity whose only mode of experience is as a fixated, bounded 'thing' cut off from other 'things' and stuck in that estranged position through fear, conceptualisation, and attachment. In the course of Zen practice one comes to realise what the self really is. Shifting from dualistic subjectivity, one undergoes a liberating expansion into the open field of experience in which what appears to be the 'self' and what appears to be an 'other' have been dwelling all along.[25] Expressed slightly differently, one realises direct or pure experience in which one *is* one's experience and, by extension, identifies with the content of the experience. This unified, non-dualistic experience is prior to and envelopes the normal dualistic view that the 'self' *has* an experience of something.[26] In this regard, Awakening is an opening of awareness, not an obliteration of it, and for this reason Abe Masao speaks of the 'expanse of Awakening' (*kaku no hirogari*).

In one respect, the Mahāyāna concept of *śūnyatā* (emptiness or emptying) indicates this dissolving of entrapment in bounded dualistic subjectivity. Awakening to *śūnyatā* does not entail a grasping of some ultimate 'thing' called *śūnyatā* as the ground of Being or a void apart from actuality. In Hisamatsu's metaphor, one drops out of individual subjectivity as a particular, formed wave and awakens to the pervasive water that is formless yet inseparable from the myriad waves (forms) rising and falling here; out of a full realisation of the dissolution of the wave into formless water, one reemerges as true wave, an individual grounded in a realisation of the inseparability of the part and the whole, of non-duality as the dynamism between plurality (waves, dualistic view) and unity (water, monistic unity with 'other'). In more standard Zen terminology, one 'sees into one's nature' (*kenshō*). One cannot objectify this awakening, for it is like an eye that works behind conscious seeing but is never seen. From another angle, one *is* this awakening when one is fully merged with immediate experience and hence not reflecting on experience. Nishida Kitarō clarifies this unobjectifiability of Awakening as follows,

> In the Zen sect, people speak of 'Seeing into one's [Original] Nature and thereby realising Buddhahood.' But we must not misunderstand these words. 'Seeing' does not indicate our seeing something outside ourselves as an object, or seeing the self introspectively within us. The self cannot see itself, just as an eye cannot see itself. But this does not imply that we see the Buddha transcendently. If such a thing were seen, it would be an apparition. 'Seeing' refers to an overturning of the self.[27]

This overturning of subjectivity that objectifies things is simultaneously a realisation of the 'Mind that arises without abiding anywhere',[28] the awareness that is often likened to a mirror, which reflects all things without clinging to or distorting them.

This description points to the *prajñā* (wisdom) said to be realised in Awakening. *Prajñā* plays a key role throughout the Buddhist tradition.[29] In early Buddhism, *paññā*, the Pali equivalent to *prajñā*, indicates the first two components of the Noble Eightfold Path: right understanding and right intention, which signify a recognition of the truth conveyed by Śākyamuni's teaching and the aspiration to practice it. In some formulations of the Eightfold Path, these two components indicate salvific wisdom realised on the basis of the practice of morality (*śīla*) and concentration (*samādhi*), and hence they come as the seventh and eighth steps. One scholar writes:

> The ideal Buddhist way of dealing with one's karma is patterned directly on the Buddha's experience. It begins with *śīla*, a set of moral rules to purify, and begin the transformation of, one's nature. *Śīla* increases the individual's self-insight and mindfulness (*smṛti*), essential since karma cannot be counteracted without its being brought to full consciousness. Then, *samādhi*, the cultivation of meditative calm (*śamatha*), and finally one-

pointedness of concentration, comes [sic]. Only from a state of mental control can the third step, *prajñā* (wisdom), be attained.[30]

In more general terms, early and Theravāda Buddhist teachings portray *paññā* as designating an insight into and realisation of the Four Noble Truths and the pivotal concepts of suffering, impermanence and no-self. In the *Aṭṭhasālinī*, Buddhaghosa (5th century C.E.), one of the greatest Abhidhamma[31] thinkers, writes:

Knowledge [*paññā*] is so-called because it knows. And what does it know? It knows the Four Noble Truths, beginning with the statement that 'all this to which we are attached is transitory and unable to give lasting happiness and spiritual contentment and hence is miserable.' . . . It makes known the verifiable fact of transitoriness, miserableness [*dukkha*] and the absence of a persistent personality or individuality.[32]

These texts also set forth the thesis that dependent co-arising (P., *paṭicca-samuppāda*) can be known only by *paññā*.[33] As a theory of the interrelationship of the various constituents (*dharmas*) constituting 'things', dependent co-arising has been expressed in terms of the Twelvefold Chain of Causation, a formulation of how ignorance leads to suffering and rebirth and then to further ignorance in an ongoing series of births. Without *paññā*, one will fail to grasp how the 'link' of ignorance connects with the eleven other links (*nidānas*) to generate rebirths and hence will fail to break out of the chain.

Given the Buddha's emphasis on 'no-self', *paññā* is a wisdom without a wise self, a discernment without a discerner. One Theravāda Buddhist writes, 'it is wisdom (*paññā*), realisation, that realises. There is no other self behind the realisation'.[34] Contemporary Theravāda scholars have variously translated *paññā* as 'penetrative insight',[35] 'spiritual knowledge',[36] 'intellectual clarity',[37] and 'understanding'.[38]

In the establishment of the Mahāyāna tradition on the basis of the *Prajñāpāramita sūtras* (Perfection of Wisdom Sūtras) and interpretations of them, *paññā* takes on a new connotation. Nāgārjuna (c. 150–250), the Indian thinker whose writing on *śūnyatā* laid the philosophical basis for Zen and other Mahāyāna schools, goes beyond the Abhidhamma idea of the 'emptiness' of self (*pudgala-śūnyatā*) and argues also for the emptiness of *dharmas* (*dharma-śūnyatā*), the various factors constituting the 'self' and other 'things' in the empirical world. From his perspective, one's knowing arrives at *prajñā* when one quells normal 'discriminating cognition' (*vikalpa*) that 'essentialises'[39] things; this clears the way for the realisation that all *dharmas* – including such *dharmas* as space and *nirvāṇa*, which certain Abhidhamma thinkers regarded as 'unconditioned' – are 'empty' (*śūnya*), in the sense being devoid of any independent, unconditioned existence or 'own-being' (*svabhāva*). Expressed more dynamically, 'Wisdom is, in part, a concentrative exercise which dissolves the mental and emotional attachment of the apparent mind to "things" (including ideas or assertions), for it is the awareness that all "things" are empty.'[40] This means that the awakened Mahāyāna Buddhist regards not only objects of experience but also all of their constitutive factors (*dharmas*) as arising co-dependently[41] and hence as existing only in – and by virtue of – a matrix of interrelationship.

The 'eye' of *prajñā* thus opens up through an overcoming of ignorance, of the tendency to substantialise oneself or objectified things and then become attached to them. This wisdom emerges through relinquishment of the conventional mode of experiencing (*saṃvṛti-satya*) that reifies 'self' and 'other' and the opening up of a higher-order mode of experiencing, *paramārtha-satya*, grounded in the awakening to *śūnyatā*. It is important to note here that from Nāgārjuna's perspective, *paramārtha-satya* does not constitute a correct theory or standpoint opposing other standpoints, for it negates *all* theoretical standpoints that attempt to delineate reality conceptually.[42] D. T. Suzuki writes that '*prajñā* reinforces the awareness that all ideas stand on emptiness – a gap that conceptual thinking cannot span'.[43]

As a 'higher' religious wisdom, however, *prajñā* does not indicate a one-way move from the secular, practical realm to a separate religious realm. As stated in the *Prajñāpāramitā Sūtras*, it is a wisdom that realises that 'emptiness is none other than form',[44] that *śūnyatā* is the mode of 'be-ing' of the events that constitute the ongoing process of reality. *Prajñā* reveals the rich scope of 'empty' interrelating and the creative possibilities this field offers.[45] That is to say, *prajñā* discerns an open, fluid, ever-dynamic emptiness that is none other than the fullness of reality presenting itself in and around us.

Nāgārjuna does not concern himself with these epistemological or philosophical issues for their own sake. In that the realisation of wisdom promoted by Nāgārjuna's philosophy is none other than the dissolution of ignorance and clinging, *prajñā* plays a central religious role in the Mahāyāna Buddhist tradition:

Wisdom is the presupposition for, and the cultivation of, the negation of self-sufficient entities. The aim of wisdom is to melt the chains of greed and thirst for possession of 'things.' Or to state the same thing from the viewpoint of a religious goal, its aim is to relate oneself to all 'things' in an empty relationship, i.e., in total freedom.[46]

Prajñā, too, is said to be 'empty'. Nāgārjuna argues that this wisdom is not a positive knowledge *of* somethng or a definitive *cognitive* handle on an objective Reality. Frederick Streng summarises Nāgārjuna's view:

Prajñā (wisdom), which permitted one 'to see things as they really are,' was significant from a religious point of view since one 'became' what one knew. In summary we would say that the insight into the emptiness of all things destroyed illusion; for this illusion was created by positing self-existence on 'things' distinguished by perception or imagination. Wisdom was not itself an ultimate view, nor was it an assertion about an absolute being. Wisdom was the practice (*caryā*) of dissolving the grasping-after-hoped-for-ultimates either in the phenomenal world or the realm of ideas. To know 'emptiness' was to realize emptiness.[47]

Several hundred years after Nāgārjuna's death and the introduction of his thought to China through translations by Kumarajiva (344–413) and the writings of one of Kumarajiva's disciples, Seng-zhao (374–414),[48] the Chan tradition arose, drawing heavily from earlier Mahāyāna formulations of *prajñā*. One historian of Zen writes, 'The chief elements in the doctrine of Transcendental Wisdom [*prajñā*] – negativism, paradox, religious experience in the intuitive cognition, the comprehension of things in their thusness – all flowed from the *Prajñāpāramitā Sūtras* through Nāgārjuna into Zen, embedding themselves deeply in its substance.'[49]

Zen writers often describe *prajñā* as a direct experiencing of things 'just as they are', independent of personal distortion.[50] In such experience, as Shibayama Zenkei writes, 'Everything is revealed as it is. There is no discriminating mind or self-consciousness on the part of the mirror. If something comes, the mirror reflects; if it disappears, the mirror just lets it disappear.'[51] A slightly different way of expressing *prajñā* is to say that this way of experiencing is direct, with no value judgment or conscious distance between the seer and the seen. Contrary to dualistic experience in which one grabs and pulls in objectified things from an idiosyncratic perspective, *prajñā* is said to function through a movement in the opposite direction, in which one is 'ever thoroughly negating the self and becoming the thing itself; becoming the thing itself to act'.[52] One is not cut off from reality here, for as expressed in the current paradigm of physics, 'You are not an observer, you are a participant.'[53] D. T. Suzuki states that

> one who stands against the object ceases to be the one outside that object but transforms himself into the object itself. This identification enables the painter to feel the pulsation of one and the same life animating both him and the object. This is what is meant when it is said that the subject is lost in the object, and that when the artist begins his work it is not he but the object itself that is working, and it is then that his brush, as well as his arm and his fingers, become obedient to the spirit of objects. The object itself makes its own picture. The spirit sees itself as reflected in itself. This is also a case of self-identity.[54]

Historically this has been expressed in the Japanese religious and aesthetic tradition as a 'seeing without a seer', as the act of seeing the 'form of the formless'. And as indicated by the actions of the painter, this 'seeing' is nothing passive or dead. In Suzuki's words:

> The wonder *prajñā* performs is to catch the actor in the midst of his action; he is not made to stop acting in order to be seen as actor. The actor is the acting, and the acting is the actor, and out of this unification or identification *prajñā* is awakened.[55]

Prajñā thus diverges from any sort of trance or unconsciousness, for it is awareness at its sharpest, and an awareness that acts. As expressed in Nishida Kitarō's examples of 'pure experience' in his first major work, *An Inquiry into the Good*, this taut awareness emerges in such activities as an expert mountaineer's ascent of a precipitous cliff or an accomplished musician's performance of a mastered piece of music.[56] Zen scholar Thomas Kasulis offers an example from the world of sports:

> The Zen Buddhist . . . would emphasize the *time* at which the distinction [between the activity of an intentional consciousness and the content toward which the consciousness is directed] can be made: although we can retrospectively look at a previous experience, analyzing its subject and object, that experience, while it was being lived, was not so divided. While it is correct in a certain sense to say that 'I hit the baseball,' for instance, this expression, with its division into subject and object, is the result of a retrospective analysis. At the moment of the original event, there is only an unbroken hitting-of-the-baseball. In fact, as anyone who plays the game knows well enough, the thought of *I* as something that must *hit* the *baseball* is an obstruction to hitting the ball well. Having developed the technical mastery of the swing, the batter best performs by *not* thinking about hitting – that is, not by reflecting on what was learned or on what must be done, but rather by simply being alert. Then, at the moment when the ball is to be hit, one can react spontaneously.[57]

Although these examples are of particular trained activities or arts, Zen attempts to foster this direct, open awareness throughout the range of human activities constituting the 'art of life'.

In the traditional Mahāyāna formulation of the six *pāramitās* (perfections) embodied by a *bodhisattva*,[58] *prajñā* also functions as a discernment of the genesis of suffering. This discernment is an 'emptied' wisdom, in that a *bodhisattva's* viewpoint lies beyond attachment to substantialised 'things'. As the *Vajracchedika* states, if 'Bodhisattvas should have perception of either a dharma, or a no-dharma, they would thereby seize on a self, a being, a soul, or a person'.[59] This way of experiencing, in which a person is seen as devoid of enduring essence (and yet for that reason able to be an individual), is the basis for a clear realisation of how people become trapped in fixated selfhood and how they can break out of that entrapment.

With this character, *prajñā* serves as the basis for *upāya*, skilful means of freeing people from unnecessary suffering, in that *prajñā* enables a *bodhisattva* not only to discern suffering but also to intuit what might be unique and often paradoxical responses. Perhaps

no other Mahāyāna text expresses *upāya* more fully than the
Saddharma-puṇḍarīka (Lotus Sūtra), which includes the famous
parable of the father who lures his children out of a burning house
by telling them that an assortment of carts awaits them outside the
gate. Referring to this action, the historical Buddha reportedly
describes *upāya* to his disciple Sariputra as follows:

> Sariputra! Even as that elder, though with power in body and
> arms, yet does not use it but only by diligent tact resolutely saves
> [his] children from the calamity of the burning house and then
> gives each of them great carts made of precious things, so is it
> with the Tathagata; though he has power and fearlessness, he
> does not use them, but only by his wise tact [*prajñā* and the
> techniques based on it] does he remove and save living creatures
> from the burning house of the triple world . . . .[60]

Zen texts follow suit here by reiterating the importance of this
'tact' as the basis of skilful means to help others awaken. The
ability to discern another person's state of mind and respond to it
on the spot is often attributed to Zen teachers. In the *Linji-lu*, Linji
(J., Rinzai, d. 866) says to his disciples, 'Whoever comes to me, I do
not fail the person: I know exactly where the person comes from.'[61]
From this insight spring immediate Awakening-directed actions,
which may include shouting or striking. This discernment into the
other's situation and the ability to respond to it in creative ways are
the crux of the *bodhisattva's* compassionate activity (J., *bosatsu-gyō*),
which brings this discussion to the next facet of Awakening, compassion (*karuṇā*).

Zen claims that its practice frees people from entanglement in
dualistic subjectivity and, in fostering *prajñā*, brings about an
identification with and greater responsiveness to what was originally seen as the 'other'. This open responsiveness constitutes a
major part of compassion. As one *rōshi* writes, 'The practice of
"being with them" converts the third person, they, it, she, he, into
the first person, I, and we . . . . This is compassion, suffering with
others.'[62]

Sanskrit scholars have translated *karuṇā* as pity and compassion.[63]
Karuṇā is usually expressed in Chinese and Japanese with the
character, *hi* (悲). In Japanese Buddhism, *karuṇā* is often conveyed by
the compound, *jihi*, which literally means *maitrī-karuṇā*, *maitrī* being
the Sanskrit form of the Pali term, *mettā*, translated by T. W.

Rhys-David as love, sympathy, friendliness and active interest in others.[64] One scholar of the *bodhisattva* ideal writes that *karuṇā*

> consists in realising the equality of oneself and others (*par-atma-samata*) and also practising the substitution of others for oneself (*paratma-parivartana*). When a *bodhisattva* cultivates the habit of regarding others as equal to himself, he gets rid of the ideas of 'I and Thou' and 'Mine and Thine.' He learns to feel the joys and sorrows of others like his own, and does not prefer his own happiness to that of others.[65]

In short, *karuṇā* is said to be an unbiased openness to and identification with others and the responsiveness through which one can function skilfully to eradicate that suffering.

Buddhist scriptures distinguish *karuṇā* from ordinary feelings of sadness or pity for another person, arguing that such feelings are usually a product – and support – of fixated subjectivity (the 'ego', as it were) and the emotional energy invested in it. Such feelings may entrench a person more deeply in narrowly self-serving attachments, whereas in contrast, 'True compassion is utterly neutral and is moved by suffering of every sort, not tied to right and wrong, attachment and aversion.'[66] The person expressing compassion is like a highly competent healer. In embodying and expressing compassion one 'must be clear and knowledgeable, not distorted by emotion nor attached by involvement'.[67] This undistorted nonattachment to egocentricity leads to

> a state of complete emotional neutrality on the part of the saint, who extends to all beings an impartial, unattached, universal will-to-their-good; and because his [or her] consciousness is not walled in upon itself nor darkened by any taint of preference, emotion, self-attachment or even mine-thine distinction, it penetrates clearly and cleanly into the minds and hearts of others.[68]

Although *karuṇā* may appear to be a type of radical self-sacrifice for the sake of others, modern interpreters of *karuṇā* have emphasised that part of the initial cultivation and practice of compassion is self-nurturance or 'self-compassion'. Though looking primarily at Theravāda Buddhism, Winston King aptly points out that 'one's first ethical duty is to properly love'[69] oneself, to direct *maitrī-karuṇā* toward oneself. This compassionate regard for oneself is nothing self-indulgent or narcissistic. 'Self-directed metta aims not at the selfish advantagement of one's own interests and desires, but at the destruction of the narrowly personal elements of selfhood and the eradication of greed and hatred.'[70]

In Zen and other forms of Mahāyāna Buddhism, the 'saint' who most embodies wisdom and compassion is the *bodhisattva*.[71] Bodhi derives from the root *budh*, to discern or awaken, and *sattva* from the root *sat*, to be, giving a literal translation of 'being of wisdom'. The term implies a spiritually advanced person, buddha-in-the-making, or heroic warrior[72] who aspires to lead all other sentient beings to Awakening before entering full *nirvāṇa (parinirvāṇa)* himself or herself.[73] This orientation of the *bodhisattva* begins when one 'arouses a mind of aspiration' to help others awaken and makes vows *(praṇidhāna)* to realise this goal. Perhaps the most famous vows in the Mahāyāna are the 48 vows of Dharmakara, as recorded in the *Sukhavātī-vyūha*. Dharmakara vows 'not to obtain the highest perfect knowledge' until all other beings have fully realised the Buddha's teachings and achieved liberation. One of the most commonly recited vows in Zen practice is the Fourfold Great Vow:

> However innumerable sentient beings are,
>   I vow to save them;
> However inexhaustible the binding passions are,
>   I vow to extinguish them;
> However immeasurable the Dharma-teachings are,
>   I vow to learn them;
> However unsurpassable the Buddha-Way is,
>   I vow to attain it.

Using a slightly different English rendering of this vow, Ken Jones writes,

> . . . if delusion is separation and alienation from other beings and if, to the extent we are freed from an egocentric level of consciousness, we experience a greater sense of oneness with them, then we become compassionately at one with their suffering and their afflictions. And at this level of consciousness the notion of self-liberation has become delusive, because there is no longer a sense of separate selfhood from which to be liberated. Liberation thus becomes the liberation of all beings from suffer-

ing; hence the first vow of the aspirant bodhisattva (Buddhist saint) is: 'Beings are innumerable, I vow to free them.'[74]

Certain Mahāyāna texts outline the 'career' of a bodhisattva. It spans a series of stages (bhumis), each involving insights, virtues, or faculties developed through specific practices. Research by Har Dayal led him to conclude that the 'bhumis of the Mahayana are now supposed to be ten in number, but it is almost certain that they were only seven in the beginning.'[75] The Catasahasrika Prajñāpāramitā outlines ten bhumis, in the course of which the bodhisattva cultivates the four brahmavihāras (loving kindness, compassion, sympathetic joy, equanimity), preaches to people, maintains congruence between speech and action, masters Śākyamuni's teachings, practices self-control, uproots various hindrances, eliminates belief in a permanent self, acquires paranormal modes of knowing, preserves aspiration and becomes a buddha.[76] At this point the bodhisattva is fully qualified to lead others to Awakening, even though he or she has been engaged in this endeavor all along.

Most expositions of the path of the bodhisattva stress the practice of six or ten perfections (Skt., pāramitās). The six perfections are dāna (giving), śīla (moral behaviour, precepts), kṣānti (patience), vīrya (vigorous endeavor), dhyāna (concentration) and prajñā (wisdom). To these are sometimes appended four others: upāya (skilful means), praṇidhāna (aspiration, vows), bala (strength) and jñāna (knowledge). The domain of the first perfection, giving, overlaps with that of compassion. Dāna assumes its traditional form in giving gifts to friends and relatives, helping the poor, offering alms to monks,[77] aiding others by teaching the Dharma through preaching and serving as an example, and, in some strands of Buddhism, transferring merit (P., puñña; Skt., puṇya) to others. One scholar writes that karuṇā, as 'an attribute of a perfect Buddha and of a budding bodhisattva, is exhibited, practised and developed chiefly by dāna. It is also intimately associated with the dānapāramitā, though it is also the guiding star of a bodhisattva's entire career.'[78] Śīla is sometimes characterised as 'the control and restraint of kāya (body), vac (speech) and manas (mind)',[79] the three modes of karma. As a perfection of mental, verbal and physical action, śīla moves the practitioner away from ignorance, greed, and hatred and provides a basis for the higher pāramitās of dhyāna and prajñā.[80]

Also important in the relationship between the pāramitās and compassion is the seventh *pāramitā* in the ten-*pāramitā* scheme. As sketched above, 'skilful means' most commonly serves as the English rendering of *upāya*, which derives from a Sanskrit root meaning to use or employ. What the *bodhisattva* employs are ways of giving Śākyamuni's teaching an expression appropriate to the suffering of the 'other'. In fact, some Buddhists regard Buddha's overall teaching as a form of *upāya*; in his detailed study of *upāya*, Michael Pye observes, 'In Mahayana Buddhism the various forms of Buddhist teaching and practice are declared to be provisional means, all skilfully set up by the Buddha for the benefit of the unenlightened.'[81] Using a medical metaphor, Har Dayal writes, 'A *bodhisattva* should always adapt his teaching to the capacity of the audience. He is like a physician, who prescribes different remedies for different diseases and different persons.'[82] In this regard, compassion works hand in hand with *prajñā*, the clear discernment of the situation of the 'patient'.

Some have asserted that the *bodhisattva* ideal is just that, an ideal. Kenneth Inada writes:

> The Bodhisattva, of course is a philosophic myth that depicts the perfected individual who 'delays' his entrance into *nirvāṇa* because he is cognizant of the fact that he and others are related or involved in such a way that there is openness on the one hand and extensiveness on the other. It is the perfect model of social concern and action, somewhat akin to what Western religionists allude to as the spirit of ultimate concern.[83]

In this regard many statements about the *bodhisattva* and his or her compassion may best be seen not as descriptive of actual beings but as fundamentally prescriptive or motivational.[84]

In short, *karuṇā* emerges in Zen Awakening as an openness and responsiveness to others, an ability to enter into their suffering without being entangled in oneself. Further, to suffer with others is to act for them, just as we act to relieve our own suffering. In the words of Thich Nhat Hanh, 'When you understand, you love. And when you love you naturally act in a way that can relieve the suffering of people.'[85] One is now acting compassionately as a *bodhisattva*, leading others beyond suffering to Awakening.[86]

This chapter has offered a preliminary answer to the question, 'What is Zen?' Based in part on the thought of Nāgārjuna, Zen religious life revolves around Awakening and its two main facets, wisdom and compassion. Granting this religious character of Zen, the question now calling for an answer is 'What are the ethical dimensions of Zen life?'

2

Ethical Dimensions of Zen Practice and Philosophy

While recognising the religiously transformative impact of Zen practice and Awakening with its facets of wisdom and compassion, some observers carry doubts about the ethical nature of Zen. These doubts tend to revolve around several aspects of the tradition: the overwhelming emphasis on Awakening as the basis of a truly ethical way of life; the apparent tension between *śūnyatā* and ethics; the stress on immediacy, non-discrimination and suchness; and the espousal of 'transcending good and evil'. Using these three areas of criticism as a catalyst for discussion and as an organisational framework, this chapter considers what Zen Buddhists themselves usually advance as ethical dimensions of Zen practice and its accompanying philosophy.

THE ZEN EMPHASIS ON AWAKENING

Many Zen writers devote their attention to *satori* and the enlightened actions of Zen 'masters'. The tradition often contends that one can first understand Zen, express it and judge other expressions of it only after one has a profound experience of *satori*.[1] This contention suggests that practice yields religious and ethical fruits only upon *satori*.[2] Moreover, depending on how the ethical elements of awakened Zen experience are expounded, the compassionate activity of a *rōshi* – in effect, the Zen version of a *bodhisattva* – may seem worlds removed from the daily life of the 'unawakened'. And in extreme cases, the Zen critique of the human situation suggests that one only taints society and history when grappling with ethical issues prior to Awakening.

Assuming for the sake of argument that Awakening is indeed a distinct event, however, does Zen practice bear ethical fruits only upon Awakening? Or do such fruits emerge on 'this side' of Awakening as well? And if such fruits emerge in the process of

Zen practice, do they extend beyond *personal* transformation and facilitate broader *social* transformation as well? In general, Zen authors have not addressed these questions, primarily because of the focus on monastic attempts to lead people to Awakening and the emphasis on Awakening as the *starting point* of a truly ethical life.

As Zen writers are starting to acknowledge more explicitly,[3] wisdom, compassion and ethical change do not totally elude 'unawakened' practitioners. Practice has a transformative effect from the start, gradually bearing religiously and ethically important fruits, even though the fundamental religious problem may remain unresolved. By clarifying this effect, Zen may begin to shed its appearance of being a tradition for the few, a type of spiritual elitism with a 'trickle-down' ethic.

Zen practice usually influences the practitioner in several ethically significant ways. One striking feature of Zen life is simplicity. When entering a traditional monastery, aspirants reduce their personal possessions to a minimum, retaining only certain bare essentials: a cushion, bed roll, robes, sandals, bowls, chopsticks and toilet articles. In many cases, robes have been made from rags scavenged, sewn together and dyed by novices before ordination. Food and drink are kept simple. Nothing is wasted – possessions are repaired and maintained as long as possible, all food is eaten, the little garbage produced goes to the compost pile, and human 'waste' serves as fertiliser. Words are few, especially during a *sesshin*.[4]

Related to this simplicity is the focused attention with which monks and nuns act around the monastery or, in the contemporary context, a Zen centre. As indicated earlier, the pouring of oneself into the activity at hand is a form of practice. One fringe benefit of this is that the quality of action increases when acts are done with full attention, for one avoids the confusion that may occur when, with thoughts swirling in one's head, one fails to concentrate or scrambles to do several things at once. Many people fill their days with a juggling of activities that often becomes unsettling, ineffective, irresponsible and at times destructive. Hence the aforementioned Zen admonition: 'If you walk, just walk. If you sit, just sit. Don't wobble!'

Zen contends that in this simplicity and attentiveness the practitioner comes to respect each person and object. D. T. Suzuki conceptualises this as culminating in what he calls 'secret virtue'.

It means not to waste natural resources; it means to make full use, economic and moral, of everything that comes your way; it means to treat yourself and the world in the most appreciative and reverential frame of mind. It particularly means practising goodness without any thought of recognition by others. A child is drowning; I get into the water, and the child is saved. That is all there is to be done in the case; what is done is done.[5]

This reverent attitude finds expression in the Zen saying, 'One moment, one encounter' (*ichigo-ichi'e*), which can be expanded, 'Each meeting occurs but once in a lifetime'.

Zen practice also aims to foster a reverent, nonviolent attitude toward other beings in the world. In monasteries and other centres of Zen practice, vegetarianism is nearly universal. Before meals practitioners may chant verses of gratitude for the food nature has provided. Grains of rice are left out for birds and insects – the 'hungry beasts' transmigrating along the 'six ways' (*rokudō*)[6] – and 'pests' co-exist with monks and nuns in monastic compounds.

This attitude is one facet of cultivating what is often termed 'intimacy' with nature. The traditional Zen bond with nature finds expression in the creation and display of ink paintings on natural subjects, the writing of poetry with natural content, flower arrangements in alcoves, birds sweeping in with the breeze through open *zendō*[7] doors, gardens visible from one's cushion, lush vegetable fields on the edges of the compound, and the situating of monasteries amongst mountains and streams. In *kōan* practice the *rōshi* may ask the student to 'realise a flower' or 'realise a butterfly'.[8]

Zen practice also cultivates appreciation of labour through work practice (*samu*) around the monastery.[9] The tradition holds that this engagement in predominantly physical labour as a type of practice originates in the monastic life organised by the fourth and fifth founding teachers (Daoxin (580–651) and Hongren (601–674)) and by Baizhang (J., Hyakujō; 720–814). Baizhang's style of Chan diverged from most forms of Tang Buddhism in China, which relied on lay patronage in the form of food and monetary donations. Coining the maxim, 'A day of no work is a day of no eating', Baizhang is said to have fully appropriated manual work as part of practice and in the process moved Zen monasteries in the direction of self-sufficiency. His ordering of monastic life served as the main prototype for Zen monastic codes over the centuries in China,

Korea and Japan.[10] Even today *samu* occupies a central place in Zen life. Monks or students cook meals, clean their quarters, rake gardens, sweep walks, construct monastery buildings and grow food and vegetables in the monastery's fields. Amongst other things, this emphasis on work as part of the Zen path breaks down distinctions between religious practice and 'productive' work. *Samu* can also serve the community. Discussing a statement by Zen teacher Nanquan (J., Nansen) about desiring to be reborn as a water buffalo so he could serve the lowland farmers who had supported his monastery, D. T. Suzuki sets forth a Zen 'gospel of work, which when translated into modern terminology means to serve others, to work for the general community – and this without grumbling, without theorising, without the compulsion of "ought," or of the categorical imperative, or of an external command invested with the power of punishment'.[11] Suzuki sees *samu* as expressive of a Zen activism, a call to action. He writes, 'Zen just wants us all to work, not for selfish ends but from a great compassionate heart, which comes into operation only when we realise the doctrines of *tathatā* (suchness) and *śūnyatā* (emptiness).'[12]

Long hours of *zazen*, often in the midst of physical and emotional pain, cultivate a high degree of self-discipline and perseverance, even when not assuming the extremely rigorous form of traditional monastic Zen. During a *sesshin*, with minimal sleep and long periods of *zazen*, students usually discover an inner strength that makes it possible to function effectively in the face of adversity, and this fruit of practice is significant for sustained, committed action. This is usually accompanied by deepened composure, a steadiness from which people can act with greater wisdom, creativity, and effectiveness.

Upon making a commitment to Zen practice and entering into this context of simplicity, focused attention, mindful reverence, a respectful attitude toward other things, intimacy with nature, productive work, and self-discipline,[13] the practitioner may 're-ceive the precepts' (*jukai*). The ten primary Zen precepts (*jūjū-kinkai*) are, as phrased by a contemporary *rōshi*,

1. Not killing.
2. Not stealing.
3. Not misusing sex.
4. Not lying.
5. Not giving or taking drugs.

6. Not discussing faults of others.
7. Not praising oneself while abusing others.
8. Not sparing the Dharma assets.
9. Not indulging in anger.
10. Not defaming the Three Treasures.[14]

Zen views these precepts as expressions of how a fully awakened person acts naturally and as ethical guidelines supportive of practice. They also function as a key component of the Zen monastery or centre as a springboard to action:

> Without the precepts as guidelines, Zen Buddhism tends to become a hobby, made to fit needs of the ego. Selflessness, as taught in the Zen center, conflicts with the indulgence that is encouraged by society. The student is drawn back and forth, from outside to within the Zen center, tending to use the center as a sanctuary from the difficulties encountered in the world. In my view, the true Zen Buddhist center is not a mere sanctuary, but a source from which ethically motivated people move outward to engage in the larger community.[15]

Wisdom, compassion, and other ethically significant fruits emerge throughout the process of Zen practice, not simply upon a *satori* experience, and hence *to varying degrees* play a role in the action of all Zen Buddhists, not just the 'fully awakened'. Though a vivid and full acquisition of *prajñā* and *karuṇā* may have to await *satori*, this does not mean that they are not realised at all before then, or that they are the exclusive possession of the awakened few. This gradual religious and ethical cultivation is apt to be overlooked by those of the Rinzai persuasion who emphasize abrupt *satori* as opposed to the more gradual approach of Sōtō Zen with its emphasis on 'just sitting'. Hisamatsu Shin'ichi decried the apparently endless process of *kōan* practice found in *hashigo* Zen,[16] claiming that it often fails to bring about the One Great Death. He describes this pitfall with the metaphor of a polygon and a circle. However many times we may add sides to a polygon, it never becomes a circle; to become a circle, the polygon must undergo an absolute negation (of its 'polygonness'). Although he may be correct in saying that *satori* is *ultimately* the crux of Zen, as an 'unawakened' Zen Buddhist practices, he or she may *to some extent* gradually understand Awakening and embody the two facets of *prajñā* and *karuṇā*, even though Awakening has not yet been fully realised. Metaphorically speaking, an octagon *is* closer to a circle than a triangle is, even though it has not achieved circularity.

ŚŪNYATĀ AND ETHICS

Critics of Zen focus not only on actual practice but also on the philosophical framework of the tradition. To many, *śūnyatā* seems ill-suited as a basis for a system of ethics. It does not offer a God or a divine Will that reveals the good, gives laws, directs events, or persuades people in the direction of greater value; in viewing good and evil as relative, the philosophy of *śūnyatā* postulates no absolute Good; in taking what might be called a trans-rational approach, it does not speak of a practical reason (or natural law) through which moral direction can be found; it takes ordinary moral judgements to be non-substantial and hence tentative, thereby undercutting attempts to establish universally applicable (deontological) rules; with the doctrine of no-self it calls into question the ordinary human 'self' that functions as the locus of ethical agency; and because it is not teleological it does not provide a future-oriented eschatology or a basis for hope in an evolutionary process inherent in the metaphysical nature of things.[17]

On the basis of the discussion of *śūnyatā* in the previous chapter, one can sketch briefly several facets that Zen writers have lifted up as carrying ethical significance.

A. In part *śūnyatā* signifies a thorough negation ('emptying') of entanglement in dualistic subjectivity. One overcomes this entanglement gradually through Zen practice and dramatically by 'dying' the One Great Death. In this emptying, the narrowly selfish concern and the deceit, manipulation, domination and violence that may accompany such entanglement progressively dissolve. Expressed metaphorically, a cause of what people refer to as 'evil' or as unethical action is unearthed. For this reason, Abe Masao and others have likened Zen to the 'underground working of water', in that it eradicates entanglement in dualistic subjectivity as an underlying cause of problems rather than offer a set of actions in response to those problems after they occur. Expressed by yet another metaphor, Zen eradicates the cause of the disease rather than only the symptoms.

B. The dissolving of entanglement in dualistic subjectivity is said to be an emancipation. This dissolution ostensibly frees one up for compassionate action and releases and redirects the energy that was previously invested in bolstering the fixation in that subjectivity. Moreover, in this freedom one can function courageously, for the cowardice and immobility caused by fearful self-preoccupation and the fear of death have been eliminated. As Munan (1603–76) said, 'Die once and then do what you will do.'

C. In this self-emptying, one becomes more open to the world. Given certain connotations of śūnyatā, the term can be rendered 'openness', and as noted above Abe speaks of the 'expanse of Awakening'. That which is tightly barricaded cannot be open, whereas that which is emptied is most open and can be filled by the world. Such openness is a key facet of compassion.

D. As a formulation of relational being, śūnyatā rejects substantialist views of the self, and this rejection appears in such classical Zen texts as the Record of Linji (J., Rinzairoku), where Linji sings the praises of the 'true person without rank'. Substantialist metaphysics usually depict the self as an independent entity to be promoted and affirmed in the exercise of the will, and this may lead to an emphasis on 'making one's mark', 'carving out a future for oneself', 'being all that one can be'. This emphasis proves harmful whenever it traps people in self-preoccupation and fosters destructive forms of competition and when 'doing' is closely linked with 'having' (or 'controlling') and the extent of a person's 'having' (possessions and wealth) becomes the primary criterion for the value of that person.

Expressed positively, the realisation of śūnyatā is simultaneously a realisation of no-self (Skt., anātman; J., muga) in which one discerns that at the deepest level, 'self', experience and world converge in each moment. In existential terms, one cannot exist apart from this world and one's experience of it. In more metaphysical terms, one is constituted by and also influences myriad things other than what one takes oneself to be. On the basis of śūnyatā one discerns society most fundamentally as a network of interdependent events, not as a collection of independent selves. This promotes the recognition that ultimately one's own wellbeing is inseparable from that of others. This aspect of śūnyatā is a crucial stone in the foundation of the bodhisattva ideal set forth in Mahāyāna texts.

E. The transcendence of duality in the realisation of śūnyatā also points to an emptying of the distinction between nirvāṇa and *saṃsāra*. As indicated by the Ten Oxherding Pictures and accompanying verses,[18] in the end the Zen Buddhist 'returns to the marketplace with bliss-bestowing hands', for she now discerns the everyday world (*saṃsāra*) as the realm of Awakening (*nirvāṇa*) and proceeds to work compassionately in it.

F. In awakening to *śūnyatā*, the practitioner is also said to realise that all views are partial and tentative. This leads to a loosening of attachment to preconceptions, categories and theories and by extension to a shift from disdain and prejudice to greater empathy and appreciation. A person becomes less judgemental and more understanding, and at the social level this implies a shift away from the self-righteousness, antagonism, and conflict that arise through attachment to ideology and the collective desire to be right or on the side of Buddha, God or the Emperor.

G. As a shift away from conceptual overlays to immediate experience, the realisation of *śūnyatā* frees people from captivity in the cognitive dichotomies they may rigidly apply to experience, such as mind and body, spirit and flesh, reason and intuition, humans and nature, man and woman, us and them, right and wrong. This, too, promotes flexibility and a greater ability to deal honestly with the gray areas that characterise so much of the ethical realm.

It is important to note here that apparently negative connotations or implications of *śūnyatā* have led many people to believe that Zen is thoroughly iconoclastic and haphazardly spontaneous, rooted in an exhaustive negation that leaves nothing positive. This image of Zen also derives from nineteenth-century views of Buddhism as nihilistic, from episodes in Zen history concerning monks who burnt sutras and commentaries or called on people to 'kill the Buddha, kill the founding teachers', and from the element of negation found in such other Zen teachings as non-discrimination and the One Great Death. But is historical Zen devoid of positive content, of 'goods'? Is Zen purely a stripping away of psychological encumbrances in order to generate a mode of experience with no describable moorings? Does Zen negate *everything*, leaving nothing on which to build a metaphysics or ethic?

A close look at Zen reveals a range of positively valued elements, including the forms and formality of practice, the *rōshi* and his or her understanding, loyalty to the *rōshi*, the sect's lineage, faith in the Zen path, dedication to the monastery or centre, wisdom and compassion, and the *bodhisattva* ideal. Though Zen may talk of an awakened person rejecting the forms of Zen practice, such a denial genuinely occurs only after the person has, so to speak, crossed over to the far shore of Awakening. The boat involved is a 'good' in the practical, expedient sense. Over on the far shore, one leaves the boat rather than carry it around on the shoulders. To use the metaphor of the teachings as a finger pointing to the moon (Awakening), one can become attached to the teachings and other 'goods' (in the sense of *upāya*) and end up taking the finger for the moon. Yet as components of a system of religious transformation, the forms, teachers, attitudes and values are important; without them, the practice and the tradition as a whole may become diluted or degenerate into confusion and shabby imitations of Awakening.[19]

For Zen to become genuinely self-critical, open to further evolution, and socially engaged, it must not muddle claims about there being 'nothing sacred' with simultaneous piety toward Zen personages, lineages, rituals and property. By clarifying, distinguishing and juxtaposing the negative thrust and positively-valued elements of the tradition, Zen can more successfully uncover and criticise blind spots in individuals and institutions. And all along the way Zen needs to *turn toward itself* the eye of *prajñā* that sees through self-attachment, self-deception and self-aggrandisement.

IMMEDIACY, NON-DISCRIMINATION AND SUCHNESS

Many Zen texts and teachers emphasise the immediacy of awakened subjectivity as Zen Buddhists 'live fully in the here-and-now'. This appears to deny reflective consideration of the past or future and any possibility of or value in planned, goal-oriented action over time. This appearance gives rise to the question of whether Zen produces only immediate actions on a small scale which may – or may not – yield valuable social results. Many have asked whether Zen offers any avenue to long-term, large-scale plans of action in response to complex systemic problems. Though a *rōshi* might be able to respond freely, creatively and effectively to a disciple in a *kōan* interview, how, if at all, is the *rōshi* equipped to respond to political policies, economic structures and ways of life supportive of Apartheid or the destruction of rain forests? Zen has yet to elaborate how immediacy relates to consideration of the past and future, to critical reflection and to sustained action over time.[20] When pressed on this issue, Zen Buddhists usually state that 'immediacy' does not indicate that one is stuck in the present moment with no memory of the past and 'no thought for the morrow'. Practice gradually releases the practitioner from entrapment in the restlessly anxious morass of thoughts about the future and past, the mental static – in Zen terminology, 'monkey mind' – that fills lives with unnecessary anxiety and struggle. But this does not mean that *all* thought about past and future ceases. Immediacy indicates a clear and expansive awareness in the present, and what arises in that awareness as content may be memory or anticipation. As practice continues over time, one does recall things or look ahead, yet increasingly one does this only when necessary – without unnecessary obsession – and in calm, focused attention. In more philosophical terms, when Zen speaks of immediacy in the present, it is referring not to the normal objectified present standing apart from past and future in a linear series, but to the awakened Present, which includes past and future – and the normal objectified present – within itself.

Zen discussion of 'non-discrimination' and 'suchness' may seem to imply a metaphysical, perceptual, or valuational uniformity that precludes differences, discrimination or critical appraisal of concrete situations. In his exposition of suchness ('as-it-is-ness'), D. T. Suzuki often contrasts *prajñā* ('*prajñā*-intuition') with the discriminating intellect to such an extent that some of his readers have interpreted Zen to be a thoroughly anti-intellectual or anti-rational system. The following statement may lead the unwary reader to this interpretation.

Buddhists often speak of the 'Great Death,' which means dying to ordinary life, putting an end to the analyzing intellect, or laying aside the idea of the self. Slay, they would say, with one stroke, this meddling intellect, and throw it to the dogs. This is a strong statement, but the idea is plain; it is to transcend the intellect, to go beyond the world of distinctions. For the spiritual world of non-discrimination will never open its door until discriminating mind is destroyed to its foundations. Then only takes place the birth of *prajñā*, the illumination, all-transcending wisdom. *Vijñāna*, that is, the discriminating, self-centered mind, is now enlightened and becomes *prajñā* which will move in its own straight path of non-distinction and non-discrimination.[21]

Further, in outlining the eight 'chief characteristics of satori',[22] Suzuki prefaces his assertion that 'Zen is Suchness – a grand affirmation' with the remarks:

> Though the satori experience is sometimes expressed in negative terms, it is essentially an affirmative attitude toward all things that exist; it accepts them as they come regardless of their moral values. Buddhists call this *kshanti*, 'patience', and more properly 'acceptance', that is, acceptance of things in their suprarelative or transcendental aspect where no dualism of any sort avails.[23]

This type of statement has caused some readers to think that Zen rejects all distinctions and sees everything as the same and equal, whether a breeze or a tornado, a mischievous child or a serial murderer. Insofar as Zen fails to clarify the proper role of distinctions, judgments and decisions, it can hardly be expected to express itself fully in the realm of social ethics, where, inevitably, various factors must be objectified, distinguished, analysed and weighed as one formulates responses to issues at hand.

The tradition needs to clarify how seeing things in their suchness is neither a monistic 'unity experience' in which all distinctions disappear nor an advanced stage of ethical relativism. Though an 'affirmative attitude' and realisation of an 'aspect where no dualism of whatever sort avails' is crucial, Zen claims it does not stop there. Abe Masao stresses that the affirmation of things in their suchness is 'not an uncritical affirmation of the given situation. On the contrary, it is a great and absolute affirmation beyond – and thus not excluding – any critical, objective, and analytical distinction.'[24]

More specifically, suchness involves two aspects: equality and difference. In that all things (events) lack independent existence, are constituted by the process of dependent co-arising (one sense of *śūnyatā*), possess uniqueness as focal points of that process, and exist 'just as they are', they are equal. One might say that all things are the same or equal in their 'mode of being': they all arise 'just as they are' through complex interaction with each other, and they all can be experienced – Zen claims – 'just as they are' in their shared givenness or 'presencing' (*genjōkōan*). Yet while their *mode* of being is the *same*, the *content* or concrete particularly of each thing is *different*. No two people are alike, for each person is affected by a unique set of conditioning factors. Or, more precisely, all things affect other things, though to differing degrees. A conditioning factor may have a major influence on one thing while having only a minor influence on another, usually as a function of proximity in time or space. Because each person (or thing) is constituted by a particular set of factors – including genes, early experiences, diet, acquaintances, climate, culture, etc. – each is unique. And because new combinations of factors are continuously emerging from the infinite reaches of dependent co-arising, each thing is novel (to varying degrees) in each moment. Thus, all things *equally* emerge just as they are through dependent co-arising, but each thing is *different* from all others.

In more experiential terms, suchness is similar to what is being referred to when, for example, I say about an idiosyncratic action of my cat, 'Oh, Rusty is just being Rusty', or, 'That's Rusty for you'. This may be deepened when I happen to experience my cat with the kind of vivid immediacy that leads to statements like 'I had never before looked at Rusty in that way. I feel like I truly saw her for the first time. She was so beautiful, so precious. And yet, it was just my old cat, sitting there in the sun.' Though such exclamations may cause people to wonder what has 'gotten into' me, from my perspective the world suddenly abounds with beauty and wonder. These vivid experiences that are analogous to the realisation of suchness leave us with an enhanced appreciation of the 'little' things in life – which in these moments may be realised as 'great' things – and an enhanced sense of belonging to the world, to a larger reality of which everything is part.

Given this meaning of suchness, then, Zen would regard a mischievous child and a serial murderer as arising in the same way – 'just as they are' through interrelationship – while realising that their 'content' is quite different. Further, although they are equally products of dependent co-arising, they will affect me to differing degrees. If I live in the neighbourhood with the young rascal, I will be affected more by that child – when, for example, she knocks over my trash cans – than by the serial murderer creating tragedy in another town. This may all change, of course, if the murderer drifts into my town and targets me or my neighbourhood. Likewise, I affect my neighbour much more than I affect workers in Soweto, though my actions do affect Africans as I work, shop, vote, or travel in certain ways.[25]

By extension, although *prajñā* is often described in terms of non-discrimination and sameness, most fundamentally it constitutes a way of experiencing things in their equality *and* difference. *Prajñā* is the ability to embrace the other through direct experience prior to any thought or awareness of self as opposed to other. Zen claims that *prajñā* is the ability to *merge* with the other without the least separation of subject and object. But one does not stop there, for one then emerges from that unobjectifiable unity and sees the other as an 'other', discriminating and reflecting as necessary, though not losing awareness of the not-two-ness of the merging. In other words, I experience myself and the other non-dualistically: *not one* and *not two*. I am fully me and you are fully you, and yet at the same time we are inseparable from each other and able to be who we are because of the myriad 'others' in our world. *Prajñā* is the experiential dimension of *śūnyatā* and suchness; it is a type of wisdom, insight, or discernment issuing forth from the existential – not just intellectual – realisation that reality is neither monistic nor atomistic but dynamically non-dual, relational and organismic.[26]

Through *prajñā* as this mode of experience, the other is seen increasingly 'as it is', for practice cultivates immediate experience prior to reflective conceptual overlays on the other and hence increasingly reduces distortion due to biased perception and value judgements. One discerns the uniqueness and concrete particularity of things in historical time and space. Though some of his statements imply a contrary stand, Suzuki writes, '*Prajñā*'s all-illuminating light . . . does not obliterate distinctions but will make them stand out more boldly and clearly in their spiritual significance . . . .'[27]

Expressed in more technical Buddhist language, by virtue of the 'not-two' aspect of non-dual *prajñā*, one achieves an experiential unity with other things in the world, realised through the dissolution of fixated subjectivity and of the distance and distinctions usually created and valued by that subjectivity; and by virtue of the 'not-one' aspect of *prajñā*, one can discern the myriad components of reality in their particularity in complex, concrete contexts.[28] One realises the inseparability of these two aspects by awakening to *śūnyatā*, the dynamism in which specific parts of reality interrelate, being neither identical (as in monism) nor essentially separate (dualism and atomism).

TRANSCENDING GOOD AND EVIL

In discussions of non-discrimination and suchness, Zen Buddhists often exhort practitioners to disentangle themselves from dualistic thinking and its distinctions between good and evil, right and wrong. One of the classic expressions of this is Huineng's query, 'Without thinking of good and evil, what is your Original Face before your parents were born?' Like many religious traditions, Zen considers the realm of religious liberation to surpass the ethical realm. In promoting its soteriological aims by emphasising the need to 'transcend' distinctions between good and evil, Zen often gives the impression that one leaves such distinctions in the dust, never to enter again into consideration of what might be good or evil. In short, the tradition has yet to articulate sufficiently how one returns to 'good' and 'evil' and regrasps the realm of ethics.

Some recent Zen Buddhists have asserted that Zen talk of 'transcending' good and evil does not indicate a *permanent* negation of the ethical realm and distinctions between good and evil, for even though the practitioner in a certain sense does move beyond the ethical realm, he or she ultimately 'returns' to it. As a religious system, Zen functions to overcome alienation by promoting a realisation of the seamless whole of reality – a network of interdependent events – which eludes the grasp of dualistic subjectivity and its accompanying dichotomies or projected boundaries: us and them, mind and body, humans and nature, right and wrong, good and evil. Given that the ordinary ethical realm revolves around certain of these dichotomies, it is transcended when practice leads one beyond dualistic subjectivity to Awakening prior to the separation of subject and object and prior to dichotomies. It is primarily in this sense that Zen 'transcends' good and evil.

Zen goes beyond the ethical realm in one other respect. The mode of experience opened up in Zen practice differs from reflective consciousness, which is the ordinary locus of ethical agency and the basis on which we make distinctions, judge situations and act.[29] In promoting a shift to non-dualistic experiencing, Zen practice requires a negation of this ethical agency rather than positive efforts by the agent to achieve greater moral purity or sanctity. For this reason Zen usually argues that Awakening is a negation that can occur in any place, time, or situation, not a state to be reached through moral action or personal efforts in a gradual purificatory process leading from an impure or immoral state to a pure or moral state. According to traditional Zen, such moral action or efforts are of no avail, for the very agent behind them constitutes the central problem. Of course, most people who experience *satori* have spent many years in Zen training, but classical Zen texts usually portray *satori* as occurring abruptly upon the 'death' of the self.

Yet as indicated before, Zen does not advocate a one-way journey of self-dissolution, formlessness, unity or no-good-or-evil, for Zen argues that in *true* Awakening, the practitioner immediately returns to the thinking self, form, plurality and distinctions, though no longer stuck in dualism. What does this process involve?

Abe claims that 'all dualism or conceptual distinction is reconstructed in the realisation of Emptiness without any possibility of clinging to distinction'.[30] Distinctions between good and evil are now seen as 'empty'; they are not based on something essentially or independently good or evil. Good and evil are interdependent, shifting concepts that do not possess any independent status. In one Buddhologist's words:

> The moral values of good, evil, and neutral do not exist in themselves or for themselves with any independent metaphysical status, because they are nothing more than the temporary configurations consequent upon infinitely complex interactions of conditions.[31]

In fairly poetical terms, Huineng says, 'Although you see . . . evil and good . . . you must not throw them aside, nor must you cling to them, nor must you be stained by them, but you must regard them as being just like the empty sky.'[32] To attain this way of seeing one opens the eye of *prajñā* which no longer substantialises the pragmatic, conventional concepts of 'good' and 'evil', which recognises that good and evil are relational and hence 'empty' of independent existence. In short, although distinctions must be broken through to open up Awakening, they are said to be reestablished in their proper place: as pragmatically useful distinctions rather than unchanging, metaphysically grounded essences.[33]

This 'emptying' and regrasping of distinctions does not lead to chaos. Evaluating Dōgen's recognition of the centrality of emptiness, Hee-Jin Kim writes that 'this recognition does not lend itself to moral relativism or anarchism as far as Dōgen is concerned, because his concern is how to live relativity without falling into the trap of relativism, or how to realise absolute freedom and purity amid relationality.'[34] A. D. Brear writes,

> Before enlightenment, behavior is seen as good or bad, interpreted absolutely; after enlightenment, behavior is seen to be neither good nor bad absolutely, but still so relatively. 'Good' actions, rather than 'bad' continue to be performed, but their nature is truly seen – they are merely 'actions,' without qualities of goodness or badness.[35]

The Zen transcendence of good and evil, then, does not indicate a *permanent* rejection of morality or *absolute* dissolution of the distinction between good and evil. For Zen, 'The problem is how to save morality from legalism, conformism and moralism so as to attain authenticity, freedom and purity without retreating from moral involvement.'[36] Zen is hence not antinomian or amoral, despite what many observers, especially Confucians, have claimed over the centuries.

In fact, Zen may even be compatible with certain facets of Confucianism.[37] In discussing such terms as 'no-mind' and 'non-abiding', Charles Wei-hsün Fu writes:

> In reality, all these terms are used to point to the non-duality of the Buddha-nature or One-mind (*ekacitta*), which is totally free from the duality of right/wrong, good/evil, etc., in the mundane (relative) sense. It does not follow from this that the authentic Zen Buddhists would not engage themselves in everyday moral practice. On the contrary, they would rather think that only by means of breaking off the dualistic shackles constructed by the ignorant mind is one able to work real wonders in handling human affairs. They could even say that the real Zen mind of nonabiding is no more than the Mencian moral mind transcended, not denied.[38]

Zen talk of overcoming good and evil thus signifies several things. First, Zen starts with the subjectivity that operates *primarily* in terms of the self–other split and sets up things in the world as objects of attraction or aversion, as good or evil. To liberate oneself from this subjectivity and the suffering it causes, and to enable oneself to function freely to eradicate 'evil' without being hindered by certain forms of self-attachment, one must move beyond discriminating consciousness and its distinctions, including the distinction between good and evil. Second, in breaking beyond such consciousness to non-distinction, one awakens to the larger context of existence which has no inherent good or evil and which is will-less and spontaneous, but one does not linger there: one reemerges as a 'self', as subjectivity able to reflect and discriminate, yet grounded in the realisation of the larger matrix. Third, one gains an understanding of normal distinctions between good and evil and right and wrong as pragmatically important though not indicative of essences.[39]

By virtue of the self-emptying in this process and the accompanying ability to see reality more clearly when one 'returns' to good and evil, one is less apt to apply labels rigidly to people or events, which implies less self-righteousness and condemnation of others. And given the accompanying release from narrow self-centredness, one can move critically away from certain arbitrary or socially determined delineations of good or evil that do not support emancipation in its various senses; one can begin to rid oneself of destructive bias, whether personal, ethnic, class, national, or anthropocentric.

To this point the discussion has been largely theoretical and ahistorical, leaving unanswered the questions of whether Zen Buddhists historically have accepted, changed, or rejected specific systems of conventional morality in their 'return' to good and evil, and whether 'returned' Zen Buddhists have offered alternative, Zen-based formulations of what might be good for individuals or society. Examination of specific ethical reflection by renowned Zen figures and their actual socio-political stances in Japanese history provides an initial answer to these questions.

3

Ethical and Political Stances in Japanese Zen History

Zen writers have recently started to highlight ethical elements in Zen practice and philosophy, but what has been the actual sociopolitical role of the tradition in Japanese history? What actual social stances have Zen practice and philosophy generated in the Japanese cultural context? Given that critics have pointed to the relationship between Zen and ruling powers as ethically problematical, discussion of Zen and ethics requires an answer to these questions. To determine the actual ethical stances 'awakened' Zen Buddhists have taken in the past, this chapter provides an overview of the history of Zen in Japan, focusing on ethical reflection[1] by prominent Zen figures.

Although the monk Dōshō (628–670) introduced *zazen* to Japan and the great Tendai Buddhist priest Saichō (Dengyō Daishi; 767–822) studied it, the individuals usually regarded as pioneers of Japanese Zen are Myōan Eisai (1141–1215)[2] and Dōgen Kigen (1200–1253), who introduced the Rinzai (Linji) and Sōtō (Caodong) strands of the tradition.

Originally a Tendai monk trained at Miidera and Enryakuji, Eisai introduced Rinzai Zen to Japan in 1191 upon his return from the second of two trips to Song China. Central to his introduction of Zen was an emphasis on precepts. While a monk at Enryakuji on Mt. Hiei Eisai received Tendai precepts, the *endonkai* (complete and fundamental precepts), which were praised as 'the wondrous precepts permeating the true and the provisional' (*shinzoku-ikkan-myōkai*).[3] These precepts included '*bodhisattva* precepts'[4] but not the 'precepts of the lesser vehicle' (*shojōkai*), the Theravāda precepts laid out in the *Vinaya Pitaka*. While studying in China under Xuan Huaichang (J., Koan Eshō; n.d.), a Zen master in the Huanglong (J., Ōryō) lineage of Rinzai Zen, Eisai came to realise the importance of both the *vinaya* precepts and the *bodhisattva* precepts of

51

the Mahāyāna. As Martin Collcutt writes, 'Hsu-an [Xuan] . . . stressed the importance of the *Vinaya* and insisted that Eisai, before proceeding with his studies of Ch'an, should formally profess both the Mahayana *bodhisattva* precepts and the Hinayana precepts.'[5]

Upon his return from China Eisai echoed his teacher in advocating that the study of Zen must be preceded by the observance of precepts. In Kyushu and then in Kyoto he made this case largely in opposition to the monastic laxity of the time (especially concerning prohibitions about alcohol and eating after noon) and the increasingly popular notion that in this final period of the teaching (*mappō*)[6] observance of precepts and monastic discipline cannot be pursued successfully by struggling humans, who require the compassionate power of Amida to grant them rebirth in the Pure Land, where true practice and realisation are possible. As Heinrich Dumoulin observes, 'Eisai's determination to bring about reform was an important factor in his turn to Zen Buddhism, convinced as he was that the renewal of Buddhism in Japan would have to rest on a strict observance of rules and precepts (J., *kairitsu*).'[7] And as Akamatsu Toshihide writes, 'in arguing that the observance of precepts comes first, Eisai maintained fixed standards. In this connection, Japanese monastic Buddhism came to develop in the 13th century around the pivot of transmitted Zen.'[8]

While preaching the importance of precepts on his travels through Kyushu, Eisai encountered opposition from the Tendai monk Roben there and from the Enryakuji monastery[9] on Mt. Hiei overlooking Kyoto. In 1194, Tendai monks pressured the court to ban the 'Daruma School', as Zen was widely known then.[10] In response to Enryakuji pressure, Eisai began to formulate several arguments: that Saichō himself realised the importance of Zen meditation; that Rinzai Zen conveys the essence of Buddhism; and that Zen is based on and inseparable from the precepts.

These arguments took their strongest form around 1198, the year Eisai completed his *Kōzen-gokoku-ron* (Treatise on the Propagation of Zen for the Protection of the Realm) after having moved to Kyoto.[11] Eisai detailed the importance of precepts and outlined the relationship between the 'Sovereign's Law' or secular law (*ōbō*) and the Buddha's Law or the Dharma (*buppō*). He quoted the Song monastic code, *Chanyuan qinggui* (J., *Zen'onshingi*; 1103):[12] 'For the practice of Zen and investigation of the Way, precepts and rules [*kairitsu*; Skt., *śīla-vinaya*] come first – without taking leave of offenses and avoiding prohibited actions, how can one become a buddha and act like the patriarchs?'[13]

This argument served as a response not only to Enryakuji criticisms of Zen but also to Eisai's contemporary, Dainichi Nōnin. Eisai criticised Nōnin in the 'Gateway of Resolving the Doubts of Worldly People' (*Sejin-ketsugi-mon*) section of *Kōzen-gokokuron*, where he denounced the view that because fundamentally there are no binding passions (J., *bonnō*) but only enlightened wisdom (J. *bodai*), people do not need to practice – all they need to do is to 'eat when hungry and lie down when tired'. Eisai leveled his criticism: 'This [view] is of the sort that does not include our not doing evil. What are referred to in the holy teachings as false views are like this. You should not talk with or sit together with such people; you ought to avoid them by the distance of a two-thousand-day walk.'[14]

This advocacy of closely observing precepts emerged from Eisai's conviction that precepts are the foundation of Zen life, that Zen is a true expression of the Dharma, and that the Dharma parallels and supports secular law. From this perspective, he introduced Rinzai Zen as in part a support for the political realm, and this approach is reflected in the title his major work: 'The Propagation of Zen for the Protection of the Realm'.

Like Eisai, Dōgen regarded the ethic embodied in precepts and monastic codes as a central component of the Zen he introduced. In his systematic study of Dōgen, Hee-Jin Kim asserts, 'Dōgen is vehemently opposed to a popular interpretation of Buddhist ethics as "beyond good and evil."'[15] Dōgen admonished his disciples to 'discard the inferior and adopt the superior – relentlessly pushing them towards moral and spiritual excellence'.[16] From Dōgen's perspective, the path to this excellence lies in the pursuit of regulated monastic life, especially on the basis of precepts and monastic codes. His treatment of precepts, found in such fascicles of the *Shōbō-genzō* as '*Jukai*' (receiving the precepts), revolved around the sixteen *bodhisattva* precepts his monks received. These precepts are (1) faith in Buddha, (2) faith in the Dharma, (3) faith in the Sangha, (4) to eradicate all evils, (5) to exert oneself for all things that are good, (6) to liberate all sentient beings, and the ten major Zen precepts.[17]

Dōgen grants these precepts greater specificity by formulating guidelines covering the minutiae of monastic life. As Martin Collcutt points out, 'Of the 90 or more chapters of the *Shōbō-genzō*,

nearly a third are devoted wholly or in part to the detailed regula-
tion of such everyday monastic activities as meditation, prayer,
study, sleep, dress, the preparation and taking of meals and
bathing and purification.'[18] The end-product of this analysis was a
set of monastic rules codified in the *Eihei shingi* (Eihei Code).[19]

Dōgen's precepts and monastic rules provided an organised
framework for the smooth performance of monastic life. Yet there
was a deeper dimension as well. Paralleling his view of practice
and attainment, Dōgen saw observance of precepts and other
guidelines not merely as a means to enlightenment but more
importantly as an expression of original awakening, of Buddha-
nature or the right Dharma (*shōbō*). As he writes in the '*Senmen*'
(literally, 'face washing') fascicle of *Shōbō-genzō*, 'All these actions
express the right Dharma of the Buddhas and the Patriarchs of the
three eras.'[20] Just as zazen is an expression of one's innate 'Original
Awakening' or Buddha-nature, actions based on the precepts
express – rather than lead to – Awakening. Hee-jin Kim writes,
'Scrupulous instructions, exhortations and admonitions with respect to rules, manners, virtues and behavior, are not codes that
bind the monastic's outward movements, but are ritualised expressions and activities of Buddha-nature and absolute nothingness.'[21] Kim also writes, 'Purification is not an attempt to be
liberated from pollutions, sins, or guilts, whether physical, moral,
or spiritual, but the self-affirmation of original purity or emptiness
undefiled by dualism.'[22]

Setting aside the question of what specific type of observance –
mechanical, wholehearted, composed, etc. – truly expresses
'Buddha-nature', one might ask whether the ethic Dōgen offers
serves as little more than a prop to monastic Zen practice, as a
narrow situational ethic. Insofar as one of the *bodhisattva* precepts
concerns exerting oneself for that which is good, what exactly is
good? A possible answer lies in the fascicle of the *Shōbō-genzō*
entitled '*Shoaku makusa*' (not to do evil), which is the first line of the
Shichi-butsu-tsūkai-ge (The Song of the Precepts Preached by the
Seven Buddhas).[23] In his study of this fascicle, Takahashi Masanobu asserts that Dōgen sees the practice of 'refraining from evil
and doing good' (J., *shiaku-shūzen*) as central to Zen life.

> Buddhism would lose its truth, he argues, if *shiaku-shūzen* were
> not emphasised as its essential precept. *Shikan-taza*, if it had
> nothing to do with the deeds of good and evil, would become a

ritual *zazen* not a part of Buddhism but only a type of mental exercise. Of course *zazen* as a way of controlling and heightening as well as transcending the mental faculties is not categorically denied, but without ethical underpinnings it is incomplete.[24]

Remaining here is the issue of what is good or evil in a general sense. Takahashi writes, 'The first question is that of a standard by which we should decide what is good and what is evil. Dōgen found it difficult to decide such a problem absolutely with only public morality as a norm and ended up saying that "the standard of good and evil is undefinable."'[25] Takahashi does, however, regard Dōgen as going at least one small step further. 'Dōgen seems to insist that there is no way to judge good and evil except according to one's own discernment, which involves consulting and weighing the opinions and moral teachings of others.'[26]

Yet this still fails to offer an explicit concrete formulation of the 'good'. One can turn, however, to Dōgen's writings, including the *Zuimonki*, to gain at least a general sense of what type of 'good' emerges from the values conveyed in his approach. Dōgen extended the notion of filial piety to include all sentient beings, and he emphasised simplicity, detachment from self-preoccupation, and the great aspiration to serve and bring to Awakening all other sentient beings. In the '*Raihai tokuzui*' (Attaining the Marrow through Worship) fascicle of the *Shōbō-genzō* he points out that nuns have achieved enlightenment and argues that Zen surpasses distinctions between women and men and laypeople and monks or nuns.[27] Though in his later years Dōgen increasingly cloistered himself with his monks at Eiheiji, his willingness to assist others is said to have surpassed distinctions of gender and class. 'Just as he himself aspired to what was highest, what he prized most in his followers was the quality of their efforts, which he found to cut across the lines of social class. The circle of disciples that formed around Dōgen included high class and low, young and old, men and women, laity and monks.'[28] Several Buddhist teachers and scholars have recently begun to elaborate on the ethical implications in Dōgen's thought. In English, Robert Aitken and Francis Dojun Cook have offered provocative discussions of the concrete ethical ramifications of Dōgen's expression of Zen, partially in relation to contemporary issues.[29]

Needless to say, Eisai's and Dōgen's reflection did not occur in a vacuum. As indicated before, Eisai's treatment of precepts was not divorced from society and politics. He drew parallels between Buddhist precepts and the laws and regulations in the *ritsuryō* system of administration.[30] Precepts and codes guide monastic life just as laws govern society. Moreover, they complement each other, with the monastic Zen tradition and its magical formulae[31] providing security for the state while the state protects and patronises Zen. Along these lines Eisai argued in the *Kōzen-gokoku-ron* that the relationship between Zen and the state is such that the sovereign's (secular) law (*ōbō*) is the lord of the Buddha-Dharma (*buppō*) and the Buddha-Dharma is the consummate treasure (*shihō*) of the state. This relationship between Buddhism and the state was nothing new. Many earlier Buddhists had solicited patronage from those in power and in return performed ceremonies for the protection of the state or its rulers. Temples had opened their gates to members of the imperial family who decided – or were impelled – to renounce the secular realm of court politics; these temples carried a special designation (*monzeki*) and they benefitted greatly from the imperial connection. Certain monasteries had exerted an even more direct influence on politics. Notorious in this regard were the warrior-monks of Kōfukuji in Nara and Enryakuji on Mt. Hiei. With military prowess, major monasteries had been ready and willing to defend their interests in land holdings, moneylending, trade guilds, pawnshops and other commercial interests.[32]

Eisai's *Kōzen-gokoku-ron* should not, however, be seen as simply a call for Buddhist support of the state. Rather, many scholars contend that the text's primary purpose was protection of the Rinzai tradition Eisai was in the process of introducing and revitalisation of precepts and monastic codes as the cornerstone of a reformed Japanese Buddhism.

In conjunction with the writing of his treatise, Eisai solicited the patronage of the ruling Minamoto and Hōjō families. Following the death of Minamoto Yoritomo (1147–1199), the warrior who established the Kamakura government, his widow, Hōjō Masako (1157–1225), designated Eisai the founder of Jufukji, a monastery in Kamakura. Yoritomo's successor, Minamoto Yoriie (1182–1204), provided land and funds for the construction of Eisai's Tendai-affiliated monastery, Kenninji in Kyoto. While serving as abbot there, Eisai wrote his *Kissa-yōjōki* (1214; dated 1211 by Dumoulin), a treatise on the medicinal properties of tea, and sent a copy to the third Minamoto *shōgun*, Sanetomo (1192–1219), who was ill at the time.[33] Again, in appealing to secular power, he was following a pattern set long before the introduction of Zen.

Like Eisai, Dōgen concerned himself with the relationship between Buddhism and the state. After returning from China in 1227 convinced of the centrality of *zazen*, Dōgen wrote the *Fukan-zazengi*, which heralded a break from his Tendai background with its eclectic approach to religious practice. This caused monks on Mt. Hiei to exert pressure on Kenninji, at which Dōgen was residing. In response, Dōgen moved to southern Kyoto and built Koshōji; while residing there for over a decade he attracted followers from more established Buddhist sects in the capital area.[34] This drew fire from leaders of those sects. In the midst of this pressure, Dōgen submitted to Emperor Go-Saga a treatise entitled *Gokoku-shōbōgi* (Principles of the True Dharma for the Protection of the Realm) 'in an attempt to justify his teaching and defend his community'.[35]

Although he, too, wrote a treatise about Zen and the state, Dōgen apparently created a relationship with the ruling elite that diverged from Eisai's. In 1243 Dōgen retreated from Kyoto to Echizen, built the great Eiheiji monastic complex and while there resisted the overtures of the Kamakura government. He reportedly turned down gifts from the warrior-rulers in Kamakura and invitations to visit them there. After several years of declining invitations, Dōgen finally accepted one from *shōgun* Hōjō Tokiyori and spent the winter of 1247–1248 at Tokiyori's residence in Kamakura.

In conjunction with his treatise on protecting the realm, this fact indicates that although Dōgen was committed to monasticism, he was not as aloof from the politics and social values of his day as Sōtō Zen Buddhists have made him out to be. In fact, his writings include statements about elders, authority, hierarchy and respect. For example, in the '*Shōji*' (living–dying) fascicle of the *Shōbō-genzō* he applauds 'respecting those over you and pitying those below you, without any detesting or desiring, worrying or lamentation . . . .'[36] In the Japanese cultural context, this amalgamation of Confucian and Buddhist virtues seems to indicate the advocacy of accepting the hierarchical status quo.

Through the efforts of Eisai and Dōgen, Zen received patronage from the Kyoto aristocracy, members of the imperial family and, most importantly, the newly emergent warrior-rulers in Kamakura. As mentioned before, the Minamoto and Hōjō warrior families offered patronage to Eisai and Dōgen, and this established a pattern that lasted through the Kamakura period (1185–1333) and into the subsequent Muromachi period (1333–1573).

The ruling warriors in Kamakura patronised both Japanese monks and Chinese immigrant teachers who could transmit the flowering Song artistic traditions of the time. Hōjō Tokiyori, the first Hōjō shogun to follow the Minamoto line, installed Lanxi Daolong (J., Rankei Dōryū) as first abbot of Kenchōji (founded in 1253). The next shogun, Hōjō Tokimune (1251–1284), built Engakuji (1284) for Wuxue Zuyuan (J., Mugaku Sogen). Many of these Zen teachers from China were quite strict, basing their monasteries in Japan on Song models. Lanxi's Zen centred around meditation and *kōans* in monasteries ordered by strict observance of monastic regulations.[37] A key event in this growing connection between Zen and the warrior class occurred when Tokimune went to Engakuji to confer with Zuyuan about the Mongolian fleet that was about to attack Japan. Tokimune exclaimed to the abbot, 'The greatest event of my life is at last here.' Zuyuan asked in response, 'How would you face it?' Expressing the awakened shout of Linji, Tokimune replied, 'Kah!' Approving of this, Zuyuan said, 'Truly a lion's child roars like a lion.'[38]

A number of factors account for this patronage: the learning and vigor of the monks, respect for Zen discipline, contact with Song culture, possible use of Zen to offset the power of earlier Buddhist sects and the warriors' need for 'cultural credentials' in competition with aristocratic Heian culture.[39] Constantly faced with the prospect of battle, some warriors were also drawn to the rigorous training in Zen, the martial benefits of the sharp attention ('mirror mind') cultivated in Zen practice, and Zen resolution of the fear of death.

The prominent Rinzai monasteries built through the support of warrior-rulers came to be organised in the *gozan* or 'five mountain' classification scheme. This encompassed five main monasteries in Kamakura and five in Kyoto. The list of the monasteries in the ten 'mountains' changed periodically through the Kamakura and Muromachi periods, and at times Nanzenji in Kyoto was situated above the ten. Ranked below these main Zen monasteries were *jissetsu* ('ten temples') and *shozan* ('various mountains'). The *gozan* monasteries started to play an important religious, aesthetic, economic and political role in the late Kamakura period.

As Martin Collcutt outlines in his work on the *gozan* system, leaders of the *gozan* monasteries were usually quite supportive of the political status quo. Though Lanxi criticised scholarship and literature, he followed other Song Zen teachers in equating the observance of the laws of the land with observance of religious laws.[40] When Japan faced Mongol invasions in the late twelfth century, *gozan* monasteries in Kamakura and Kyoto offered prayers and performed ceremonies for the protection of the country.[41]

The importance of *gozan* monasteries continued to grow in the Muromachi period, in part through patronage by Ashikaga Takauji, the warrior who moved the center of government back to Kyoto in 1336. Without doubt, the key monk in the Zen-Ashikaga connection was Musō Soseki (1275–1351). In addition to being a master garden architect and central figure in 'five-mountain literature' (*gozan bungaku*), Musō served as abbot of Tenryūji, the temple Takauji erected in memory of Emperor Go-Daigo.

Like Eisai and Dōgen, Musō Soseki worked to guide the ethical life and practice of Zen monks in the several monasteries he presided over during his career. He wrote the 'Rinsenji Code', which covers such areas of monastic life as *zazen*, ceremonies, precepts, leaves of absence, the settlement of disputes, the spatial layout of monastic buildings, bureaucratic organisation, roles of the members of the monastic community, and other rules.[42] More than Eisai and Dōgen, however, Musō was deeply involved in the politics and economics of the day.

First, he was instrumental in getting the Ashikaga shogunate to establish 66 regional 'temples for the peace of the realm' (*ankokuji*) and 'pagodas for the Buddha's favor' (*rishōtō*; translated by Dumoulin as 'pagodas for the welfare of sentient beings'). Ostensibly these structures served as memorials for those who had died in the struggle between Emperor Go-Daigo, Musō's early patron, and the Hōjō shogunate during the Genkō era (1331–1333).[43] Recent scholarship has indicated that the Ashikagas intended for them to serve as fortifications and surveillance centres and thereby strengthen their hold on outlying areas of Japan.[44] Through such activities, Musō and his fellow monks played a supporting role in a dictatorial political system. As Dumoulin writes:

> The shogun made ample use of the *gozan* monks for their political purposes. Highly educated and with excellent social skills, the monks were ideally suited for diplomatic missions, and with their popular and highly respected spiritual image they

were effective means for quelling unruly elements among the populace.[45]

Second, Musō and other *gozan* monks first introduced Song Neo-Confucianism to Japan, and as a result Zen monasteries often functioned as centres of Neo-Confucian studies. Dumoulin writes:

> It was the Zen monks of the Kamakura and Muromachi periods who brought back from the mother country of China a large body of Confucian ideas and literature, which the monks then propagated staunchly . . . . For a long time, there was such a symbiosis between Zen and Confucianism that anyone interested in pursuing Confucian studies would go to a Zen monastery to study.[46]

The emperor Hanazono (reigned 1308–1317) combined study of Zen and Confucianism.[47] Daisetsu Suzuki claims that the following emperor, Go-Daigo (reigned 1318–1339), was inspired to challenge the power of the Kamakura government by his study – with the guidance of Zen monks – of the great Song Neo-Confucianist Zhuxi's history of China.[48] Later, Musō's disciple Gidō Shūshin (1325–1388) lectured to an emperor on Confucianism.[49] Another *gozan* monk, Keian Genju (1427–1508) taught Neo-Confucian philosophy to Shimazu feudal lords in Satsuma (in present-day Kyushu) soon after his return to Japan from China in 1473, and later he started a school of Chinese studies there.[50] This symbiosis occurred in other provinces, and in some cases pre-existing academies were revitalised by the Zen dissemination of Confucian learning, as was the case with the Ashikaga Gakkō.[51] This dissemination was not directed only at the elite. 'Buddhist priests, mainly Zen monks, conducted their temple schools and cared for the simple people, teaching their children to read and write and explaining for all the principles of Confucian ethics.'[52] This participation in Confucian educational activities contributed to the rise of Confucianism as the reigning political philosophy of the day, especially in the Tokugawa period (1600–1867) when it became the ideology behind Tokugawa control over Japan.

Third, Musō played a key economic role by working with the Ashikaga shoguns to send merchant ships to China. The first voyage was undertaken in 1342, ostensibly to raise funds for the construction of Tenryūji to commemorate Go-Daigo. The venture was successful, and trade developed through further voyages led by Tenryūji monks. These ships (*tenryū-bune*) benefitted the Ashikagas and brought wealth and influence to the monastery. The economic activity of *gozan* monasteries was not limited to trade with China. Following in the footsteps of such earlier Buddhist centres as Tōdaiji, Kōfukuji and Enryakuji, *gozan* monasteries functioned as proprietors of manors (*shōen*), earned rents in the form of rice, vegetables and cash,[53] and engaged in moneylending.[54] Their financial strength was promoted further through the performance of memorial services and direct patronage by warriors, Kyoto nobility, and members of the imperial family. Over time, as the *gozan* monasteries became stronger and the Muromachi government[55] weaker, the Ashikagas regulated the monasteries more and established laws that charged fees for certificates of appointment when monks assumed new positions in the complex monastic organisation.[56]

During the latter half of the Muromachi period, Rinzai Zen began to expand beyond the *gozan* system. Two non-*gozan* monasteries, Daitokuji and Myōshinji, became particularly powerful. The Daitokuji line produced Ikkyū Sōjun (d. 1481), a Zen teacher of the Muromachi period who often appears in discussions of Zen and ethics. In addition to being a discerning teacher and dynamic calligrapher, Ikkyū proved himself an iconoclast in his criticisms of institutionalised Buddhism. He travelled extensively, preaching to a wide range of common people in language they could understand. Dumoulin contends that 'Ikkyū went far, perhaps too far, in his efforts to reach the people. He had little regard for monastic rules and even broke basic laws of Buddhism, eating fish and meat, loving sake and women.'[57] Concerned about the condition of the poor, Ikkyū reportedly returned in his formal robe to a wealthy home that had given him little when he begged there earlier in old clothes, and upon receiving a grand meal, he set the robe in front of the food, exclaiming that the feast was served not for him but for his robe.[58]

The ascendency of Daitokuji and Myōshinji parallels a decline in *gozan* power. As the Muromachi period unfolded, the fortunes of the Ashikaga bakufu and the Kyoto *gozan* temples became increasingly intertwined. The power of the *gozan* monasteries eventually waned together with Ashikaga power in the late fifteenth and early sixteenth centuries. One major point in this decline was the destruction of four of the five Kyoto *gozan* temples in the Ōnin War

(1467–1477), one of numerous civil wars stretching across the next hundred years.

During this period of civil war and the subsequent Tokugawa period, not only the economic but also the social and political situation of Zen changed. Although Zen monasteries continued to perform an educational and administrative function for the government, Neo-Confucianism developed away from Zen monasteries and caught the ear of the ruling shoguns. Hayashi Razan (1583–1657) and other prominent Confucian scholars started centres of Confucian studies from which they advocated Neo-Confucian approaches to society and politics and served as advisors to Tokugawa Ieyasu and his descendents. They also engaged in polemics against Buddhism, many of which were based on Chinese treatises that attacked Buddhism on ethical grounds. This process led to increasing separation between Zen and formal Confucian studies.

Though they encountered Confucian attacks and lost their privileged position in advising the rulers and conducting Confucian studies, Zen teachers at this time continued to integrate Confucianism into their teachings. Dumoulin writes:

. . . it was particularly painful for Zen when Confucian scholars at the beginning of the Tokugawa period consciously began to remove Confucianism from the embrace of the Zen school . . . . Although the Zen monks could no longer be considered the main advocates of Confucianism, they continued to preserve and carry on the Confucian heritage among the common people.[59]

Takuan Sōhō (1573–1645) presented Neo-Confucian thought from his Zen standpoint, avoiding the polemics of other Zen figures who were reacting more directly to Confucian criticisms of Buddhism at that time.[60] He exhorted 'the four classes of warriors, farmers, artisans, and merchants to fulfill their duties faithfully and to practice the social virtues.'[61] He criticised merchants for their greed and the rich for their 'lack of kindness'.[62]

The Confucian approach to society was not propagated only by Rinzai monks. Suzuki Shōsan (1579–1655), a renowned samurai who became a Sōtō monk, chose 'to equate the self-renunciation of Zen, based on the Buddhist teaching of the non-substantiality of self (*muga*), with absolute loyalty to one's lord'.[63] With this emphasis on the key Confucian virtue of loyalty, he followed Takuan and others in combining Confucianism and Buddhism in his teachings.[64] On the basis of the view that all work in society is the work of the Buddha in that it comes from the Buddha-nature in all people, Shōsan offers practical ethical advice not only to samurai but also to peasants and merchants in *Banmin tokuyō* (Meritorious Way of Life for All). Concerning Shōsan's words to farmers, 'when you train your body and mind by doing your harsh and toilsome work, then there are no disturbances or troubles in your mind', Dumoulin writes:

> In Tokugawa Japan such an ethic would have special meaning for the suffering and needy rural population. When times of drought or heavy taxes oppressed the farmers and threatened to precipitate peasant revolts, the Sōtō monks, who were always close to the people and who took part in the social movements of the time, offered the people practical assistance.[65]

This Sōtō connection to the common people was nothing new. Situated largely outside of the urban areas where Rinzai *gozan* temples and older sects held sway and influenced politics and the fine arts, Sōtō monasteries produced monks who responded more to the needs of the peasants. They prayed with the people for safety, fertility, and other blessings, and they officiated at funerals.[66] 'The monks were always ready to help with social projects such as building bridges, irrigating rice fields, draining swamps. In this they were being faithful to their Buddhist heritage, for the bodhisattva ideal had always been proven in concrete acts of service.'[67] Yet, the Sōtō focus was not entirely rural. Concerning the world of business, Shōsan argued that merchants should not get entangled in self-serving desires but should direct success in business to serving the common good.[68]

While many Zen figures in the Tokugawa period continued to emphasise monastic practice with its rules and precepts and continued to interact with the ruling elite, certain teachers followed the earlier examples of Ikkyū and Bassui Tokushō (1327–1387) and devoted much of their time and energy to revitalising Zen by criticising the flaws in institutionalised Zen and, like Takuan and Suzuki, reaching out to the common people in their teaching. Two of the key figures in this regard were from the Myōshinji line: Bankei Yōtaku (1622–1693) and Hakuin Etaku (1685–1768).

Bankei is known for giving 'Dharma talks' in ordinary Japanese for the common people and expressing Zen in terms of the 'unborn' (*fushō*). Hakuin travelled in both urban and rural areas, talking with the people he met along the way. 'With his gift for translating the Buddhist precepts into moral values for everyday life, he constantly urged the faithful to live a morally virtuous life both at home and in the marketplace.'[69] His moral guidance derived from Buddhist stories about good and bad *karma* and from his studies of Confucianism. In his 'In Praise of Filial Love', Hakuin advocated respect for parents based on gratitude for their giving oneself a body.[70] He called on feudal lords to renounce their extravagant lifestyles and govern humanely, especially with regard to the poor. In addition, Hakuin reformed Rinzai Zen by offering a new approach to *kōan* practice, and his reforms constituted the most important event in Zen history in the late Tokugawa period and the following Meiji period (1868–1912), the first fully modern period of Zen history.

The close connection between Zen and the political realm continued in Meiji period, although at the beginning of the period Zen and other stands of Japanese Buddhism encountered persecution, for Meiji reformers rejected the Tokugawa shogunate and elevated the Imperial system, with its Shintō underpinnings, in formulating a new political system and national identity. Attacks on Buddhism did not last long, however, and Buddhists soon displayed their conservative colors once again. Imakita Kōsen (1816–92), teacher of D. T. Suzuki's *rōshi* Shaku Sōen (1859–1919), wrote *Zenkai ichiran* (A Wave on the Zen Sea) in 1862 for Confucian scholars and samurai,[71] where he argued that Confucianism and Buddhism are fundamentally the same. Zen figures also supported Japanese militarism.[72] Shaku Sōen reportedly refused to work with Leo Tolstoy on a peace appeal during the Russo-Japanese War (1904–1905).[73] Like their cousins in other sects, Zen Buddhists contributed to the anti-Christian and anti-socialist climate in the early twentieth century. (A rare exception to this is Uchiyama Gudō, who was executed for his political protests in 1911.) Certain Zen figures supported growing Japanese militarism in the 1920s and 1930s by directing Zen practice for soldiers as a preparation for combat, and a large meditation hall was erected in Tokyo for this purpose. Yamazaki Ekishū stressed unity with the emperor and fulfillment of sacrificial duty in what has been termed 'Imperial Way Zen' (*kōdō-zen*). Harada Sogaku (1870–1961) reportedly said:

Forgetting [the difference between] self and others in every situation, you should always become completely one with your work. [When ordered to] march – tramp, tramp; [when ordered to] fire – bang, bang; this is the clear expression of the highest Bodhi-wisdom, the unity of Zen and war . . . .[74]

This area of recent Japanese history has received little attention in Japan. The only Zen writer to investigate and criticise it in detail is Ichikawa Hakugen, whose views will be discussed in Chapter 4.

Since World War II, monasteries have continued to function, though with fewer monks and nuns than in the past. Contemporary observers have criticised the use of Zen monasteries for special corporate training programmes. Pointing out that such 'corporate Zen training' may occur in conjunction with (or parallel to) temporary employee service in the Japan's Self-Defense Forces, Daizen Victoria states, 'It seems unlikely that employees would be made to undergo military training if the company's goal were truly their enlightenment!'[75]

Numerous themes and issues emerge from this brief overview of Zen in Japanese history. First, ethical reflection passed through several stages. As founders of newly introduced sects and, by extension, as reformers, Eisai and Dōgen devoted themselves to laying a firm foundation for Zen practice in Japan and to criticising laxity in other Buddhist sects at the time. To this end they focused on guidelines for Zen religious life, which include precepts and monastic rules. They drew from Theravāda *vinaya* precepts, rules, and regulations, from various formulations of '*bodhisattva* precepts' in the Mahāyāna tradition, and from Chan monastic codes. These guidelines provided moral guidance in the sense of regulating the actions of Buddhists through sanctions against lying, stealing, sexual misconduct, and the use of intoxicants, through exhortations, and through calls for humility, respect and altruism. Although this guidance has important ethical significance, there are shortcomings. Eisai and Dōgen made general statements about promoting the good and avoiding evil, yet they offer little in the way of an explicit definition of what might be good overall. One might surmise that the 'good' is the observance of precepts or the making of vows to save others and promote the Dharma. Yet to what extent is there an implicit stance about the 'good' in a larger, more concrete, social sense? Given their emphasis on authority and smooth relations with the state, did their implicit social ethic consist of a general call to take a stance of submission and obedience toward those in power while acting altruistically in accordance with the *bodhisattva* ideal in the narrow religious sense? Insofar as this appears to have been their view, based on native, Confucian, and Buddhist elements in their cultural milieu at the time, one might say they *did* have a social ethic. Although this implicit social ethic followed the lead of earlier forms of Japanese Buddhism with support of and from the state, one is still left with the question of whether their stance was true to the spirit of Zen teachings or the Buddha's original message.

The second phase occurred in the late Kamakura and Muromachi periods when political involvement became even more distinct and the Confucian connection stronger. *Gozan* monks deepened the relationship between Zen and ruling powers, increased Zen involvement in the economic realm, and drew together Zen and Confucianism. Though Sōtō Zen was active in rural areas and such Rinzai figures as Bassui and Ikkyū reached out to the common people, the main way *gozan* Rinzai Zen moved into the countryside was through the *ankokuji* and *rishōtō*, which have been characterised as a controlling arm of the Ashikaga government. Musō and other monks do attend to precepts and monastic codes, but apparently less than Eisai and Dōgen did, for by this point Zen had set down roots and become secure to the point of being the most influential sect of the age.

In the third stage, roughly corresponding to the Tokugawa period, many prominent monks preached to and worked with the people. They gave Buddhist precepts and Confucian values a popular expression. This guidance, however, did not call into question the social structures of the time. Although Hakuin reportedly pleaded the case of peasants to those in power, much of the preaching tended to offer guidance about how to make the best of one's lot in life, of one's social and economic standing. As seen in Suzuki Shōsan's writings, Zen monks called for people to respect hierarchy and do their work without complaints as a way of expressing their Buddha-nature. Although Sōtō monks did help peasants improve their general comfort and well-being, they apparently did not question publicly the political and economic systems in place at the time that influenced dramatically the situation of the peasants. And by this stage Zen had lost the ear of the rulers.[76]

The fourth stage is the period from the time of the persecutions of Zen and other forms of Buddhism in the early Meiji period through World War II. Though at first thrown on the defensive by the elevation of Shintō, the restoration of imperial rule (at least on paper), and attacks on Buddhist institutions, Zen regained its footing and resumed its active support of the government as Japan militarised. In the early twentieth century it joined the clamor against Christianity and socialism and supported the imperialistic crusade that emerged soon thereafter. The fifth stage is the postwar period, in which monasteries and temples function less politically and with fewer practitioners, though they have been criticised for supporting corporate training.

As Ichikawa Hakugen, Daizen Victoria and others have pointed out, the most conspicuous theme in this history is the close connection between Zen and the political status quo. Of course, one might argue that the historical social acquiescence of Zen and other types of Buddhism is a natural outgrowth of conditions in traditional Asian societies over the centuries. In such societies, criticism and social action do not readily emerge, for traditional sources of authority and undemocratic political processes are often accepted as part of the familiar status quo. And even when Zen Buddhists may have disagreed with the status quo, oppressive political forces could have rendered social activism extremely difficult. Throughout most of Japanese history Zen has existed under a series of repressive leaders, including the Minamoto warriors, Hōjō regents, Ashikaga warriors, the Tokugawa shoguns, anti-Buddhist Meiji reformers and militarists during World War II. Under such conditions, existing political structures and practices may have been accepted as the only or the proper order of things, with no notion of alternatives. Or, Zen figures may have decided to remain silent and direct their energies toward religious transformation, thinking that risky activism aimed at some sort of social or political change could jeopardise efforts to promote higher-order religious emancipation. If this is indeed what occurred, one may ask whether this was an act of cowardice or an act of compassion, amounting to either escapism or religious commitment.

In any case, throughout Japanese history Zen Buddhists have pursued monastic practice but have not stood aloof from the social world. In fact, one may argue that Zen did have a social ethic. Though never systematically set forth, this de facto ethic took a pro-government, largely Confucian approach to society. In short, it exhibited a conservative stance, despite images of Zen iconoclasm. There are several possible responses to this stance. One can accept it as reflecting the true spirit of Zen or Buddhism as a whole; one can criticise it as a deviation from the true teachings and principles of Zen; or one can simply view 'true' Zen as an abstraction and argue that there is no Zen apart from the various concrete forms of the tradition at different times in different cultures or that to criticise Zen from the outside or on the basis of external criteria constitutes intellectual, moral, or cultural imperialism. What is invaluable and constructive in this discussion, however, is the presence of contemporary critics *within* the tradition, of Japanese and non-Japanese Zen Buddhists who have responded critically to their tradition.

4

Recent Critiques and Developments

Zen Buddhists have recently begun to reflect critically on traditional Zen in Japan and to give more explicit attention to ethics and the various problems confronting humanity. In part, this concern derives from the introduction of Marxism and other forms of Western thought after the Meiji Restoration (1868), the shock of World War II, and dialogue with Christianity.

A prominent Zen thinker in this regard is Hisamatsu Shin'ichi (1889–1980). Following his studies of Buddhism and philosophy under Nishida Kitarō[1] at Kyoto University, Hisamatsu reportedly experienced Awakening in a traditional Rinzai retreat at Myōshinji, a temple in western Kyoto.[2] He taught at Kyoto and Hanazono Universities, started a lay Zen organisation and became an accomplished master of tea ceremony.[3]

Although his Zen experience was rooted in *kōan* practice with Ikegami Shōzan Rōshi, Hisamatsu did not fully accept Zen in its traditional form. He criticised Zen as falling short of true Buddhist religiosity, for in its predominantly monastic form it has focused overwhelmingly on *satori*, at the expense of due attention to actual problems in the socio-historical world. He expressed this criticism as follows:

> If, as has been the case with Zen, activity starts and ends only with the so-called practice of compassion involved in helping others to awaken, such activity will remain unrelated to the formation of the world or creation of history, isolated from the world and history, and in the end turn Zen into a forest Buddhism, temple Buddhism, at best, a Zen-monastery Buddhism. Ultimately this becomes 'Zen within a ghostly cave.'[4]

In his talks and writings Hisamatsu recognises that 'Rinzai Zen decries becoming entangled in oneness, describing this in such ways as being "attached, degenerating in a dark cave," or practicing "the evil Zen of silent illumination (*mokushō*)".[5] Yet he contends that Zen in *all* of its forms in Japan generally fails to address historical problems and contribute to the creation of what he refers to as a 'postmodern' world. Moreover, he observes that there even are 'cases when people feel that *not* having an interest in such problems is a condition for true Zen practice'.[6] But to emphasise only Awakening is to practice an incomplete, imperfect Zen, for that alone falls short of 'perfect awakened functioning'.[7]

Hisamatsu's criticism of Zen practice extends to actual forms of practice as well. He claims that work with *kōans* does not always lead to a total Awakening. In many cases, the practitioner proceeds 'quantitatively', slowly passing through *kōans* in the manner of *hashigo* or 'ladder' Zen but never realising a final and decisive Awakening. Hisamatsu expresses this pitfall through the aforementioned metaphor of a polygon and a circle. However many sides we may add to a polygon, it will never become a circle, even though it will look more and more like one. To become a circle, the polygon must undergo a total negation; there must be an absolute, qualitative disjunction.[8]

Confronting this pitfall in Zen practice, Hisamatsu seeks to establish a *kōan* that not only includes all other *kōans* but can serve as a way of practice leading all people – including the laity – to true Awakening. To this end, he sets forth the 'Fundamental *Kōan*':

I would like to establish a method for 'Cornered, one passes through; passing through, one changes,' in the simple form, 'Right now, if nothing you do is of any avail, what will you do?' If all our ways of being and all our actions are of no avail, what do we do? The expression, 'all our actions,' refers to our total actuality, but the situation where nothing will do is an absolute predicament, the last extremity.[9]

According to Hisamatsu, this fundamental *kōan* – 'Right now, if nothing you do is of any avail, what will you do?' – includes all traditional *kōans*, and its resolution is none other than complete Awakening.[10]

In looking for a genuine way of practice, Hisamatsu does not aspire to improve Zen in its predominant historical form of monasticism. He rejects monastic Zen as antiquated and urges Zen to evolve into 'Zen for all people' (*taishūzen*). By applying themselves to the Fundamental *Kōan* and becoming the Great Doubt Block,[11]

all people – not only monks and nuns – can awaken to what
Hisamatsu calls the Formless Self.[12] A direct relationship with a
Zen master in a monastic setting is not absolutely necessary –
Great Faith, Great Resolution and a Great Doubting Spirit consti-
tute a sufficient basis for working with the Fundamental *Kōan* and
becoming the Great Doubt Block.[13]

Hisamatsu argues that true practice goes beyond zazen or work
with *kōans*. Zen has suffered from an overemphasis on religious
discipline in the narrow sense at the expense of various studies
necessary for effective action in response to problems in the world.
True practitioners of Zen must study such areas as politics, economics, history and the natural sciences in order to understand
more fully the issues facing humanity and to work out skilful
means (*upāya*) of responding to them. In short, practice without
such study is blind.

At the same time, from the opposite angle, Hisamatsu criticises
Buddhologists. From his perspective, 'Modern Buddhology, while
taking in new Western ways of study, has tended to follow in the
footsteps of traditional Chinese methods emphasising the doctrinal study of the different schools [of Buddhism]. Practice has
become an object of research. Living practice has been all but
ignored.'[14] Consequently, Zen scholars 'have become strangers to
practice, and because of that, to satori itself'.[15] What, then, constitutes the proper methodology of scholarship? 'It is not the objective and impartial study of ethical, philosophical, or religious
phenomena, but gaining knowledge of how to "live" morality,
philosophy, or religion, that must be the essential concern.'[16]
Buddhist scholarship thus requires practice, and the overall goal
'must be that fundamental human subjectivity should come to be
the totally and ultimately unified self'.[17] To Hisamatsu, then, just
as Zen practice without study is blind, study without practice is
powerless.

Because practice without study is blind ('has no eyes', to use a
Zen expression) and study without practice is powerless ('has no
legs'), Zen Buddhists must create, test and polish methods[18] of
'negotiating the Way'[19] that include both religious practice and
academic study. Hisamatsu thus advocates what he terms the
'unity of study and practice' (*gakugyō-ichinyo*).

In summary, then, Hisamatsu calls traditional Zen into question
by arguing that it has focused almost exclusively on *satori* and
has not paid due attention to the world and history. It must

develop beyond the confines of the monastery and become Zen for all people in all societies, a change that calls for a new type of practice: the Fundamental *Kōan* in conjunction with *zazen*. Further, practice must be linked with study of a variety of disciplines and of actual conditions in the world, while Buddhologists must link their scholarship with practice.

On the basis of his criticism of contemporary Zen and Buddhist scholars, Hisamatsu establishes his own standpoint – what some have called 'Hisamatsu Zen' – and encapsulates it in the three-dimensional framework of F, A and S:

Awakening to the Formless Self, the depth dimension, the Self as the ground of human existence;

Standing on the standpoint of All Humankind, the width dimension, human being and the world in its entirety;

Creating history Supra-historically, the length dimension, awakened human history.[20]

Hisamatsu's discussion of the first dimension of his philosophy, Awakening to the Formless Self, begins with an analysis of ordinary human existence. In an essay entitled 'Ultimate Crisis and Resurrection', he raises the question of the *raison d'être* of religion, asking, 'Where in people does one find the "moment" whereby they need religion?'[21] Focusing on the Christian and Buddhist traditions, he argues that the two critical issues facing people are sin and death, the fundamental limitations of human existence which finite selves never overcome. Some theologians regard sin as an evil action contrary to the good action called for in a given situation, and in morality one can strive to avoid such sins and may be relatively successful. Yet no matter how hard or how long a person struggles, he or she can never overcome *sin itself*.

To Hisamatsu, however, sin is not limited to the tension between good and evil or the human response to the will of God. He writes, 'Even if we could get rid of sin in a moral sense, we could not be free from the contrast between ugliness and beauty in the world of art, or opposition between falsity and truth in the world of science.'[22] Just as we never realise goodness totally independent of evil, we can never rid ourselves of ugliness and falsity by standing in beauty and truth. Nevertheless, in morality, art and science, people often strive to enhance one side of the dichotomy and eliminate the other, aiming at absolute Good, Beauty, or

Truth. It is in this sense that people are caught in sin as the fundamental inseparability of the two poles and the resultant dilemmas in the realm of the will (good–evil), anguish in the realm of feeling (beauty–ugliness) and contradiction in the realm of the intellect (truth–falsity).

Hisamatsu next argues that 'sin ought to be extended to include the problem of reason per se',[23] for sin as the inseparability of the poles in each dichotomy is 'indubitably based on the structure of reason itself'.[24] From his viewpoint, 'The opposition of rational and irrational is basic to the structure of reason, so that to remove what is irrational and leave behind only what is rational is, one must say, impossible.'[25] By focusing on the dilemma of the rational and irrational, Hisamatsu offers a novel exposition of the predicament to which Zen responds. Unfortunately, he does not fully clarify how the dichotomies of good and evil, beauty and ugliness, and truth and falsity are *based on* or can be *deepened to* the problem of reason, of rationality and irrationality. Some might argue that reason pertains to the intellect, which wrestles with the polarity of truth and falsity, not the other two polarities.

Hisamatsu treats death in much the same manner as sin. From his perspective, a finite human does not first have life and then die in the future, with life and death being two ontologically and temporally distinct realities. Rather, life and death are inseparable – it is impossible to live without dying. From this traditional Zen vantagepoint, mere physical death is not the central religious issue; instead, 'our sharing in the nature of life-and-death comes to be the basic problem of our life . . . . Therefore, the meaning of death ought to be deepened to the extent that not mere death but life-and-death is death.'[26] In more philosophical language, Hisamatsu asserts that 'at the bottom of life there exists the antinomy of life-and-death'.[27] Just as he construes sin as the paradoxical inseparability of good and evil rather than as evil alone, he treats death as the inseparability of life and death rather than as mere physical death.

As a finite self, then, a human struggles to find goodness, truth, beauty and life at the exclusion of evil, falsity, ugliness and death. But such one-sided fulfillment is impossible. Given the inseparability of the poles, one cannot arrive at a pure or absolute form of one pole at the exclusion of the other. Although someone might find temporary, relative satisfaction, the negation of that satisfaction soon arises. Expressed with the metaphor of waves, insofar as people exist as waves on the agitated surface of an expanse of water, they are eternally unsettled, for waves continue to rise and fall in endless opposition.

In expanding the idea of sin to the contradiction of rationality and irrationality, and death to life-and-death, Hisamatsu sketches the axiological and ontological aspects of what he terms the 'ultimate antinomy', the paradox constituting the crux of the human situation. He further develops this perspective by conceiving of sin as the opposition of value and anti-value,[28] and death as the opposition of existence and non-existence (*sonzai-hisonzai*):

> In both aspects of value and existence, the human contains insolvable contradictions in himself or herself at the starting point or basis of life. Besides, in the concrete human being, the two contradictions are found to exist in an indistinguishable, inseparable way. In that sense, they are non-dual contradictions, an absolute, ultimate contradiction. That is, they are considered to be ultimate worries, the moment in humans which requires ultimate deliverance.[29]

As stated here, value and existence are inseparably related and constitute an absolute contradiction. Value does not exist in isolation; it is always related to being. Nor is human existence unrelated to value; life and death are anything but value-free. In arriving at this notion of the ultimate contradiction, Hisamatsu answers his initial question about the *raison d'être* of religion:

> Such ultimate antinomy really pressing upon us is the true 'moment' of religion. A death or sin which one can look upon is an abstract one, a mere object of thought. We are confronted by ultimate death, ultimate sin. This ultimate antinomy is the very self-awareness in which existence and value are one; it is not anything to be known objectively. It is original to people; it is at once my way of being and that of all human beings.[30]

To suffer from the absolute antinomy is to be striving to do good but always succumbing to evil, to be living but unable to rid oneself of death. This antinomy is fully manifest in 'self-awareness' of inseparable sin and death. This awareness is not an objective mode of knowing but a subjective realisation of the most unsettling kind.

In its extreme form, this 'self-awareness' constitutes the Great Doubt Block. To Hisamatsu, one becomes liberated from it not by arriving at an absolute Good or eternal life as distinguished from evil or death, but by breaking through the contradictory structure of one's existence. This breakthrough occurs when one penetrates to the depths of the ultimate antinomy, becomes the Great Doubt Block, and then dies as the 'self' caught up in this fundamental antinomy. At this point the Formless Self 'awakens to itself', and in this Awakening one breaks free from the dilemmas, anguish, and contradictions of the will, emotion, and intellect and from the antinomies of good-and-evil and life-and-death. Hisamatsu claims in a conversation with Carl Jung, 'The cure in psychoanalysis is to . . . treat isolated diseases individually. But, in Zen, as indicated by the expressions "*do-issai-kuyaku*" (save all from suffering) and "*kyūkyō gedatsu*" (absolute freedom), it is to be awakened to the "Self" not enmeshed by things, and to get rid of all diseases at once.'[31] In terms of the metaphor of waves and water, to overcome the struggling self and awaken as the Formless Self is for one to awaken as the underlying water and realise true peace beyond yet in the midst of the ongoing dialectic of synthesis and antithesis, peace and anguish.

This transformation does not indicate, then, a withdrawal to some sort of unchanging oneness. In 'Hisamatsu Zen', Awakening is the basis for genuine action in the world (standing in the standpoint of All Humankind) and in history (creating history supra-historically), the arenas of social ethics. Hisamatsu discusses the relationship between the Formless Self and the dimensions of *A* and *S* as follows:

> The Formless Self, which is no-birth-and-death freed from birth-and-death, must function and give rise to all things in actuality. This is the True Self (*F*), which constitutes the source of *A* and *S*. It is Self-Awakening. In that it is spatially boundless [formless], it is the basis of All Humankind, and in that it transcends the three periods of past, present, and future, it is the basis of Supra-historical history. Since this Self is no-thought (*munen*), no-mind (*mushin*), and the true reality of no-boundary, one can stand in the standpoint of all humankind and create history while transcending history.[32]

The second dimension of Hisamatsu's paradigm, All Humankind, is the dimension of width, the socio-political world of humanity as a whole. Hisamatsu asserts that Zen must function to resolve not only supra-mundane suffering (the absolute antinomy) but also 'mundane' suffering. He proclaims that all people must join together irrespective of nationality, race, ethnicity, class, or sex and strive to solve the overlapping social, political and economic problems facing humankind.

On what basis, however, are people to link together? As might be expected, this query brings us back to the depth dimension, to the Formless Self. The dimension of All Humankind is not something appended to the dimension of the Formless Self; rather, Hisamatsu construes it as part and parcel of it. He argues that the true Awakening of one person is at the same time a realisation of the Awakening of all beings. One realises that all people are originally awakened,[33] although most people do not know that they are. This Awakening provides a point of departure for working to have those who are unaware that they are fundamentally awakened become 'objectively' awakened. Only in this realisation of Awakening prior to the suffering of antinomic existence can one truly stand in the standpoint of all humankind and work compassionately to awaken others and transform the world.

Hisamatsu's emphasis on all humankind is not theoretical or political in the narrow sense. To stand in the standpoint of all humankind is to express the Great Compassion (Skt., *maha-karuṇā*) realised in Awakening. But the concern manifested in Great Compassion does not begin at the time of Awakening; from the start one must embody concern for others. As Hisamatsu points out in his talks and writings, the Fourfold Great Vow begins with the line, 'However innumerable sentient beings are, I vow to save them', and only thereafter moves to the apparently individualistic vow, 'However inexhaustible the binding passions are, I vow to extinguish them.'[34]

As implied here, from the beginning one must strive to awaken oneself and others rather than look to receive the salvific compassion of God or Amida. Hisamatsu states, 'True religious life lies not in a human being receiving compassion, but in a turning over of that view to our practicing compassion.'[35] He calls this practice the 'temporal functioning of eternity'.[36] This is the functioning of a *bodhisattva* (*bosatsu-gyō*), in which, as it were, the 'Christian God becomes immanent, and all people consequently possess this transcendent entity within themselves, and all people then join together through that transcendent entity'.[37] In this functioning, what links up with others is not the ego but a 'transcendent Person or transcendent Humanity',[38] that is, subjectivity awakened to the larger whole of humanity and the world. The standpoint of all humankind thus presupposes Awakening to the Formless Self, in that 'the ultimate basis of the expression, "same-womb" (*dōbō*), is found in the whole of humankind as width and such transcendent humanity as depth'.[39]

Further, in that the 'transcendent humanity' at the base of the standpoint of all humankind is found in the depth dimension of the Self, the accompanying compassion or love does not originate from a Buddha or God standing above people on a higher plane; love for others does not derive from being loved by a transcendent Being. The structure of Hisamatsu's universal concern hence differs from the notion of universal brotherhood (and sisterhood) *beneath* God or universal love in imitation of Christ's unconditional love. The concern differs also because it reflects Objectless Great Compassion:

> In one's original condition . . . there is no salvation. That is to say, in one's original place there is no saving and no being saved. Saving and being saved, seen from the standpoint of distinguishing Expedient Dharma and True Dharma, are Expedient Dharma. Clearly realizing that one is originally saved, that saving and being saved are originally non-existent, and then saving those who do not realise this fact – this amounts to Objectless Great Compassion. Therefore, if one is unawakened to the True Self, one cannot understand this point and in ignorance is convinced one must be saved.[40]

This statement reflects Hisamatsu's debt to Mahāyāna Buddhism, which, as outlined in Chapter 1, claims that a *bodhisattva* functions salvifically without acknowledging a 'self' to be saved.

According to Hisamatsu, one of the greatest barriers to having all people stand in this standpoint of all humankind is the modern nation-state. Although he does not advocate eradication of global cultural diversity, he rejects the nation-state as the locus of political and economic power. He sets forth his critique of the nation-state in a 'Postmodernist Manifesto'. With regard to this manifesto, Hisamatsu claims, 'The second point [All Humankind] lies in transcending the fatally deadlocked egoistic structure of the nation-state, and in creating a universal and unified sovereignty for all humankind.'[41] This unified sovereignty is 'a world system in which all of the world is one, not a state system or a nation system'.[42] Unfortunately, Hisamatsu does not lay out how humanity can move beyond nation-states to a world system, how the world system might be organised, or how regional disputes are to arbitrated.

The creation of a new world system is an issue in the dimension of length: time and the 'supra-historical' creation of history. Awakened to the Formless Self and standing in the standpoint of all humankind, the 'True Person'[43] functions creatively to bring about a history of liberation. In Hisamatsu's idiom, the Formless Self creates history 'supra-historically'; that is to say, while functioning, the Formless Self is in history but not of it, for it is freed from existential entanglement in the dichotomies discussed before and it is awakened to the Present, inclusive of past, present and future. Like the spatial dimension of all humankind, the temporal dimension of the 'supra-historical' creation of history is thus based on and inseparable from the depth dimension of the Formless Self.

According to Hisamatsu, through the probing of the contradictions inherent in human existence and the turning over of consciousness in the One Great Death, 'antinomic history' is turned over as well.

> The casting off and self-dissolution of the ultimately contradictory subject of history and its freeing of itself with the emergence of the unhindered, self-abiding, fundamental subject is not achieved in the movement of history, that is, through the historical dialectic. It is accomplished at the root-source of history, which is prior to the birth of history. In living in history itself there is an ultimate contradiction, and thus, this ultimate contradiction cannot be resolved by means of living in history. It can only be resolved through the self-dissolution of history itself. Therefore, though the term 'the casting off and self-dissolution of history' has been used, this means that history 'casts itself off' and returns to what is prior to its own birth.[44]

In this passage, Hisamatsu advances several of his more provocative and abstruse ideas, including the 'self-dissolution' of history and history's returning to a point prior to its own 'birth'. Yet he does not fully explain what it means for history to 'cast itself off'.

Does history somehow have the ability to do this? In what sense? Or is history to be equated with the totality of human experience as encapsulated in each individual? Several points can be made as a partial response to these questions.

First, when Hisamatsu discusses history or its creation, he is not viewing it from an external position. In the dualistic way of thinking, one conceives of oneself as being born into the flow of history at a certain point in time and then leaving it upon death at another point. This position outside of time from which history is objectified is an abstraction, removed from concrete experience. When Hisamatsu sees history as a dynamic, concrete actuality here and now, he is standing squarely in (or moving with) history yet not entangled in it, seeing history not simply as a linear flow but also as something fully subsumed in the Present.

Second, Hisamatsu argues that the Awakening of the Formless Self is not an event within the temporal process of history, but an event at its very source. It consists of a shift beyond the historical self (dualistic existence as the locus of history) and its contradictory nature. In breaking beyond the inherent contradictions of human existence, one also overcomes the contradictions at the base of history, which are inseparable from the existence of dualistic subjectivity. Accordingly, the awakening to one's 'Original Face prior to the birth of one's parents' is said to be none other than an awakening to the root-source of history which lies prior to the 'birth' of history, with 'prior' referring primarily to ontological priority rather than to mere temporal priority.

In elaborating this Hisamatsu often quotes the *Vimalakīrti-nirdeśa Sūtra*, especially the phrase, 'creating without parting from Awakening'. The awakened human creates history *within* the temporal process, but *from* Awakening. Here, too, the Formless Self, the transformed existence realised in the dissolution of the 'self', is free from suffering in history yet working in history as it assumes various 'forms', as it acts in various compassionate ways (*upāya*). This awakened creativity involves a dynamism of two directions: *to* Awakening and *from* Awakening, and Zen refers to these two aspects as the 'sweeping-away gate' (*sōtōmon*) and the 'establishment gate' (*konryūmon*). In contrast to many other views of history and salvation, then, the creation of history does not simply end in religious emancipation but proceeds from it. Salvific Awakening functions here in the Present, not 'over there' in the future. It must be realised right now *as both the goal and the starting point*.

Further, this creative functioning of the Formless Self is not caught up in that which it creates, or even in the creative activity itself. Only subjectivity free from entanglement in self-fixation and self-attachment can create history supra-historically. This freedom from self-attachment is essential, for 'it is only when we are free from our very action of creation that we can really create history'.[45]

Although Hisamatsu does not sufficiently explain the 'self-dissolution of history', he does convey a sense of his goal when he criticises the modern age. He contends that the modern world has collapsed for two reasons, one phenomenological and the other ontological. Concerning the former, he writes in the 'Postmodernist Manifesto', 'We can no longer trust absolute sovereignty to nation states . . . . Because of egoism, in the realm of politics peace is impossible, in the realm of economics, the free circulation of material and spiritual wealth is obstructed, and in the realm of ethics, universality for all humans is lost.'[46] The ontological reason for the collapse of the modern world is the loss of unity and integration:

> . . . the modern age itself collapsed as a consequence of excessive 'multiplication.' Accordingly, the method for the resurrection of the modern world lies neither in a restoration of the medieval world, which is lacking in multiplicity, nor in a further intensification of the approach of the modern world, which is completely devoid of 'unity.' Rather, it must be realised in the thoroughgoing actualization of existence itself as the non-dualistic oneness of unity and multiplicity in which multiplicity is realised in unity and unity in multiplicity. Herein, unity is the root-source to which multiplicity must return, while multiplicity is the expression of unity. Thus unity and multiplicity do not consist of a mere static relation, but rather a dynamic and creative one.[47]

To Hisamatsu it is the Formless Self that functions without getting caught in the one or the many, without becoming attached to unity or multiplicity, for it is awakened to *śūnyatā* as the dynamism operating in the inseparability of the two poles. Depending on the circumstances, the creation of history moves freely in the direction of the one or the many, never ignoring the opposite pole.

Contrary to what one might imagine, Hisamatsu does not conceive of the postmodern world as lying in a line of extension from antiquity, the Middle Ages and the modern era. Rather, he speaks of a fundamental discontinuity between the modern and postmodern periods, which parallels the discontinuity between the ordinary human self and the Formless Self. 'The postmodern world does not signify something merely coming after modern humanity in the temporal sense, but rather, in an ontological sense, the creative realisation of being itself in history, whereby the two indispensable conditions for existence [unity and multiplicity] will be equally . . . fulfilled.'[48]

More specifically, Hisamatsu claims that the transition from the medieval to the modern age was one from heteronomy to autonomy based on the rational ego. In the modern world, many people work rationally on the basis of idealistic, progressive humanism in an attempt to solve various problems. Although it is important to work in this way to overcome contemporary problems, one must ask whether this approach gets at the root of the problems. As might be expected, Hisamatsu contends that idealistic humanism, with its anthropocentric faith in the rational ego, cannot penetrate to the source of the problems, however successful it may be at *relative* improvement of the human lot, for the presupposed rational ego with its antinomic way of existence and deep-rooted self-centredness is the source of the problems. Because this ego does not usually reflect on its structure of existence, 'idealistic humanism is a false endlessness (*schlecte Unendlichkeit*). It never overcomes the two poles [of existence and nonexistence]. It tries to take only the existence side of existence–nonexistence . . . . This is the standpoint of the delusion that it can reach an eternally unreachable goal.'[49] In short, although the modern rational ego works at the phenomenal level of actual problems in an attempt to solve them one by one as they arise, this attempt is endless, for the ego fails to confront the basic contradiction and anxiety within itself from which the external problems arise. To achieve true historical change, one must turn to the fundamental problem from which relative problems emerge, a shift in orientation that leads to the realm of religion.

Humans need to discern, then, the standpoint from which they are to approach actual problems. To use a metaphor used by Hisamatsu, people must realise which of the two standpoints to take: the unsettled wave or the formless water. To use another one of Hisamatsu's metaphors, they must work like a spider, which does not get caught up in that which it creates, not like a silkworm, which ultimately becomes more and more entangled in its creation.

In collaboration with his students, Hisamatsu summarised his standpoint in the 'Vow of Humankind':

> Keeping calm and composed, let us awaken to our True Self, become fully compassionate humans, make full use of our gifts according to our respective missions in life, discern the agony both individual and social and its source, recognise the right direction in which history should proceed, and join hands as brothers and sisters without distinctions of race, nation, or class. Let us, with compassion, vow to bring to realization humankind's deep desire for Self-emancipation and construct a world in which everyone can truly and fully live.

Though his writings and work with the F.A.S. Society generated a general outline for a Zen social ethic, several questions need to be addressed. First, can the 'postmodern' world be established *only* by means of an absolute discontinuity, an absolute death of egoism? This question harbors several issues, religious and secular. As for the former, a Christian might contend that grace, the salvation it makes possible, and the actions springing from an experience of grace do not necessarily presuppose a thoroughgoing 'death' of the self; the experience of grace may free people from selfish concerns and empower them to address the problems of the world and history just as much as – if not more than – the Zen 'death' of the self does. Historically, at least in terms of observable acts, Christians have engaged in more social and political activism than have 'selfless' Buddhists.

As for the secular issue, many of the people making committed efforts to create a peaceful world that provides for the satisfaction of global human needs do not follow or even affirm religion, much less Hisamatsu's form of it. Most of them are thinking in terms of a gradual transformation involving structural change, and the notions of the absolute death of the self and radical discontinuity between the modern and postmodern worlds do not necessarily enter into their thinking. Are their efforts not efficacious? Is Hisamatsu begging the question from a Zen perspective when he claims that Awakening is essential to the creation of a postmodern world in his sense of 'postmodern'? Or is he advancing a tautology which simply states that a world that is postmodern in the sense of involving Awakening requires Awakening?

This relates to a second issue. Hisamatsu's system is based on his own Awakening, and when he discusses the world and history he apparently does so from that perspective. His exposition indicates that only the awakened individual can truly stand in the standpoint of all humankind and create history 'supra-historically'. Is his standpoint intelligible and accessible in the true sense only to those who have experienced *satori*? In regard to Zen art he states that 'to determine which calligraphic style or which style of painting or which music expresses a Zen style, one must have a thoroughly vivid Zen realisation. If one lacks this realisation, one probably will not be able to understand why a certain calligraphic style . . . expresses Zen meaning.'[50] With regard to the creation of a 'postmodern' world he seems to be saying, in effect, that 'to determine which political style or which style of action expresses a Zen style (creates history supra-historically), one must have a thoroughly vivid Zen realisation'. Although Hisamatsu provides a new form of Zen practice for the laity, does he not end up offering another ethic for the elite, for the awakened few?

A third question concerns the concrete programs or techniques the 'supra-historical' creation of history requires. Hisamatsu discusses the problem of the nation-state and the need to go beyond it to a 'world system', but how might humanity actually establish that system? What other areas of human living does the creative functioning focus on? What about such issues as racism, sexism, child abuse, pollution, resource depletion, the threat of nuclear war? Although Hisamatsu exhibits an insight into what might indeed be the fundamental cause of these issues, his thought does not address them directly in terms of concrete socio-historical factors and specific steps that might be taken in response. Nor does he set forth the specific political, economic and cultural forms his postmodern world would assume. He works only at the level of general principles and does not introduce the concreteness and specificity needed in a viable social ethic. He sometimes seems to be assuming that once all people are awakened, actual concrete problems will automatically disappear. Yet even if we assume such a widespread awakening could be accomplished, we must ask whether such an awakening will be in time, given the looming threat of nuclear and environmental suicide.

Hisamatsu's student, Abe Masao, provides some of the needed concreteness in his reflection on the ethical nature of Zen. In line with the Mahāyāna tradition as a whole, Abe maintains that ethical issues are to be grappled with on the basis of an Awakening to one's 'Original Nature', which is beyond good and evil. He claims that 'to distinguish good and evil and to think of matters on the basis of this discrimination is itself evil or illusory thinking'.[51] Although the good is to be desired, 'Good has no priority over evil. The priority of good over evil is an ethical imperative but not an actual human situation . . . . The Buddhist shares the Pauline thought that the more we try to do good, the more we become aware of evil in ourselves.'[52] Like his predecessors in the Kyoto School of philosophy, he acknowledges the ethical demand to promote good and eliminate evil, yet perceives ethics as leading inevitably to religion. 'However strong the ethical imperative may be, we cannot *actually* fulfill it, but rather must fall into a conflict, the dilemma of good and evil. Human nature cannot be completely controlled and regulated by ethics, which is why we must go beyond the realm of ethics and enter that of religion.'[53]

Abe ascribes the cause of this dilemma to *karma*. 'Since our present existence is the fruit of a beginningless karma, we are involved in the conflict between good and evil.'[54] He defines *karma* as not simply 'mere physical movement, but physical or mental activity oriented by volition, which is based on free will'.[55] 'Free will' is the blind thirst to live (P., *bhava-taṇhā*), to affirm and protect oneself. The karmic effects (*vipāka*) of action by this 'free will' are 'not determined solely by the act itself, but also by many other factors, such as the nature of the person who commits the act and the circumstances in which it is committed'.[56] The action influences not only the actor's future but that of others as well. Moreover, responsibility extends beyond the actor's action and its fruits, and includes 'everything caused by *human avidyā* universally rooted in human nature'.[57] The vastness of the influence exerted by actions and shared responsibility constitute the two main facets of 'collective *karma*'.

In Abe's interpretation of Buddhism, *karma* and free will constitute the central problem facing humanity: 'the problem of human free will is grappled with in terms of karma which must be overcome to attain enlightenment or awakening and thereby to achieve real freedom.'[58] In response to this problem of good and evil and the will, Zen 'enjoins us "to awaken to the purity of one's original nature" or "to awaken to the original purity of one's nature" which is beyond the duality of good and evil [and free from *karma*]. The problem of good and evil must be coped with on the basis of awakening to the original purity of one's nature . . . .'[59] Abe sees this awakening as predicated upon the 'death' of the ego.

In the final and deepest realization of the dilemma between good and evil, the structure of my ego collapses and I come to the realization that I am not simply good, or simply bad. I am nothing whatsoever. However, this realization is not negative but positive, because in the full realization of Nothingness we are liberated from the dichotomy of good and evil, life and death. At this point we awaken to our true nature prior to dualistic consciousness.[60]

In this liberation, one overcomes *karma* and fundamental *avidyā*. In Abe's words, 'If we . . . completely abandon our attachment and clinging, and empty our conception and its objects, that is, if we do not substantialise the self and its objects any longer and awaken to their nonsubstantiality, karma ceases and *avidyā* is overcome.'[61]

Using Hisamatsu's language, Abe claims that in Buddhism, which sees good and evil an antagonistic yet fully interrelated principles, 'what is essential for salvation is not to overcome evil with good and to participate in the Supreme Good, but to be emancipated from the existential antinomy of good and evil and to awaken to Emptiness prior to the opposition between good and evil'.[62] This is 'the awakening to Sunyata, which is entirely beyond any type of will. It is a realisation of suchness or *jinen*, primordial naturalness or spontaneity without will.'[63]

On the basis of this Awakening, good and evil are realised as completely relative to each other, as interpenetrating and reciprocal. 'They always co-arise and co-cease so that one cannot exist without the other. There is, then, no supreme good which is self-subsistent apart from evil, and no absolute evil . . . apart from goods. To Buddhists both the supreme good and absolute evil are illusions.'[64] Further, in awakening to *śūnyatā*,

(1) the distinction and opposition between humans and nature, which is caused by anthropocentrism based on the emphasis on

the free will peculiar to human existence is fundamentally overcome; (2) the struggle between flesh and reason in making
decisions based upon free will, which is inevitable in human
existence as the subject of free will, is also overcome; (3) original
sin as the disobedience of human free will against God's will
involved in theocentrism does not emerge in Sunyata as suchness or *jinen*.[65]

The central question needing an answer here is, in Abe's words,
'how ethics then can be established on the realisation of *śūnyatā*?
Having transcended the duality of good and evil, to what moral
principles may one appeal that are in keeping with the spirit of this
liberating experience?'[66] Abe addresses this issue by making three
points.

First, he argues that the realisation of *śūnyatā* must be grasped as
'not merely a goal to be reached, but the ground on which everything in life is established'.[67] If projected outward as a goal, it
becomes divorced from us, and we become eternally frustrated in
our attempts to realise it.

Second, when we understand *śūnyatā* as this 'ground', 'the
duality of good and evil is viewed in a new light . . .'.[68] One comes
to realise a 'relativisation and reversion' of good and evil not unlike
Kierkegaard's 'teleological suspension of the ethical'. To Abe,
however, this occurs in a context quite different from that of
Western theistic religions, for 'the "transvaluation of values" is
realised not within a certain established framework of ethical life
nor under the rule and judgment of the all-good and all-powerful
God, but in and through the realisation of the boundless openness
of *śūnyatā* in which there is no One God'.[69] Ethical action springs
from Awakening rather than a set framework or a heteronomous
criterion of judgment and action.

Third, through Awakening to *śūnyatā* and the relativisation of
the good–evil distinction, 'the basis of the ethical life is not destroyed but is rather preserved, clarified and strengthened'.[70] More
specifically, 'This ultimate experience makes the distinction between good and evil clearer than before because of the fact that the
distinction is thoroughly realised without any limitation in the
awakening to the boundless openness of *śūnyatā*.'[71] And 'Once we
return to that point of suchness, everything is realised in its
distinctiveness. The distinctions between self and other, good and
evil, life and death, are *regrasped* in the new light of suchness.

Accordingly, it becomes the real point of departure for our lives and for our activity.'[72] Expressed in language used elsewhere in this book, 'Herein, Buddhist ethical life is established in light of *prajñā* (wisdom) and *karuṇā* (compassion) where, without the distinction of good and evil, the distinction is clearly realised.'[73] Yet is Abe arguing here that Awakening enables us to see pre-existing distinctions between good and evil more clearly? Or does it provide a new distinction or at least a basis for judging existing ethical distinctions?

To Abe, compassion must be active compassion, a *karuṇā-pāramitā* (compassion of the far shore, perfected compassion) accompanying *prajñā-pāramitā* (wisdom of the far shore, perfected wisdom). This activity is based on a will purified in the realisation of emptiness. 'The implication is that unlike one's self-centered free will involved in karma, pure and free will revived in the locus of Sunyata is self-emptying and self-negating. This pure and free will revived in, and realised as the center of, Sunyata, functions in terms of a "vow" . . . .'[74] The vow here is *praṇidhāna*, the vows made by aspiring *bodhisattva*, such as the 'Original Vow' made by Dharmakara (prior to becoming Amida) in Pure Land Buddhism.

The vow alone does not constitute true compassion, however. 'Just as Sunyata must empty itself and turn itself into vow, it must empty even the vow and turn itself into the "act" or "deed" which is traditionally called *carita* or *carya*.'[75] Moving in this direction, Abe arrives at a criterion for value judgments: 'The vow and act realised through the self-emptying of Sunyata provide not only the center of boundlessly open Sunyata but also the ultimate criterion of value judgment. This judgement is made in terms of whether or not a thing or action in question does accord with the vow and act to make oneself and all others awakened.'[76] Abe's general discussion here would benefit from consideration of what else might be necessary for making such these value judgements, especially in response to large, complex issues. Expressed differently, what is necessary beyond the immediate use of *prajñā* by a *rōshi* in the one-on-one encounter with a disciple?

Abe contextualises the vows and acts of a *bodhisattva* in a discussion of history. He states that Buddhism regards time as beginningless and endless, and past and future as reversible; as a result, 'Buddhism is relatively weak in its view of history . . . . since time is understood to be entirely beginningless and endless and thus reversible, the unidirectionality of time and the uniqueness of each moment essential to the notion of history are not clearly expressed in Buddhism.'[77] In the face of this obstacle, Abe begins to sculpt a Buddhist view of history in terms of how emptiness 'empties itself' into vow and act. An awakened person equipped with *prajñā* realises Original Awakening, suchness, and temporal reciprocity while at the same time functioning in compassion through time toward the future to help innumerable beings overcome their ignorance of Original Awakening and awaken to 'their suchness and interdependence with other things'.[78] When regrasped in this context, 'history is no longer a "history of karma" in which persons are transmigrating beginninglessly and endlessly. It becomes a "history of vow and act" in which wisdom and compassion are operating to emancipate innumerable sentient beings from transmigration.'[79]

This is possible on the basis of *śūnyatā* as a 'self-awakened cosmology'. In Abe's words, 'on the basis of this new cosmology, a Buddhist teleology can be established which, on the realisation of Emptiness or Suchness, provides meaning, purpose and direction for human society and history'.[80] This teleological aspect calls for further elaboration, especially given claims by Abe in other writings that Buddhism is not teleological and given the possible role such a teleology might play in the articulation of a Zen social ethic.

Another issue arising here is how the realisation of emptiness links with the vow and act, parallel to the issue of how, in Hisamatsu's system, the Formless Self (F) links with all humankind (A) and the creation of history supra-historically (S). Abe writes that *śūnyatā* 'must' empty itself, giving rise to the vow and act, but does this word 'must' mean that *śūnyatā* will *necessarily* give rise to them, or does it mean that *if* we are to be ethically engaged in the world after Awakening then *śūnyatā* will have to empty itself? Given that to Hisamatsu and Abe the social involvement of Zen Buddhists traditionally has been rather limited – which might indicate the lack of a necessary connection between *śūnyatā* and acts – this question demands attention (unless, of course, one restricts 'vow' and 'act' to their original, limited, soteriological connotations).

In his writings, Abe applies his framework to several specific ethical issues. He argues that the Holocaust, resulting from collective *karma* working through the ages, is all of our responsibility. He states that 'even such an atrocious event as the Holocaust in Auschwitz, which is relatively unrelated to me, must be grasped as a matter of my own responsibility in terms of sympathetic and collective karma which reverberates endlessly and is unfathomably deep'.[81] In that we must take collective responsibility at the religious level (rather than at the human ethical level) for the *karma* rooted deeply in humanity, the solution to such a problem as this takes on a collective character. Abe also calls on us not to 'substantialise and cling to it [the Holocaust] as a fixed separate entity unrelated to the rest of the vast and endless network of human history'.[82] 'While in a human, moral dimension the Holocaust should be condemned as an unpardonable, absolute evil, from the ultimate religious point of view even it should not be taken as an absolute but a relative evil.'[83] Abe's approach here provides a basis for a Buddhist response to systematic evil, but several questions need to be asked. Is an awakening to collective karmic responsibility a sufficient response to large-scale evil? Does one not also have to focus on concrete, historical causes and respond actively in specific ways?

In other essays Abe discusses tolerance and human rights in Buddhism. He sets his discussion on a 'trans-homocentric, cosmological basis', and asserts that 'in Buddhism human beings are grasped as a part of all sentient beings or even as a part of all beings, sentient or nonsentient, because both human and non-human beings are equally subject to transiency or impermanency'.[84] This leads him to a important ecological stance. He states that 'the ethics of mankind must have two aspects: an interhuman aspect within mankind, and an aspect which concerns human responsibility to the non-human universe'.[85] The underlying metaphysical ultimate here is 'the transpersonal, cosmological dimension common to the human and nature: the *Dharma* or suchness (as-it-is-ness) of everything in the universe'.[86] With this starting point, awakened humanity 'does not consider such things as land, water, air, the sun and all kinds of energy only as the common resources of mankind but considers them as the common blessings on behalf of the myriad phenomena of the universe'.[87]

In an essay entitled 'Sovereignty Rests with Mankind', Abe also develops Hisamatsu's critique of the nation-state. He writes, 'A human society must be built in which present-day sovereign states are negated, and in which it is precisely "mankind" as a living, self-aware entity that has the sovereignty.'[88] Elaborating on this sovereignty, he contends that 'it must be a sovereignty which takes wisdom and compassion as its principle rather than authority and justice'.[89] In his treatment of justice, however, Abe usually considers one view of justice: justice as judgment, by either a divine Judge or 'His' human judges here on earth. Because this aspect of justice does not exhaust the meaning of the term, justice in a certain sense may be more compatible with Buddhist principles than Abe makes it out to be.

In his writings Abe grants more concreteness and specificity to the general framework offered by his teacher Hisamatsu, though his largely philosophical approach does not provide treatment of ethical issues in concrete historical contexts or of the actual historical stance of Zen. For this, one must turn to other Zen writers.

A modern Zen thinker who has written about ethical issues in greater historical detail and about the historical posture of Zen is Ichikawa Hakugen (1902–1986). He sets forth his ideas most systematically in Zen to gendai-shisō (Zen and contemporary thought; 1967) and Bukkyōsha no sensō-sekinin (Buddhists' responsibility for war; 1970). In the former, he observes that the realisation of śūnyatā and the accompanying wisdom and compassion entail in one respect a 'freedom from morality', especially in the conventional sense. In modern Japan this morality includes the Imperial Rescript on Education (kyōiku chokugo; 1890), the Fundamental Principles of National Polity (Kokutai no hongi; 1937) and the unity of religious observance and governance (saisei itchi).[90] According to Ichikawa, however, Zen has not always been free from such morality. For example, Zen took a generally critical view of Christianity and socialism in the nineteenth and early twentieth centuries, and during World War II Zen figures promoted 'Imperial Way Zen' (kōdōzen). Tracing the roots of these stances, he writes, 'In the Edo Period a Zen deepening of Shintō was undertaken by Munan, Hakuin and Tōrei [1721–92], and in conjunction with this the assimilation of Zen in Japan was promoted. This assimilation accompanied the establishment of the imperial system's authority and in the process Zen came to lose almost all of its autonomy.'[91]

Ichikawa attributes this accommodating stance of Zen to the Zen ethic of harmony (wago), which includes nonresistance and tolerance. More specifically, the problem lies in the actual substance of this harmony. He writes:

With what has modern Japanese Buddhism harmonised itself? With State Shintō. With state power and authority. With militarism. Accordingly, with war.

To what has modern Japanese Buddhism been nonresistant? To State Shintō. To state power and authority. To militarism. To wars of invasion. Toward what has modern Japanese Buddhism been tolerant? Toward those with whom it harmonises. Toward personal responsibility for the war.[92]

The narrowness of this tolerance is readily apparent in the severe Buddhist criticism of Uchimura Kanzō, the renowned Christian leader of the Meiji Period who in 1891 refused to bow to the Imperial Rescript on Education in the school where he was teaching.[93] This narrowness also crops up in the conservative Buddhist response to socialism, especially when that school of thought expressed itself in a plot by Miyashita Takichi (1875–1911), Kōtoku Shūsui (1871–1911), and other radical socialists to assassinate the emperor in 1910.

In *Bukkyōsha no sensō-sekinin* Ichikawa maintains that the ethical pitfalls latent in the Zen approach to society derive from interpretations and applications of key Buddhist ideas. First, the notion of 'seeing the universal in the particular' can lead to an overemphasis on such institutions as the *ie* or 'home'. The universal here is the imperial system, and the particulars are individual homes with Shintō shrines (*kamidana*), and they interrelate like an organism and its cells. The ideological stance that the home is a microcosm of the nation (the macrocosmic whole) or its imperial system facilitates unification of citizens behind the agenda of the imperial system or those who co-opt it to achieve certain ends. Second, the Mahāyāna idea that 'discrimination is sameness', that all things express suchness in their respective ways, can serve to justify or mask social discrimination and validate possibly unjust social systems. Third, D. T. Suzuki's logic of *sokuhi* and Nishida Kitarō's logic of 'absolutely contradictory self-identity' can be interpreted as meaning that 'to be servant of every situation' by dedicating one's life to the emperor in a holy war is, through paradoxical negation, what the *Record of Linji* (J., *Rinzairoku*) means by 'to be master of every situation'. Fourth, Ichikawa argues that the Buddhist goal of *anshin* or peace of mind has been distorted into an advocacy of *anzen*, safety or social order.[94]

In *Bukkyōsha no sensō-sekinin* Ichikawa also sets forth twelve issues that emerge in the relationship between Japanese Buddhism and society.

1. The state and Buddhism. Ichikawa points out that Japanese Buddhism has emphasised its role as protector of the state, an orientation originating in Indian Mahāyāna *sūtras* and developed in Japan. From his perspective, this orientation became a bit less pronounced when new sects of Japanese Buddhism emerged in the Kamakura period, but it eventually became more noticeable as those sects actively supported the system of administration and ordinances the shogunate executed through temples in the Tokugawa period and as they participated in the policy of banning Christianity. Consequently, Buddhism 'ossified into a religion of the *ie* [home], a religion for funerals and memorial services, a type of ancestor worship, and in this way became mixed with Shintō and in part turned into a national teaching. This led to the intolerance and hostility toward Christianity, with its modern and transnational character.'[95]

2. Buddhist views of humanity and society. Ichikawa argues that despite the doctrine of shared Buddha-nature as a basis for equality in society, the doctrine of *karma* can lead to discriminatory views, such as the idea that women are more ignorant and hence more entangled in passion-driven *karma* than men are. Needless to say, *karma* in this way can be used to justify the status quo. 'The theory that individual distinctiveness due to the law of cause and effect spanning past, present and future constitutes true equality and justice came into being, and this theory provided a foundation for social orders with people in proper places.'[96]

3. Encouraging the good and chastising evil. This is the heading of the sixth article of Shōtoku Taishi's 'Seventeen Article Constitution' (604). Ichikawa regards modern Buddhism as integrating Confucian ethics into itself when it supported law and order and conservative policies in the Meiji Period. This trend was nothing new, for it originated in Shōtoku Taishi's constitution, which provides a template for the relationship between Buddhism and the state in Japanese history. Ichikawa notes that the Constitution includes the lines, 'When you receive the imperial commands, fail not scrupulously to obey them. The lord is Heaven, the vassal is Earth . . . . If the Earth attempted to overspread, Heaven would simply fall into ruin.'[97]

4. The problem of human rights and justice. Ichikawa states that the Buddhist doctrines of dependent co-arising and no-self did not provide a foundation for notions of autonomous, individual human personalities and as a result

did not advance a principle equivalent to natural law for establishing a basis for modern human rights and justice. The maxim from the Seventeen Article Constitution, ‚[Let us] turn away from that which is private and set our faces towards that which is public', connected directly with an expression in imperial-system fascism: 'self-annihilation for the sake of the public'.[98]

Along these lines, according to Ichikawa, 'The doctrine of no-self became a theory and ethic serving Mikado imperialism.'[99]

5. The lack of dogma. Given the negation of substantialist notions and resultant lack of pivotal dogmas, and given its emphasis on the inner, subjective dimension, Buddhism in Japan generated an 'ethic of the emotions' (*shinjō no rinri*) as opposed to an 'ethic of responsibility' centered on the results of external actions.

6. The philosophy of debt (*on*). *On* connotes a debt or obligation carried in conjunction with something – a gift, favor, or service – received from another. Ichikawa writes:

With the perspective of dependent co-arising as its backdrop, the philosophy of debt was the center of Buddhist ethics, but out of the four types of debt (to parents, ruler, sentient beings, and either heaven/earth or the three treasures (Buddha, Dharma and Sangha)), the debt to one's parents changed into debt to the emperor in the context of Japanese patriarchal theocracy, and the debt to sentient beings became less important.[100]

7. The theory of interdependence. Ichikawa claims that the theory of interdependence became a theory supportive of problematical relations between the whole in the form of the state or society and the part in the form of the individual, between the capitalist and the laborer, and between militarists and citizens. In this way it became a theory supportive of 'big-family-system cooperation' (*daikazoku-sei kyōchōshugi*).

8. The doctrine of the Middle Way. Ichikawa argues that the political middle ground occupied by Buddhism was not a product of confronting oppositions and tensions in society but a vague, 'social-improvement' approach stemming from a safe, compromising stance taken before any confrontation with oppositions.

9. The tradition of ancestor worship. In the process of becoming assimilated into Japanese culture, Buddhism participated in the conventional morality of ancestor worship within the 'great-family'

Buddhism of Japan. With this stance Buddhism came to support the holy-war morality reflected in the expression, '[bring] the whole world under one roof' (*hakkō-ichiu*).

10. The spirituality of aging. To Ichikawa, the doctrine of tranquility (*jakumetsu*) and the medieval Japanese culture of *yūgen*, *wabi*, and *sabi*[101] led to an emphasis on that which is older and subdued, and this in turn led to a view of the aged as nonconflictual, desireless, obedient and tolerant. This has moved Japanese away from criticism of actuality to an acceptance of it, especially given the deference extended to one's elders.

11. Peace of mind rather than justice. Given that Buddhism is a religion based on the notion of *śūnyatā* rather than God, it has tried to rebuild society 'through the establishment of individual peace of mind rather than through prayers or resolutions to bring about the justice of the kingdom of God here on earth'.[102] This orientation has blunted Buddhist responses to injustice in society.

12. The theory of *soku*. Viewing *soku*[103] as roughly equivalent to suchness and non-duality, Ichikawa contends that it leads to a static, aesthetic perspective, a detached subjective harmony with things rather than a dynamic theoretical framework from which to confront actuality. In this way 'it weakens interest in political and social liberation for people'.[104]

Although Ichikawa points out these pitfalls in Japanese Buddhism, he sees Buddhism as offering resources for a social ethic. From his perspective, responsibility can be based on a clear discernment of society from the vertical dimension of religious freedom (*śūnyatā*), a standpoint beyond the status quo, not co-opted by it. This vertical freedom is embodied by individuals cleansed of the absolutism of the self and the will to power and authority. This religious freedom connects with horizontal or socio-political freedom, and it can give rise to a criticism of the power of nation states and a rejection of capitalist systems based on private property.

Ichikawa encapsulates his stance with the acronym S.A.C., standing for *śūnya*, anarchism and communism, although the Japanese expression he renders as communism is *kyōdō-shugi*, communalism, not *kyōsan-shugi*, communism.[105] Unfortunately, Ichikawa does not develop this to a high degree of specificity. Here, too, one is offered a general framework and some guiding principles but not a fully elaborated system of social ethics.

Hisamatsu, Abe, and Ichikawa are not alone in their reflection on Zen and ethics. Non-Japanese Zen Buddhists have in recent decades started reflecting on ethics and have started developing the tradition in new directions.

A group of Vietnamese Zen monks in the Tiep Hien ('interbeing') Order, founded during the Vietnam War, have reworked the traditional Ten Precepts. Their fourteen precepts offer a valuable case study of how Zen has expressed itself in an extreme state of affairs: war in Southeast Asia. Abridged from Thich Nhat Hanh's listing of them, the precepts are:

1. Do not be idolatrous about or bound to any doctrine, theory, or ideology, even Buddhist ones.
2. Do not think that the knowledge you presently possess is changeless, absolute truth.
3. Do not force others, including children, by any means whatsoever, to adopt your views.
4. Do not avoid contact with suffering or close your eyes before suffering.
5. Do not accumulate wealth while millions are hungry. Do not take as the aim of your life fame, profit, wealth, or sensual pleasure. Live simply and share time, energy and material resources with those who are in need.
6. Do not maintain anger or hatred . . . . Learn to look at other beings with the eyes of compassion.
7. Do not lose yourself in dispersion and in your surroundings.
8. Do not utter words that can create discord and cause the community to break. Make every effort reconcile and resolve all conflicts, however small.
9. Do not say untruthful things for the sake of personal interest or to impress people. Do not utter words that cause division and hatred . . . . Always speak truthfully and constructively. Have the courage to speak out about situations of injustice, even when doing so may threaten your own safety.
10. Do not use the Buddhist community for personal gain or profit, or transform your community into a political party. A religious community should, however, take a clear stand against oppression and injustice, and should strive to' change the situation without engaging in partisan conflicts.
11. Do not live with a vocation that is harmful to humans and nature.
12. Do not kill. Do not let others kill. Find whatever means possible to protect life and to prevent war.

13. Possess nothing that should belong to others. Respect the property of others but prevent others from enriching themselves from human suffering or the suffering of other beings.
14. Do no mistreat your body.[106]

Here the 'cardinal precept', as it were, is said to be awareness: 'The most basic precept is to be aware of what we do, what we are, each minute. Every other precept will follow from that.'[107] This awareness takes the form of mindfulness in the present, as one attends to the impact actions, utterances and thoughts (inclusive of feelings) have on the world around oneself. For example, 'When we eat a piece of meat or drink alcohol, we can produce awareness that 40,000 children die *each day* in the third world from hunger and that in order to produce a piece of meat or a bottle of liquor, we have to use a lot of grain.'[108] One other Buddhist writes about the Tiep Hien precepts, 'it could be said that these fourteen precepts issue a clarion call of Emptiness and Non-ego in action . . . . Each precept enjoins a form of moral action that is based on non-separation and an unceasingly aware state of compassion.'[109]

Introduced to Europe and North America in the late nineteenth century, Zen is once again assuming a new form. Like other sects of Buddhism sinking their roots into North American soil, the tradition as a whole is embracing social concern. To a large extent, this trend reflects traditional concern about human rights, personal freedom, democratic forms of government and traditions of protest and social action in North America.

Recently Zen social engagement has emerged, partly in conjunction with the Buddhist Peace Fellowship (BPF), which is based in Berkeley with branch chapters in approximately eighteen other US cities and in England and Australia. The BPF serves as an umbrella group for a variety of socially active[110] Buddhists. The most prominent Buddhist activist connected with the BPF is a Vietnamese Zen teacher connected with the Tiep Tien order, Thich Nhat Hanh, who served as a chairman of the Vietnamese Buddhist Peace delegation to the Paris Peace Talks and has worked extensively in the U.S. to run peace workshops and organise letter-writing campaigns to assist political prisoners in Vietnam.[111] The BPF and its members have assisted refugees, organised peace events, held retreats for Vietnam veterans and children, withheld the military portion of Federal taxes, participated in Ploughshares and other nonviolent protest groups, joined Witness for Peace trips to Central America, worked to stop the massacre of tribal Buddhists in Bangladesh, drawn attention to human rights abuses in Burma, publicised the protest efforts of fasting Vietnam veterans, and published numerous books and pamphlets on social issues. In conjunction with the BPF, the International Network of Engaged Buddhists took shape in the late 1980s.

In addition to work with the Buddhist Peace Fellowship, Zen Buddhists in North America have engaged in a variety of other social activities and movements. Robert Aitken, Zen leader of the Diamond Sangha and Maui Zen Center and one of the founders of the Buddhist Peace Fellowship, has led nonviolent protests at military installations in Hawaii. Zen Buddhists in New York started a prison meditation program, calling it the Green Haven Prison Zendo. Students from the Minnesota, Rochester and Providence Zen centers sat in *zazen* for several days in a park near the United Nations building during the second UN Special Session on Nuclear and General Disarmament. In May 1986 a conference on Buddhism and Nonviolence was held at the Rochester Zen Center. The San Francisco Zen Center and its sister centres in Green Gulch and Tassajara. have been active in nuclear protests and various forms of community work. Issan Dorsey of the Hartford St. Zen Center started Maitri Hospice for AIDS patients. This parallels the work of the L.A. Buddhist AIDS Project and the San Francisco Zen Center Hospice. Bernard Glassman-sensei of the Zen Community of New York started the Greyston Family Inn project to provide 'housing, job training, counseling and childcare for single homeless mothers and their children'.[112]

This active character of Zen connects with the lay orientation of the tradition in North America. Zen teachers and students have been adapting traditional Zen forms of practice in an attempt to create a new practice appropriate for practitioners there. Some teachers have stayed close to traditional monastic patterns, while others have improvised new forms less rooted in the monastic approach. These improvisations include altering traditional meditation schedules to accommodate working students, creating new *kōans* suited to non-Japanese mind-sets, doing away with or altering robes, organising training settings for couples, providing care for children of parents in training, and running acupuncture clinics, organic farms and bakeries. Several of the major centres have built rural meditation centres to function as monasteries for those who want to engage in longer-term intensive practice. Though many practitioners engage in extended periods of practice as monks or nuns, the orientation is toward the laity, which is another reason why the connection between practice and social issues has attracted greater attention in North America than in Japan, where the monastic form has held center stage.

One area where distinct change has occurred is the role of women in Zen. Partly in response to traditional Zen attitudes toward women,[113] to male-dominated Zen institutions, and to abuse of authority on the part of certain male Zen teachers, women have worked to change existing Zen centres or have branched off to create new centres with greater gender equality and other conditions supportive of women's practice. Some of these changes in North America have been outlined in a recent book by Sandy Boucher, *Turning the Wheel: American Women Creating the New Buddhism.* Several conferences about women and Buddhism have been held at the Providence Zen Center (Korean Zen) and other locations, and women associated with the Diamond Sangha in Hawaii publish *Kahawai,* a journal about women and Zen.[114]

As Zen sinks new roots in the West, divergence from the Asian forms of the tradition is inevitable. Of course, change across cultures is nothing new for Buddhism. The tradition changed when it entered Chinese culture in the first few centuries of the common era. After being introduced to Japan in the sixth century, the various sects of Buddhism soon assumed uniquely Japanese forms. As part of this development, Eisai, Dōgen, Hakuin, Hisamatsu and others have given Zen a Japanese character, naturally different from that of Chan. Similarly, Zen is changing in the West, and Zen Buddhists need to monitor these changes with due caution, yet without rigid adherence to traditional forms.

Part II
Toward a Zen Social Ethic

5

Wisdom, Suffering, and Practice

With a focus historically on religious 'goods' in the context of monastic life, Zen Buddhists have not developed systems of social ethics. Although Zen life does contain significant ethical components, Japanese Zen Buddhists have often deferred to Confucianism or conventional Japanese ethics. Usually failing to reflect critically and exhaustively on the ethical components of Zen life in the context of the larger Buddhist tradition, Zen Buddhists in Japan have exhibited a wide range of political stances and behaviours, some of which appear to diverge from basic Buddhist values. For example, as outlined in Chapter 3, certain Japanese monks whose monastic life was guided by precepts and regulations led social lives characterised by close collaboration with the political status quo, which often involved violence and oppression and was headed by warriors most Buddhists would be hard pressed to equate with *bodhisattvas*.[1]

In short, although Zen does have a religiously transformative effect with ethically significant fruits, it has not generated a systematic Zen social ethic.[2] Without careful reflection – grounded in self-critical examination of Buddhist texts, principles, and values – Zen may continue to wander through a range of social orientations, some of which may run contrary to the spirit of the tradition.

Building on Part I, this chapter highlights several further issues concerning Zen and ethics and points to directions in which Zen concepts may be expanded as an initial step toward a Zen social ethic. The issues discussed here are the scope of *prajñā*, the distinction between religious and mundane suffering, the connection between religious practice and social praxis, and the nature of compassion and *upāya*, especially in light of recent ethical problems in Zen.

Over the centuries Zen has concerned itself primarily with the immediate existential state of the practitioner and with the expression of Awakening through poetry, painting, calligraphy, tea ceremony and temple gardens. The functioning of *prajñā* has been primarily religious and aesthetic. Granting that images of a monistic experience with no distinctions whatsoever fall short of Zen *prajñā* with its discernment of things in their immediate particularity, one can still ask whether *prajñā* is limited to the religious and aesthetic arenas or whether it can provide a way of viewing and responding to problems in society.

Through Zen practice one's view of things is said to be increasingly cleansed of distortion and prejudice and increasingly freed from the sense of the world being an alien or threatening object 'out there'. This ability to see things more clearly proves invaluable when one attempts to uncover the causes and exact nature of a specific social problem, be it abuse, poverty, pollution, resource depletion, the arms race or oppression of minority peoples. Zen can argue that *prajñā* not only provides an insight into human entanglement in dualistic subjectivity as a fundamental cause of social problems, but also provides a mode of experience that promotes discernment of the complex interaction of sociohistorical factors constituting the secondary cause of social problems. In more Buddhistic language, *prajñā* promotes insight into the dependent co-arising of the specific problems addressed by any social ethic.

For *prajñā* to function in this way, however, Zen needs to expand it. Practice and Awakening do not provide paranormal powers through which one can perceive, while sitting on a cushion in Kyoto, the exact causes of child abuse in a nearby home or of conflict in a neighboring country. With his notion of the 'unity of study and practice', Hisamatsu argued that one needs continually to augment *prajñā* by critical study, most importantly of relevant disciplines and information about actual social or political problems as well as, one might add, creative problem-solving techniques and past approaches. In this way, *prajñā* can draw on reason and its tools – that is, reappropriate critical analysis and conventional knowledge non-substantially – to address social problems in the world, and thereby evolve into what might be called 'informed wisdom'. Abe Masao points in this direction when he writes, 'Through the realization of our true Self one can properly and effectively work in the social relations between self and others. Of course, to do so one needs objective knowledge of the social environment and historical change.'[3] As an insight into human defensiveness and cognitive distortion, *prajñā* also promotes discernment of the potentially destructive self-interest latent in most approaches to problems.

By offering a discernment of social issues parallel to the discernment of a student in the *sanzen* room, Zen can begin to generate creative responses to social situations, parallel to skilful responses (*upāya*) to the student. Such responses as living a certain style of life, protesting against harmful policies, and creating new economic paradigms and programs can all function as 'social *upāya*'.

To move in the direction of formulating a social ethic, then, Zen can expand the scope of *prajñā* beyond the religious realm in the narrow sense of religious or existential suffering to the social realm and what might be termed 'mundane' or 'social' suffering. This expansion calls for a further, accompanying expansion or rectification as well. Traditionally, Zen has maintained the ideal of monastic life, of religious pursuits separate from society, and at times it has admonished practitioners not to get caught up in social concerns as long as the fundamental religious problem remains unsolved. But to what extent does this distinction between the religious and social realms hold?

Zen traditionally has focused on religious or existential suffering: the alienation and pain that result from entrapment in fixated subjectivity. Zen argues that this suffering is a universal condition insofar as all humans manifest such subjectivity, sever themselves from the larger world, become attached to various objects of attraction and aversion, and fear physical death. Whether weak or strong, sick or healthy, poor or rich, all people succumb to this type of suffering. Even if the world were free from poverty, oppression and war, humanity would, Zen claims, still experience this fundamental suffering. With this approach Zen has provided a hermeneutic for understanding a dilemma in human life and a solution to that dilemma.

From the perspective of social ethics, however, this orientation has created a pitfall for the tradition. Zen Buddhists usually treat the 'universal' religious predicament in virtual isolation from particular social situations. They tend to speak in ideal terms, usually arguing that a human being can awaken in any time and place, regardless of the circumstances. This emphasis on the possibility of Awakening in any time or place drives a wedge between the overarching religious concern and specific social concerns. As a result, social suffering is either ignored or, if considered by Zen, relegated to a distant secondary position. Historically, monastic

Zen has not studied, analysed, or responded self-critically to the full range of suffering in the social world. This lack of a critical spirit has contributed to problematical support of the status quo, whether the aristocracy, samurai dictators, militarists, or certain large corporations.[4]

In response to this pitfall, Zen can begin to delineate how 'religious' suffering contributes to suffering in what are separated out for convenience's sake as the social, political and economic realms;[5] to examine the unique historical and cultural contexts in which suffering occurs, especially in terms of how certain concrete situations cause more or less entrapment in dualistic subjectivity and how certain situations promote or hinder liberation from it; and to recognise the need for, and the intrinsic value of, the solution of particular social problems. In short, Zen needs to clarify how religious and social suffering are related in terms of their genesis and solution, and how Zen insights can be brought to bear on socio-historical suffering.

To this end several initial points can be made here. Although Zen Buddhism characterises ordinary human existence as *duḥkha*, this characterisation pertains to one way of existing, not existence per se. Living (and dying) is not something inherently bad or of negative value; the *fact* of existing in this world is not the problem. Further, Awakening is something that happens while one is living here in this world, not in a different type of existence in a different time and place. In short, the concept of *duḥkha* does not denigrate life itself but rather denigrates a way of experiencing and living that leads to existential anguish. Awakening is not an escape from this world but an eradication of a way of being that causes suffering in this world.

Zen can assert that social and religious suffering are in one respect qualitatively different, yet at the same time interrelated, each affecting the genesis and solution of the other.[6] Equipped with 'informed *prajñā*', one may discern how entanglement in dualistic subjectivity at the individual and national levels contributes to a variety of problems, such as war, economic injustice, nuclear weapons, the oppression of women, children and minorities, and the ongoing devastation of the very environment on which life depends. At the same time, from the opposite direction, 'informed *prajñā*' can uncover the social, political and historical factors contributing to entrenchment in ego-centredness in a wide range of cultural settings; it can reveal how certain conditions do in fact make relinquishment of attachment to fixated subjectivity more or less difficult. Granted, *in principle*, the malnourished villager or abused woman can experience *satori* and may actually do so. *In actuality*, however, the satisfaction of basic needs, a safe place to practice, and access to a qualified Zen teacher are crucial supports of Zen practice, even though these conditions are not absolutely necessary. Or, to offer another example, people possessing great power and wealth may succumb to greater self-fixation than do people living with 'enough', people whose basic needs are met and who are not clinging to their wealth or craving a never-ending increase of wealth.[7] Economic systems oriented toward accumulating personal wealth foster greed and hatred (two of the three Buddhist 'poisons') and in this way make people all the more self-entrenched. Political and social situations characterised by fear, mistrust and aggression do not support a loosening of self-attachment. The presence of these aspects of social life is one factor behind Zen's monastic bent, its tendency to remove itself from society rather than devote its energies to transforming society into a context more supportive of Awakening.

In any case, while making its case for the universality of the human predicament and the ability – in principle – of any person in any situation to awaken, Zen needs to discern how ignorance (*avidyā*) and suffering (*duḥkha*) influence the 'non-religious realm' and critique actual social, political and economic structures and processes as more or less conducive to ignorance and suffering or to wisdom and Awakening.

With this approach Zen can deepen its understanding of human suffering and can respond to those who argue that Zen should devote itself to resolving suffering as traditionally defined in the narrow religious sense and not waste its time and energy on issues falling outside its 'proper' domain. To discover the causes of various forms of suffering and engage in creative responses to them is to work for the emancipation of oneself and others, an approach well within the 'proper' domain of Mahāyāna Buddhism.

This approach can provide a basis for what may be called 'Buddhist realism', paralleling the 'Christian realism' advanced by Reinhold Niebuhr. This 'realism' builds upon an open discernment of the objective, concrete particularity of suffering, of its causes, of possible solutions, and of the overall goals that can be reasonably aimed for and achieved. This realism cuts through a possible perfectionistic orientation to ethics that argues that most or all people can be awakened and that such a collective awakening would solve all problems.[8] This type of realism can also mitigate the attitude that only Zen can bring about a true cessation of suffering.[9]

The line of thought followed thus far in this chapter – concerning the scope of *prajñā*, the interrelationship between religious and social suffering, and engagement in creative responses to suffering – leads to the issue of action in Zen. As indicated earlier, despite images of Zen as passive and focused only inwardly, the tradition fosters dynamic action, whether by the *rōshi* or by the artist. In a broad sense, Zen action – inclusive of practice and praxis – assumes two forms: action prior to or leading to Awakening and action emerging from Awakening.[10] When it does concern itself with ethical action in relation to others, Zen focuses overwhelmingly on the latter, usually understood as compassionate 'bodhisattva functioning', yet rarely treats the former, primarily the actions of the 'unawakened'.[11]

In the context of Zen, action leading to Awakening takes the form of religious practice. This usually entails such activities as *zazen*, *samu*, work with *kōans*, chanting, observing precepts, listening to Dharma-talks, and artistic expression. This practice aims at the practitioner's *satori* as a resolution of religious suffering and, given the emphasis in Zen texts and *kōans* on particular *satori* experiences, it stands as a type of individual religious transformation.[12]

Given the linkage between religious and social suffering sketched above, Zen can argue that the second mode of action leading to Awakening is praxis directed toward a solution of social suffering in all of its forms – economic, political and ecological. This action aims at social transformation, with the ultimate goal of group emancipation in the secular and religious senses. This social praxis is given a useful definition in a Buddhist context by Ken Jones:

> By 'social action' we mean the many different kinds of action intended to benefit humankind. These range from simple, individual acts of charity, teaching and training, organised kinds of service, 'Right Livelihood' in and outside the helping professions, and through various kinds of community development as well as to political activity in working for a better society.[13]

Concentrating almost exclusively on religious practice in monasteries, however, historical Zen has rarely taken such action into account.

For Zen to engage most fully and profoundly in action leading to liberation, it must clarify the connection between religious suffering and social suffering. Just as Zen may argue that social and religious forms of suffering interrelate in their genesis, it can make the case that they interrelate also in terms of the actions taken in response.

First, religious transformation does not occur in isolation from other people or actual social situations. Given the Buddhist notion of dependent co-arising, the distinction between the individual and social realms ultimately crumbles – all actions are social in that they impact other people, however subtly, and the 'individual' exists because of (in profound interconnection with) the 'society'. Thich Nhat Hanh declares:

> Meditation is not to get out of society, to escape from society, but to prepare for a reentry into society. We call this 'engaged Buddhism.' When we go to a meditation center, we may have the impression that we leave everything behind – family, society, and all the complications involved in them – and come as an individual in order to search for peace. This is already an illusion, because in Buddhism there is no such thing as an individual.[14]

Like all human actions, *zazen* impacts society. 'Meditation is to see deeply into things, to see how we can change, how we can transform our situation. To transform our situation is also to transform our minds. To transform our minds is also to transform our situation, because the situation is mind and the mind is situation.'[15] This stance is based on the realisation that social situations affect human subjectivity at the same time they reflect it. For this reason, 'Awakening is important. The nature of the bombs, the nature of injustice, the nature of the weapons and the nature of our own being are the same.'[16] When one discerns this one realises that Zen practice affects society at a variety of levels, some quite subtle.[17] From this perspective, to go on a true 'retreat' is not to escape but to 'advance'. In fact, insofar as one's practice influences one's society, 'it is not a privilege to meditate, but a responsibility'.[18]

Second, both everyday activities and social action can constitute forms of practice. When done with full attention, one's working, driving, and shopping are all forms of practice in that they provide opportunities to slip out of self-fixation through immersion in the action at hand. Social engagement usually comes to call the 'self' into question and demand the relinquishment of narrow self-attachment. As it confronts the practitioner with its complexity and dilemmas, social action constitutes a *kōan* of sorts.[19] In this way, both the giving of oneself to breathing in *zazen* and the giving of oneself to social action[20] are what might be called 'practice-praxis' or 'Practice'. As Zen often asserts, the deeper one goes within, the more one is brought out into the world, and the more one enters into the world, the more one is brought back to the question of the self. In short, 'We must practice in a way that removes the barrier between practice and non-practice.'[21]

As discussed further in Chapter 6, Zen can pursue 'Practice' as an activity that promotes the reduction of social and religious suffering by satisfying basic needs, supporting full participation in the world, providing a context for higher religious endeavors, and helping all people who seek Awakening to realise it. This emphasis on group liberation is central to Mahāyāna or Great-Vehicle Buddhism, with its *bodhisattva* ideal, especially as expressed in the Fourfold Great Vow.

Though this approach has suggested a Zen reformulation of action as practice leading *to* Awakening, the active self-emptying in this action also emerges *from* Awakening. That is to say, it expresses and 'manifests' Awakening in that the fixated 'self' is dissolved in the act of complete breathing, listening, speaking, writing, healing, teaching, marching, witnessing, dying. With this 'self' forgotten in complete absorption in the action and subject and object no longer standing in opposition, Awakening in one respect is expressing itself. 'Original Awakening' is expressed not only in the acts of 'awakened' people but also in giving away the 'small self' in social action, just as done with complete breathing in *zazen*. This is one way of expressing Dōgen's notion of the unity of practice and attainment, the idea that practice does not simply lead *to* Awakening but, when done as a full pouring of oneself into the action or as a total exertion (*gujin*), expresses Awakening or, radically stated, *is* Awakening.[22]

This discussion of Zen and action leads to several other issues. The focus of Zen is existential, in that it asks the question, 'Who am I?' The essential concern is the nature of the 'self', and so the pivotal question is that of what one should *be*, not what one should *do*. Zen goes a step beyond ethics in the ordinary sense in that it calls into question the moral agent rather than simply dwelling on a critique of the agent's actions. From the Zen perspective, only by eliminating entrapment in dualism and realising Awakening can one truly overcome the fundamental cause of socio-political problems and work compassionately in the ethical and religious arena; if one is not grounded in subjectivity that realises the interconnectedness of all things and can see the 'other' as oneself, one's ethical efforts will ultimately fail.

In this respect, Zen diverges from socialist thought and liberation theology, which usually regard the transformation of people as primarily a *future* goal realised *after* social transformation. Gustavo Gutierrez writes, 'The commitment to the creation of a just society and, ultimately, to a new man, presupposes confidence in the future.'[23] For Zen, the 'new [hu]man' is primarily the basis or starting point of social action, not its future result. Granted, as argued before, individual transformation and social transformation are to be striven for simultaneously, but from the Zen perspective no true social transformation can be attained without a religious transformation of the humans making up any given society.

Zen differs from socialism and other schemes of action, liberation, or progress in one other respect. Partly rooted in Taoist soil, Zen views action as problematical. Most people living in 'modern' societies emphasise hard work, competition and control as the fuel of progress. Most problems – even those caused and now exacerbated by action directed toward 'progress' – are seen as solvable by further action, be it further hard work, market activity, or technological fixes. This anthropocentric faith in human action leads a Japanese farmer influenced by Zen, Fukuoka Masanobu, to write:

The more people do, the more society develops, the more problems arise. The increasing desolation of nature, the exhaustion of resources, the uneasiness and disintegration of the human spirit, all have been brought about by humanity's trying to accomplish something. Originally there was no reason to progress, and nothing had to be done. We have come to the point at which there is no other way than to bring about a 'movement' not to bring anything about.[24]

This radical and perhaps overstated vantagepoint may irritate inhabitants of modern, 'advanced' societies, where sitting quietly without visibly acting is often seen as a waste of time or a form of laziness unless it is done to make oneself a better performer of some activity – whether tennis, sex, or work on Wall Street. Monks, nuns, and other practitioners of Zen may be seen as escaping 'reality', construed as the realm of action, or as succumbing to irresponsibility, defined as a failure to respond actively to certain situations. They may be judged as unproductive members of society who inhibit or at least fail to contribute to 'development'. What is more, Zen monks and nuns make poor consumers.

Given the chaotic attempts to win and to dominate others in the 'real world' with all of its greed, prejudice and violence, perhaps what the world needs most are monasteries and quietistic saints who do nothing in the normal activist sense, but simply engage in a different way of living, characterised by simplicity, compassion and nonviolence. And in some situations, whether in the monastery or the market, our *being*, not our *doing*, constitutes the optimal response to a situation. As Thich Nhat Hanh writes, 'Sometimes if we don't do anything, we help more than if we do a lot. We call that non-action. It is like a calm person in a small boat in a storm. That person does not have to do much, just to be himself and the situation can change. This is also an aspect of Dharmakaya: not talking, not teaching, just being.'[25]

But, does this critique of action and anthropocentric confidence imply that Zen can (and should) offer only a monastic regimen focused on a *rōshi*'s efforts to help a small number of disciples awaken? Monastic Zen practice is crucial, even in modern times, but Zen must not get stuck there. To ignore social and political problems is to fall short of full compassionate action. As Hisamatsu argues, 'If Zen ends in mere self-awakening and the awakening of others, it is not perfect awakened functioning.'[26] For the compassion accompanying wisdom to be a full compassion, it needs to be *active* compassion, which discerns the suffering of others *in all forms* and acts to alleviate it. If Zen intends to create a world supportive of human well-being and Awakening, merely the enlightened presence of highly evolved Zen Buddhists is not enough.

Abe Masao has termed *active* compassion *karuṇā-pāramitā*, the 'perfection of compassion' or 'compassion of the far shore', which must accompany the 'perfection of wisdom' or 'wisdom of the far shore' (*prajñā-pāramitā*).[27] To Abe, if true wisdom and compassion are attained, action emerges as the 'self-emptying of emptiness'. In true Awakening, one identifies with the larger, everchanging matrix of relationships out of which individual be-ing emerges; one 'merges' with others in the dissolution of fixated subjectivity and then splits apart, now seeing the 'other' as ultimately inseparable from oneself. On this basis, according to Zen, one comes to work to liberate the other-as-self just as reflexively as when one dodges an oncoming car or pulls a child out of its way. Freed from self-interest in the narrow sense, one's matrix-based interest coincides with the interest of others. Perhaps this is the gist of a story about Gandhi:

> A friend once inquired if Gandhi's aim in settling in the village and serving the villagers as best he could was purely humanitarian. Gandhi replied, '. . . I am here to serve no one else but myself, to find my own self-realization through the service of these village folk.'[28]

But a crucial issue arises here. Even after informing *prajñā*, expanding it by directing it toward social suffering, and recontextualising action, one may still ask about the end to which one directs actions? What guidelines does Zen offer? What are the Zen criteria for actions to be deemed 'good'?

Zen representatives sometimes argue that upon Awakening one innately knows the 'good', even though it cannot be formulated in words as a set of criteria, and that the good appears in any action or state of affairs that leads people to Awakening. The implication is that awakened people know and do the good at all times, and that the spontaneity and intuitive nature of this knowledge makes it difficult to articulate a clear definition of what specifically is good, although one can at least look to these figures as role models.

This view needs to be examined critically. In fact, a number of people are currently involved in this examination, primarily with regard to a specific ethical problem that has arisen as Zen spreads to the West. In the past fifteen years several highly publicised crises in North American Zen centres have unfolded involving sexual relationships between Zen teachers and their students. This has triggered a set of questions. Is there something inherently wrong with a Zen *rōshi* sleeping with a student? If not, on what basis does one determine when advances or sexual contact are acceptable? Does one need to be awakened to make that determination?

Some have argued that such contact is inherently wrong.[29] This implies an absolute ought, something universal that must not be violated and hence, to use the language of Ethics, a deontological approach. Those who argue this way need to clarify what it is about such an action that is contrary to the promotion of Awakening. Expressed differently, they need to clarify how sexual contact would *always* be unacceptable – as *upāya* or simply as an action in general – whereas a shout, a blow with a stick, or the cutting off of a boy's finger[30] might not be.

Some observers have argued that although sexual contact may in some unique cases promote Awakening, given the difficulty of determining this and given the potential for abuse it should be avoided. Unlike a universal and deontological stance, this approach is situational and utilitarian. Others have argued that such an act may promote Awakening, so one must not condemn it but strive to sort out the positive and negative instances. From this perspective, when the act is positive the teleological fruits might be immediate or long-term, and the student may not immediately realise that the act was beneficial. (There could be short-term pain or anger followed by long-term benefit recognised later.) This leads to the question of who can or should make the distinction between positive and negative instances?

Perhaps this is the responsibility of the student, who as an adult (usually) needs to decide whether to consent. Yet one might ask here whether this absolves a possible abusive *rōshi* of responsibility and whether Zen would see the student as equipped to decide clearly, which raises the further issue of whether Zen practice – at least in the traditional *rōshi*-student form with accompanying trust in and self-relinquishment to the *rōshi* – can function if the student is deemed responsible for deciding which acts by the *rōshi* are to be accepted and which rejected. This connects with the larger question of the proper way, if any, of 'surrendering' oneself to the teacher.

Discerning the difference between positive and negative instances of sexual advances or contact might be seen as the responsibility of the *rōshi*. But what is the nature of this discernment? How does the *rōshi* know when it will not be destructive? Can this be articulated – and perhaps publicly defended – or is it something intuitive, a matter of *prajñā*? If the latter is the case, people again encounter the 'one has to be awakened to judge' pitfall, and this runs the risk of abuse insofar as one defers to the judgement of a *rōshi* deemed to be awakened. This raises the further question of how one selects a *rōshi* to practice under (or *with*) – does one simply judge as best as possible and then make a trusting leap of faith?

The final possible response to sexual contact between a *rōshi* and a student would be that actions springing from *satori* are inherently good and hence if the person has been designated as a *rōshi* on the basis of an acknowledged *satori* – that is, has received *inka*, the certification of *satori* in a Zen lineage – then that action will certainly be good. Few take this stance explicitly, but it is often implied in discussions of Zen 'masters' and their discernment rooted in Awakening.

Given the pain that has arisen for many individuals involved in these incidents in North America and the apparent irresponsible abuse of power and authority on the part of the *rōshis* involved, such contact can be seen as tragic. Further, it is contrary to Buddhist principles, for the precept on illicit sexual relations certainly makes no provision for sexual contact between teacher and student, and no prominent Zen figure has ever advanced a case for the 'upayic' value of such contact. For these reasons Zen can serve its development in the West by rejecting sexual relations between teachers and students.

Regardless of the stance one takes concerning this specific, concrete ethical problem in current Zen circles, Zen still needs indicate what the overall 'good' might be, what the touchstone might be for judging actions or evaluating various social situations or possibilities. Based on the issues raised here about *prajñā*, suffering, and action, and on the way they were expanded as possible building blocks for a Zen social ethic, Chapter 6, the final chapter, sketches a possible Zen formulation of what might be 'good' in society.

6

Zen Formulation of the Social Good

Ethicists often address the question of the social 'good' in terms of justice. Zen Buddhists, however, have never set forth a systematic formulation of justice. Perhaps this is not surprising, given that the concept originated in the West and hence is foreign to the tradition. To some Zen Buddhists the idea of 'justice' is not simply foreign but also contrary to the spirit of Zen. Treating justice in terms of judgment and punishment, Abe Masao writes:

> . . . the notion of justice is a double-edged sword. On the one hand, it sharply judges which is right and which is wrong. On the other hand, the judgment based on justice will naturally cause a counter-judgment as a reaction from the side thus judged. Accordingly, we may fall into endless conflict and struggle between the judge and the judged.[1]

In place of justice in this sense, Abe advocates *prajñā* as a recognition of everyone and everything in its nonsubstantial distinctiveness or 'suchness'. From his perspective, justice and wisdom lead to very different ethical stances in society. To Abe, justice, 'when carried to its final conclusion, often results in punishment, conflict, revenge and even war, whereas wisdom entails rapprochement, conciliation, harmony and peace'.[2] Abe further argues that the linkage between justice and love[3] proves difficult, whereas the linkage between wisdom and compassion is comparatively smooth. 'Love and justice are like water and fire – although both are necessary, they go together with difficulty. Compassion and wisdom are like heat and light. Although different, they work together complementarily.'[4]

Does this characterisation of justice exhaust the meaning of 'justice'? Is Buddhist wisdom, as a recognition of everything and everyone in its distinctiveness or suchness, a sufficient basis for a social ethic? And what formulation might Zen offer in place of, for example, Reinhold Niebuhr's notion of justice as a balance of power in society requiring the use of force to maintain the balance? In a dialogue with Richard DeMartino, D. T. Suzuki draws heavily from Taoism to contend that government and the rules, institutions and exercise of power functioning to maintain justice are a problem and perhaps, in a certain sense, are contrary to religion. Suzuki claims:

> When things become separated into two, the problem of justice will always be there. It will never be able to be resolved. Therefore I think the best solution is to be found in 'anarchism' or 'non-government.' Until people are governed by non-government – or by non-doing – there will always be problems.[5]

In response, DeMartino begins to formulate a Zen notion of justice. He observes that while Zen has not considered possible connections between compassion and justice, such Christian thinkers as Paul Tillich have investigated the relationship between love and justice. DeMartino states that 'compassion – or love – always involves the duality or differentiation between one being and another being, and this differentiation always involves – within the arena of duality – the issue of justice'.[6] He continues:

> . . . insofar as the basis and the aim of justice is the establishment or preservation of balances and the redress or removal of imbalances among claims or rights as between one and another, the basis or aim of justice could be said to be the reduction or removal of the discriminatory aspect that inheres in any dualistic 'two'ness of the two.' But this discriminatory aspect of the two'ness of the two is thoroughly overcome (even as it remains) only with the actualization of the not-two'ness of the two – or of love, wherein the one is at once both itself and the other.[7]

From this standpoint, love and justice are inseparable. Love without justice is naive, and justice without love is uncompromising.

In the case of a love that would naively or blindly disregard the requirements of justice, the result tends to be an irrelevant – and perhaps even harmful – sentimentality. In the case of a justice that would . . . disassociate itself from love, the result tends to be a rigid, formalistic, dogmatic – and perhaps inhumane – legalism.[8]

The ethical agent finds his or her footing in a realisation of non-duality, which serves as a springboard for a new type of justice. In DeMartino's words, 'when justice does emerge as a mode of the Self-expression or functioning of Love within the dimension of duality, such a justice is never simply a rationalistic, a prudential, or a humanistic justice. It is . . . a Love-based-justice of a "twice-born" humanism.'[9]

These statements by Abe, Suzuki and DeMartino about justice provide a backdrop for consideration of what might be 'good' in society and, by extension, what a Zen formulation of justice might entail.

Actual Zen·practice and philosophy suggest possible directions in which a Zen social ethic can be formulated. Progressively realised in *zazen*, *śūnyatā* signifies that reality is neither monistic nor pluralistic but non-dualistic, in the sense that reality is a process of unique events (plurality, not-one), all of which are interrelated in a vast matrix (unity, not-two). Reality is 100 per cent plural and 100 per cent unified at one and the same time, with neither aspect taking precedence. This dynamism of reality does not consist of two separate facets, for they both exist together – just as, to use the Buddhist metaphor, waves cannot exist without water and water cannot exist without being in *some* form (i.e., waves).

A practicing Zen Buddhist is said to realise this dynamism when he or she recognises how fixated subjectivity 'dissolves' or 'drops off' into the matrix of relationship called the universe ('exists together with everything', as Joshu Sasaki Rōshi says) and then reemerges as a different 'self'.

This dynamism termed *śūnyatā* involves two directions: difference (the split between self and matrix, or subject and object) to unity (merging or unity of subject and object) and unity to difference. According to Zen, after surrendering self-fixation and embracing or merging with the world and the others in it, one reemerges as a reflective, thinking self, though no longer entangled in fixated subjectivity. One can now act more freely and flexibly, responsibly and responsively, as one contributes to and receives from the world. In short, neither totally subordinating or losing oneself (no sense of self, leading to excessive humility, obedience or self-sacrifice) nor totally affirming oneself (no sense of interrelationship and empathy, leading to arrogance, domination or self-aggrandisement), one *participates* fully and compassionately in the world, all the while responding to the changes encountered. By awakening to this two-way dynamism, one is liberated from self-entanglement; one is saved *to* this world, not away from it. To use the metaphor of waves and water, Zen contends that when one extricates oneself from the view that one is merely a wave, one awakens to the non-dualistic ocean of water and at the same time awakens as the true wave, the 'wave-as-water/water-as-wave' wave.

Zen further contends that, as this new 'self' balanced in nonduality, the practitioner is emptied of rigid attachment to such dichotomies as us–them, man–woman, mind–body, better–worse, right–wrong and good–evil and the judgmental labelling that may emerge from such attachment. One can see the partiality of standpoints, and can now make practical distinctions without getting stuck in them. Emancipated from rigid adherence to prejudices and vested interests, one can open more empathetically to others and their views, hopes and fears. The approach to reality becomes more tolerant and inclusive, more egalitarian, as it were. No longer entrenched in distinctions between 'me' and 'you' or 'us' and 'them', one's orientation turns more toward general well-being, not simply one's own. As one Zen Buddhist writes:

. . . I see Zen practice as subversive in the deepest sense: it overturns distinctions which have been the very foundation of our attitudes, actions, and institutions. Most fundamentally, it shatters the premise of separateness that has guided our behavior since infancy. And with this, mysteriously, a revolution of the heart begins, turning the Zen student from self-concern toward concern for the welfare of others, from concern for the small self toward concern for the Self in which there are no 'others.'[10]

This expansive awareness 'in which there are no "others"' diverges markedly from fixated subjectivity and the emphasis on competition, winning, dominance and possessiveness that may emerge from substantialist notions of the self.[11]

In this regard, as mentioned before, Zen epistemology (*prajñā*) and ethics are based on a criticism of the normal ethical agent, the thinking/acting 'self'. Zen does not rest upon the presupposition of an independent 'self' and the exercise of its will upon objective conditions to make them conform to an envisioned goal. Nishida claims that the uniqueness of Japanese culture lies 'in moving in the direction from subject to object [environment], ever thoroughly negating the self and becoming the thing itself; becoming the thing itself to see; becoming the thing itself to act'.[12] Though at first glance appearing to indicate something contrary to what Nishida describes, Dōgen expresses one and the same self-negation in terms of a self-forgetting.

> To practice and confirm all things by conveying one's self to them, is illusion. For all things to advance forward and practice and confirm the self is enlightenment . . . .
> To learn the Buddha Way is to learn one's own self. To learn one's self is to forget one's self. To forget one's self is to be confirmed by all dharmas.[13]

To view other people and nature as objects to be dominated, manipulated and changed is to exhibit ignorance; they come to be seen as 'out there', as something to be controlled and used for narrowly self-serving purposes. To take leave of this fixated and fixating standpoint, realise the dynamic web of interrelating events that constitute the world, and then discriminate anew on this basis is to enter into more compassionate interaction with what from the initial perspective was seen as wholly 'other' than oneself. In an exegesis of Dōgen's statement, Robert Aitken writes:

> The self imposing upon the other is not only something called delusion, it is the ruination of our planet and all of its creatures. But enlightenment is not just a matter of learning from another human being. When the self is forgotten, it is recreated again and again, ever more richly by the myriad things and beings of the universe . . . .
> Man-over-nature is the self advancing and confirming the myriad things, an anthropocentric delusion. It is the same mind-set as Americans over Vietnamese, or man over woman, or managers over workers, or whites over blacks.[14]

To 'forget' the self and observe how one is recreated by other things is to realise one's interdependence with them and to become responsive to them.

Zen claims that by virtue of this *prajñā* cultivated in practice one begins to discern the far-reaching and often subtle impact of actions. As reflected in verses chanted before Zen meals, one realises more deeply how decisions at the market may impact the natural world and the lives of people in distant places, just as the food on one's table derives from countless factors, natural and human. Further, one realises how groups – whether families, businesses, races or societies – with their values, behaviour patterns and histories come to exhibit *karmas* of their own, and how members partake of this trans-personal, collective *karma* when they are formed to a great extent by the group, act as part of the group, or reap the consequences of the group's actions. The recognition of personal and collective *karma* leads to a greater sense of responsibility for the effects of one's actions and the world created by them, however indirectly. Thich Nhat Hanh sketches such responsibility in a discussion of possible responses to the rape of a 'boat person' by a Thai pirate: 'In my meditation I saw that if I had been born in the village of the pirate and raised in the same conditions as he was, I am now the pirate . . . . If you take a gun and shoot the pirate, you shoot all of us because all of us are to some extent responsible for this state of affairs.'[15]

All people affect the world and must take responsibility for it, but they exert different degrees of influence on different situations. For example, a white supremacist, a black coal miner, a New York gold trader, a baker in Melbourne and a boxer in Tokyo are all connected with the system of Apartheid, although in different ways and to markedly different degrees. Accordingly, though at the deepest level all people influence the situation in South Africa, in actuality the magnitude and form of individual influence differs. For this reason, relative ethical responsibility differs as well. A South African and an Australian, or a white supremacist in Pretoria and a carpenter in Soweto, each affects the situation of 'coloureds' in South Africa, although in actuality their ethical responsibility for the injustices of Apartheid is quite different. Zen argues that given the nature of *karma* all people ultimately must shoulder responsibility for Apartheid or the Holocaust seem to imply that people are equally or in the same way responsible, which can blur necessary relative distinctions between those who are directly involved and those who are only indirectly involved, or between the oppressor and the oppressed. Indeed, can one truly say that a black infant in Pretoria must 'ultimately' shoulder responsibility for the oppressive system into which she was born? Cultivated in Zen practice, the discernment of the effects of actions heightens awareness of embeddedness in the world and enhances one's sense of 'responsibility' (in the causal and ethical senses, depending on the situation), but this does not exhaust the scope of the term. Zen can begin to formulate a social ethic by clarifying how the realisation of relationality and the consequent openness does, or may, lead to a greater 'response ability', in that one can now begin to act responsibly and responsively. Freed from attachment to narrow biases or entanglement in fear, one manifests a greater commitment to changing habitual patterns of behaviour or lifestyle; and with energy no longer trapped in self-preoccupation, one is freed into action.[16]

From a Buddhist perspective, taking responsibility and acting responsively do not pertain only to observable actions. True responsibility includes acknowledging and, when necessary, criticising one's concepts, theories and thought processes, for these inner mental factors affect the world both in subtle modes of influence and as the basis of external – physical and verbal – actions. The Dalai Lama writes:

> World problems . . . cannot be challenged by anger or hatred. They must be faced with compassion, love, and true kindness. Even with all the terrible weapons we have, the weapons themselves cannot start a war. The button to trigger them is under a human finger, which moves by thought, not under its own power. The responsibility rests in thought.[17]

Taking responsibility for thoughts and emotions – primarily by paying attention to and acknowledging them – is the first step toward taking responsibility for actions and acting anew.

In this Zen formulation of responsibility, the responsible agent and 'others' possess no unchanging essence (*svabhāva*). This viewpoint affects attitudes toward judgment and punishment. A human being is everchanging and devoid of any underlying essential goodness or evil, and hence always has the potential for psychological or ethical change. Further, all people suffer pain and disconnection and need healing. And given the nature of *śūnyatā*, we all contribute to the pain or the healing of others. In fact, a Zen social ethic might be most faithful to the tradition when it focuses primarily on ignorance, pain, compassion, and healing rather than evil, injustice, condemnation, and punishment,[18] although consideration of justice in some form is necessary for maintaining the realism called for before and hence avoiding a naive, perfectionistic ethic.

Awareness of shared ignorance, pain, and healing mitigates the tendency to build walls between ourselves as 'good, law-abiding citizens' and certain others as 'good-for-nothing criminals' or between 'us' and 'them' at the international level. Such awareness also erodes barriers between the 'sane' and the 'insane', the 'healthy' and the 'sick'.

The non-dualistic view of selfhood provides Zen with resources for a novel approach to human rights. Many formulations of human rights begin by presupposing a collection of independent selves possessing certain inalienable rights, which must be respected and defended. This may amount to the attitude, 'This is me and that is you; we both have certain rights, and I won't bother you if you don't bother me.' Atomistic selves are posited *first*, and rights become an issue when those selves enter *secondarily* into relations with each other and discover that their respective desires and claims come into conflict. This atomism lies behind many systems of social ethics and such formulations as the United States Bill of Rights.

In contrast, Zen 'selfhood' is relational. All things 'co-arise dependently'; nothing can exist apart from the matrix of interrelationship constituting reality. In Nāgārjuna's terms, things are empty (*śūnya*) of any independent, enduring essence or own-being (*svabhāva*), for they are thoroughly relational (and yet unique). What makes one feel like an independent self or soul is the ability to objectify things and remember and substantialise as a 'self' the unique series of experiences one *is* over time, yet this sense of a separate self that 'has' experiences over time and the uniqueness one *does* possess derive not from an independent essence, but from interrelationship: the interaction of such overlapping inputs as one's genetic heritage, the prenatal environment, early family experiences, diet and cultural milieu. And our happiness – both individual and collective – is possible only in and through relationship. More exactly put, one can never leave the matrix of relationship, and the *way* people interrelate determines in large part the quality of life they experience together. Further, the way people interrelate depends upon the degree to which they are awakened to their interrelationship.

Śūnyatā as this process of interrelating does not signify, however, that a person is illusory or should be subordinated to or sacrificed for the whole. The Zen notions of the One Great Death and no-self (*anātman*) do not indicate an obliteration of dualistic subjectivity forever or an erosion of concern for the individual. Zen does recognise the very real existence of each individual as something unique, unique through – not despite – interrelationship and interdependence with others. Further, Zen views its practice as enhancing the discernment of and respect for the individual – a relational, processive individual. Yamada Mumon Rōshi writes in a discussion of wasted lives that 'to have a clear realisation of absolute respect for oneself by grasping that one is living here and now and that the world is functioning in such a way as to give one life, constitutes the most important and most fundamental issue of human life'.[19]

Given the metaphysic underlying Zen, then, 'rights' begin to make sense only in an arena larger than the individual. People may speak of the rights of life, liberty and the pursuit of happiness. To lead one's life means to relate with other people and things, whose presence and co-operation is indispensable; liberty makes sense only in relation to the larger social context and the liberty of others; and the pursuit of happiness is hardly something that occurs in a vacuum, for happiness is primarily relational, whether in conjunction with one's family, a beloved cat, or the wilderness serving as home for the hermit. In short, what people usually hold dear as their inherent rights are expressed and satisfied only in a larger social context and the ecological matrix of life.

Further, because Buddhist metaphysics, epistemology and soteriology do not hinge on the uniqueness of human will and reflective self-consciousness, and because the basis of 'selfhood' is *śūnyatā* or dependent co-arising characteristic of *all* facets of reality, Zen is led away from the stance that rights are relevant only to human society divorced from the non-human domain or that rights are asserted *over and against* the non-human realm. Offering a Buddhist view of rights, Abe states, 'The self and nature are different from one another on the relative level, but on the absolute level they are equal and interfuse with one another because of the lack of any fixed substantial selfhood.'[20] Accordingly, 'In Buddhism,''human rights" is to be understood in this trans-anthropocentric, universal dimension.'[21] And as discussed in more detail later, by shifting the discussion to this larger context of the universe, Zen can expand the notion of rights to include the 'rights' of the non-human realm as well; in Abe's words, 'Under the [Buddhist] commandment, ''Not to destroy life,'' the rights of animals and plants are as equally recognised as are human rights. Not only is nature subordinate to human beings, but human beings are also subordinate to nature.'[22] Yet Abe and other Zen Buddhists need to answer several questions here. Granting the likelihood of a primary emphasis by Zen on responsibility rather than on rights, what 'rights' might still play a role in a Zen social ethic? Life, liberty and the pursuit of happiness? Do these rights apply to deer, forests and mineral deposits? Do non-human 'rights' carry the same weight as those of humans?

In answering these questions, Zen can turn to its sources. First, the Mahāyāna doctrine of *śūnyatā* implies the stance that there are no *absolute* rights. In human terms, there is no enduring self, no enduring property and no enduring wealth. Yet although selves and rights should not be reified or absolutised, Buddhism does support certain 'rights'. Given the historical Buddha's criticism of the caste system, the tradition can argue that all people have an intrinsic right to work to eliminate suffering in its various forms and attain religious liberation. The Dalai Lama advances such an argument.

> Regardless of race, creed, ideology, political bloc (East and West) or economic region (North and South), the most important and basic aspect of all peoples is their shared humanity – the fact that each person, old, young, rich, poor, educated, uneducated, male or female, is a human. This shared humanness and thus the shared aspiration of gaining happiness and avoiding suffering, and the basic right to bring these about, are of prime importance.[23]

Zen may add here that 'happiness' and the avoidance of suffering derive in large part from optimal participation in society and the natural world. 'To be' means to be in relationship, to participate in – *contribute to* and *receive from* – the whole of which one is part. The social 'good' is achieved to the extent people actualise optimal participation and mutually supportive interaction in society. Insofar as it might use the term, Zen can construe 'justice' as 'participatory justice'.

Given that Buddhist notions of *śūnyatā* and *karma* indicate that people are always participating – influencing others and being influenced by them – in society, a formulation of 'participatory justice' needs to clarify which *types* of participation are congruent with Buddhist principles. In moving to an emphasis on both religious realisation of dependent co-arising and ethical consideration of specific instances of dependent co-arising, Zen needs to specify which concrete social conditions *optimise* participation. This does not mean, however, that there is one type of optimal participation that works for all cultures. *Śūnyatā* implies formulations that are flexible within and across cultures, and an openness to experiment, reflect critically, and change as needed. Apropos here is a statement in an article on environmental ethics: ' . . . value consists in achieving an existential integration of things';[24] but this must not be a static integration, and for this reason one needs to call 'attention within process to those elements making up the general tolerance of change, the feminine, motherly, womblike patterns that both survive the special changes and provide the matrix out of which the special changing harmonies can arise'.[25] Chaos and struggle can play a valuable role insofar as they break people out of oppressive or destructive structures, contribute to more fulfilling participatory integration and keep the integrated whole dynamically 'alive'.

Granting this need for flexibility, Zen can argue that optimal participation in society presupposes the ability to participate in a significant and fulfilling way. In most societies,[26] this ability depends at the very least on education, the right to vote, and validated work. A modern, 'developed' society must foster universal education aimed at full literacy, the ability to reflect self-critically, knowledge of global cultural history, artistic self-expression and specific skills enabling individuals to participate in the economic sphere. Education needs to be promoted especially for the poor and disenfranchised, that is, people whose participation is severely limited.

Along with education, Zen might argue that the right to vote constitutes a precondition of full participation in society. Full voting rights should not be denied any adult on the basis of gender, ethnicity, race, religion, or social status (determined by income, property, criminal record, or psychiatric history). At the least, all adults must possess this form of political power. And in political life, not only the right to vote but also the ability to run for and hold public office must be guaranteed. In this regard, Zen might argue that campaign funds need to be strictly regulated and the government should monitor donations from businesses and other organisations that may influence decisions after an election victory. Ideally this would bring about a more representative government free from control by individuals or corporate entities with substantial wealth and vested interests.[27]

Full participation in human relationships, which form the skeletal structure of society, presupposes the right to speak, to communicate one's own ideas, hopes and fears, to have a say in matters affecting oneself, whether in a dyad, family, small group, organisation, society or humanity as a whole. All people have a right to this 'voice', and each voice deserves to be heard. In light of this right and in conjunction with the *bodhisattva* ideal, Zen may advocate the 'duty' of respecting the other's voice and *listening* to it. With such a stance, Zen could balance the Greek virtue of eloquence by praising the virtue of attentive listening and the receptivity, empathy, and respect it fosters.

This orientation could lead Zen to advocate the rights of self-expression and access to the expressions of others. People have a right to utilise various means of 'giving voice' to ideas and feelings and to maintain access to the voices of others. This calls for a free exchange of opinions and information, which requires, among other things, self-critical, uncensored and dynamic media, functioning not as ends in themselves or to serve (or perhaps protect) certain vested interests (such as advertisers or corporate owners), but as two-way conduits and forums for discussion. People would also have the right of artistic self-expression through such activities as literature, drama, music, dance, painting, drawing or sculpture. This might entail Zen advocacy of public support for and non-interference with the arts, so that 'voices' can find expression through a variety of verbal and non-verbal media. In more general terms, this Zen approach encompasses the right to participate in the cultural life of one's society and humankind as a whole. All people deserve a cultural voice, an input into the mythos- and ethos-making of their cultures.

Perhaps the most important arena of social participation is the economic life of a society. Primary to a Zen approach to economics is a recontextualising of 'economics'. Central concepts of modern capitalist and socialist economic thought, such as GNP, growth, profit, and labour need to be critically examined and, when necessary, either rejected or reformulated. Fundamentally, Economics[28] concerns how human beings interact with each other and their physical environment to secure objects and services necessary for, and extending beyond, the sustenance of life. Human life does not occur in a vacuum, however, for the human realm is one small part of a larger system of relationships. Humankind comes to life and sustains itself by virtue of a wider web of existence in the world. Economic activities necessarily take place in the context of the natural realm, and they succeed in the long run only when humankind maintains a sustainable relationship with that realm. To fail to reflect seriously on short- and long-term ecological consequences of economic practices constitutes a dangerous form of *avidyā* and the first step toward planetary suicide.

With awareness of this larger context of economic theory and praxis, Zen Buddhists can reconsider the guidelines and ends of economic life. The overall goal of economic activity should be the satisfaction of the most basic needs – water, food, clothing, housing, and health care – of the greatest number of people while assuring overall sustainability and ecological harmony with the larger biosphere. A truly *Buddhist* economics perhaps should – despite a widespread commitment to quantitative methods and ostensibly value-free objectivity in mainstream Economics – first determine whether the basic needs of *all* people in the world are presently being satisfied. This question cannot be divorced from questions of justice, especially that of whether the possessions and enjoyments of one group of humans (or their pets) preclude the satisfaction of the basic needs of others now and in the future. *Prajñā* and *karma* certainly imply a commitment to discern whether the self-attachment of some people causes – or at least generates apathy toward – the unsatisfied needs of others and whether economic activity promotes participation in society and by extension a realisation of larger participation in the world. On this basis Zen can enter into consideration of justice as a fair distribution of goods and services.

A primary mode of participating in the economic arena in a society is work. Work is not simply a means to certain ends (pay, the production of goods, or the rendering of services), but also an end in itself. First, work provides an opportunity to 'give the self away' to one's activity. In this sense work can be construed as *samu*, as a form of practice, not as something divorced from 'sacred' religious practice. Second, work provides an opportunity to *participate* in a common task, to clarify, affirm and deepen relationships in productive activity serving the participants and a larger whole; in this way Zen can promote fellowship and cooperation rather than antagonism and competition. In his popular book, *Small is Beautiful: Economics as if People Mattered*, E. F. Schumacher offers a similar view.

> The Buddhist point of view takes the function of work to be at least threefold: to give a man a chance to utilise and develop his faculties; to enable him to overcome his ego-centeredness by joining with other people in a common task; and to bring forth the goods and services needed for a becoming existence.[29]

For these reasons, rather than accepting a certain level of unemployment as healthy for the economy – mainly in that it guarantees a supply of cheap and often underpaid labor – a Zen Buddhist might advocate meaningful work for all people, while recognising and valuing work that often goes unpaid, such as housework, childrearing, and volunteer activity, though levelling criticisms when work of any sort involves exploitation. Overall, through work individuals are able to participate in society by *contributing* to the economic life of the society and *receiving* such things as income or goods necessary for satisfying basic needs.

In addition to work, a key value in a 'Zen' economics might be sharing based on non-attachment to possessions. Though many have held up self-interest in a free market as the key to economic balance and well-being, selfishness and self-centred motivation in large-scale economic systems have not led to economic processes that satisfy everyone's basic needs, support social and global peace, or sustain ecosystems. The simplicity, non-possessiveness and generosity seen in traditional monastic life could be advocated and materialistic self-aggrandisement rejected.

Buddhism as a whole offers a wealth of resources here, for historically it has worked to promote self-emptying and overcome greed and acquisitiveness. The historical Buddha specified that communal property should not be transferred to individuals.[30] All possessions of monks and donations to individual monks were regarded as property of the Sangha. In most Buddhist countries,

'Buddhist social ethics had little place for the economic virtues of saving, calculating and investing. The pursuit of economic gain as an end in itself was not socially sanctioned.'[31] U Nu, Buddhist leader of Burma in the early 1960s, argued that the illusion of the self as the root of suffering should be responded to by a sharing of property, which serves to reduce discrepancies of wealth reflective of greed, hatred and ignorance.[32] This traditional Buddhist aversion to acquisitiveness has provided little support for social Darwinism and such capitalist values as self-interest, competition, and the ongoing accumulation of personal wealth. One British colonial official in Burma offered a stark expression of social Darwinism in response to Buddhist values:

> The first and greatest truth is to make the best use of this beautiful world God has given us. The greatest sin is to be useless, to cumber the ground. It is our duty to sweep away the cowardly, the inefficient, the weak, who misuse it, and put in their place the strong and useful. The Burman . . . must throw off his swaddling bands of faith and find the natural fighter underneath. He must learn to be savage, if necessary to destroy, to hurt and push aside without scruple. He must learn to be a man . . . .[33]

In the context of the Buddhist tradition, Zen can argue that insofar as basic needs of some people are not being met, personal property should be held in trust for possible use and enjoyment by others. From the perspective of Buddhism and its metaphysics of impermanence and relationality, both property and the property owner are non-substantial, so we can say that, in a sense, property belongs to no one in particular. Moreover, given the underlying Buddhist psycho-religious analysis of the human condition, people need to avoid making property into an object of attachment once basic needs have been met. In fact, some have argued that it is private ownership that causes social injustice and inequality. Making this point in an effort to refute 'pseudo-Buddhist' arguments that social inequality results from *karma*, D. T. Suzuki writes, 'The overbearing attitude of the rich and the noble, the unnecessary sufferings of the poor, the over-production of criminals, and such-like [sic] social phenomena arise from the imperfection of our present social organisation, which is based upon the doctrine of absolute private ownership.'[34]

By discerning the needs of others through Zen practice, one can work with and contribute to others according to their need and one's ability to give. Basing itself on the model of traditional monasteries, Zen may argue that the resources of the group need to be pooled in ways that support people at any unexpected time of need, and that this can be promoted by simplicity, by the reduction of one's consumption to guarantee that there is and *will be in the future* enough to go around, enough to satisfy *all* basic needs of *all* people. Here the 'safety net' is not primarily *individual* wealth (private property, savings and investments, or those of close relatives) which is often supported by narrow self-interest and the hoarding and protection of wealth, but *group* wealth, accompanied by Zen values of compassion, mutuality, non-attachment and generosity. In this scheme of economic participation, though individuals have unique skills (things contributed) and unique needs (things received), that uniqueness is embedded in a matrix of relationships with social, political, economic and historical components. Along these lines Zen can raise the question of whether economic systems lead to participation as opposed to vulnerable dependence or unbalanced participation in the form of one-sided contributing (one's energies or resources) without receiving (just wages or other rewards) or one-sided receiving (from threatened corporate takeovers, forced or underpaid labor, price fixing) without a constructive contribution (actual productive labor, time, energy, etc.).

Given these attitudes toward property and sharing, a key value in a Zen-based economic system is what can be termed 'enoughness'. From a Zen perspective one can argue that both those who do not have enough to satisfy basic needs and those who have much more than enough tend to be disadvantaged in the attempt to awaken. The poor may lack the resources – time to engage in religious practice, access to teachers, etc. – supportive of overcoming religious suffering. Or as is often the case, they may lack food and other goods necessary for physical well-being and, by extension, focused religious practice. The Buddha himself is said to have attained Awakening after nourishing his body with milk following a period of extreme asceticism, and 'he saw that the milk was doing wonderful things, and he knew that once our body is strong enough, we can succeed in meditation'.[35] Realising that the satisfaction of higher spiritual needs requires the satisfaction of survival needs, thereafter the 'Buddha himself postponed preaching the Law of impermanence until his listener was fed'.[36]

One should not assume, however, that the satisfaction of those needs is *merely* an instrumental good rather than an intrinsic good or that when an individual chooses to pursue higher goals after those needs are met the quest should be Buddhist. The satisfaction of basic needs is an intrinsic good in that the fulfillment of these needs both reduces suffering and constitutes a central component of full humanity and full participation in the world. Though many Buddhists historically have taken an instrumental view of satisfying survival needs, the situation is changing. One scholar writes, 'In twentieth-century popular Buddhism[,] material well-being is frequently thought of not – or not only – as a means for the achievement of *nirvana* but also as a goal in itself.'[37]

Further, Zen might argue that the rich – those who have much more than enough – may also be at a disadvantage. When entangled in self-aggrandisement and fearful clinging to wealth, those who are rich may find it hard to overcome self-fixation. This possibility is recognised in Buddhist attitudes toward Śākyamuni's princely status and in *vinaya* regulations demanding a renunciation of wealth. Zen could respond to concentrations of wealth and promote the value of 'enoughness' by calling for concrete steps to remedy need. Relevant here is a statement by Winston King.

> A 'Buddhist' economy would be one which would moderate *its* plans somewhat as a Buddhist individual is called upon to do: avoid either indulgent or ascetic extremes and take a middle way. A Buddhist philosophy of economics would call for a moderation of those ambitious plans that would seek to make an enterprise or nation the biggest and the best in the world, or aim at ever-expanding expansion and production. Presumably also it would limit personal wealth by means of taxes . . . . And on the other hand it would limit the lower range of income so that grinding poverty would be avoided or eliminated, presumably by State action if necessary.[38]

To these ends the Zen traditions of simplicity, devoting oneself to constructive work, and communal living provide a valuable model.

The value of 'enoughness' relates to the goal of long-term sustainability. In a Buddhist economic system, an emphasis on 'enoughness' could contribute to a sustenance of the world, especially when connected with a reverent attitude toward the biosphere. It may also contribute to the solution of a problem many historians have discerned – the tragic marriage of economic greed and violence that runs throughout human history. As Nolan Jacobson writes, 'One of the best kept secrets of the most powerful civilization in history – the West – is the barbaric fact that violence has been the primary mode of sustaining its own large-scale existence.'[39]

'Enoughness' thus has two facets: personal and social. The first concerns individual well-being and religious awakening, and the second concerns group well-being – now and in the future – and a social Awakening on the basis of a set of socio-economic processes that promote fulfilling participation. 'Enoughness' finds doctrinal support in the idea of the Middle Path, which in one respect negates both austere living (economic hardship or asceticism coercively or willfully imposed) and profligate living. As conveyed in the Pali scriptures, Śākyamuni discovered an end to *duḥkha* by steering a course between the life of a prince and the extreme asceticism of a wandering *yogi*. Further, the 'economics of enoughness' proposed here is not unique in Buddhism, for it parallels the Sarvodaya notion of sufficiency, U Chan Htoon's 'economics of sufficiency', and U Tun Hla Oung's 'economics of the Middle Way'.[40]

As a first step to promoting 'enoughness' and other facets of a Zen-based economic system, Zen Buddhists could criticise reliance on narrow, materialistic measures of value in economics, which can become the henchmen of the triad of Buddhist evils: greed, hatred and ignorance. One Buddhist writes that most economists view development as a matter of unlimitedly

> increasing currency and things, thus fostering greed (*lobha*). Politicians see development in terms of increased power[,] thus fostering ill-will (*dosa*). Both then work together, hand and glove, and measure the results in terms of quantity, thus fostering ignorance (*moha*) and completing the Buddhist triad of evils.[41]

A shift away from materialistic criteria of value is especially crucial for cultures like the United States, where material wealth often functions as the criterion of value, where about 7 per cent of the world's population consumes nearly 40 per cent of the global natural resources tapped annually, and where rates of violent crime run extremely high. Needless to say, such contemporary economic indicators as GNP cannot fully measure well-being in the overall, true sense. In fact, increases in GNP – the good news most economists and policy-makers long for – may actually correlate with a decrease in human well-being. For example, reckless cutting of unreplenishable tropical rain forests is accounted for as a plus in GNP calculations, as are vast expenditures for nuclear weapons, police protection, pollution clean-up and higher costs of living in urban areas.

A new indicator is called for. Theologian John B. Cobb, Jr. and others have been working on an Index of Sustainable Economic Welfare (ISEW) which more directly reflects actual economic welfare. In conjunction with other adjustments, Cobb's group subtracts from GNP the expenditures that are regrettable necessities rather than contributions to welfare. These regrettables include such things as the cost of national defense, commuting, police protection, sanitation services and road maintenance. Also subtracted are increases in GNP attributable to rising land prices (and hence rents) due to urbanisation and the costs of pollution abatement and control. Added to GNP is the value of the change of air, water and land quality each year relative to a base year, although the figure 'added' may be negative if the quality declined that year. Cobb's group also makes adjustments related to non-market activity and income distribution (different weightings of income changes by quintiles). Further, the group has considered subtractions for resource depletion, although such calculations are quite difficult. The costs involved here include the value of non-renewable resources tapped in any given year (not simply the market value but also some other value – perhaps nearly infinite – reflecting the loss of them as nonrenewable resources) and the value (admittedly difficult to quantify) of the species and wilderness areas lost that year.

From the Zen perspective, one can augment this by creating what might be called an Overall Quality of Life Index. This would also take into account infant mortality rates, life expectancy at age one, and literacy rates, three elements of the Physical Quality of Life Index, an index used by some economists studying Third World development. In addition, an Overall Quality of Life Index would include consideration of physical health (frequency of disease, malnutrition, starvation, etc.), crime rates, protection of civil rights (degree of due process, nondiscrimination against minorities, etc.), and the frequency of military conflict. Such an indicator would not be purely numerical and hence would call for an overall appraisal (perhaps in the form of an annual report with numerical and other components). With greater openness to the complex aspects of life that elude quantification, critical evaluation of well-being could be carried out without merely a numerical bottom line.

This revamping of familiar economic indicators and equations leads to the notion of optimal consumption. Consumption fails to be optimal if it does not promote sustainability, the satisfaction of basic needs of future generations of human beings and other living things. In this regard, two sacred cows of economic thought at present – growth and technology – need to be examined critically. Does growth or development mean progressively higher levels of economic activity calling for increased resource usage (greater 'throughput', to use economist Herman Daly's term),[42] pollution, and urbanisation, or does it indicate an improvement in overall well-being? Many economists, including Herman Kahn, would argue that ingenuity and technological breakthroughs will handle such dangers as smog, acid rain, deforestation, desertification, toxic chemical waste, holes in the ozone layer of the atmosphere, the melting of the polar ice caps due to the greenhouse effect, the sudden depletion of underground aquifers, and the salinisation and erosion processes destroying much of the most fertile agricultural land on the planet. Kahn writes:

> The potential for feasible technological fixes or solutions to important issues such as energy, pollution, safety, and health should not be underestimated, although it frequently is. The astonishing history of science and technology in the nineteenth and twentieth centuries shows that solutions to the physical needs of society have usually become rapidly available when those needs were perceived as urgent and feasible . . . .
>
> An examination of the efforts now being made indicates that one or more technological solutions will become available for pollution, traffic, resource, ecology, and similar problems.[43]

Given the vast array of ills current economic activities have created, is a headlong plunge into *increased* economic activity while clutching onto faith in technology the wisest way to proceed? How would Kahn's remarks be received around Three Mile Island or Chernobyl?

Ironically, to argue against purely quantitative growth and faith in technological fixes is seen as a conservative, 'anti-progress' (or perhaps even anti-American) stand. Given the ecological effects of growth up until now – not to mention the questions of whether growth as presently understood does indeed 'trickle down' to liberate the economically depressed – critical evaluation of the growth paradigm and the capabilities of technology is of crucial importance. From the Zen perspective, 'enoughness' based on simplicity and sustenance of the ecosystem, not ever-expanding consumption and increasingly complex forms of pollution and technology, is to be the cornerstone of economic systems.

At this point one may note here that a 'Zen economics' would not correspond to a Marxist or socialist approach. Granted, Buddhism and Marxism do exhibit certain similar characteristics. In a work entitled *Buddha, Marx, and God*, Trevor Ling writes:

> Theravada Buddhism and Marxism alike embody both a critical analysis of the present human condition, and a way of changing it; both are concerned with the liberation of man from his present unhappy condition, a condition conceived in the Theravada as *dukkha*, existential suffering, and in Marxism as servitude and bondage. Both are particularly concerned, although in different ways, with the evil consequences of human egoism and greed.[44]

Despite these similarities, Marxist and socialist models diverge from the approach sketched here in that they usually fail to consider adequately the larger ecological context of economic activity, and hence can lead to environmental records as dismal as those of capitalist systems. Further, most socialist systems have been highly centralised with a lack of local self-determination. And as outlined in a booklet by Francis Story entitled *Buddhism Answers the Marxist Challenge*, Buddhism rejects the Marxist negation of religion, Marxist materialism, the coercive element of Marxism, the idea that good socio-economic systems give rise to good people rather than the other way around, the materialistic utopian hope of Marxism, and the emphasis on class struggle rather than harmony.[45]

In any case, to implement the type of Zen-based economic approach outlined here, a paradigm shift unequalled in human history proves necessary. Without a pronounced shift in subjectivity from self-centredness to a spiritual identification with and appreciation of the world, no amount of facts and explanations will be sufficient to change destructive patterns of living, especially in wealthier classes or nations, unless a major catastrophe were to shock people out of these patterns. As a process of self-emptying, Zen practice can promote this shift. More concretely, the primary shift Zen can effect is the overcoming of ignorance (self-centredness) and greed (acquisitiveness). Further, for a sustainable economic system to come into being and be widely supported, a great number of people must transform their relationship to nature from one of alienation and devastation to one of informed understanding, intimate identification and reverent nurturance. Economic and educational systems must foster respect for and protection of the ecological context of human and non-human life. People need clear information about pollution, resource depletion and the destruction of wilderness areas. As part of this educational process Zen Buddhists need to debunk the myth of the technological fix: the aforementioned belief that technology can clean up pollution, solve resource problems and even create beauty and enjoyment when global ecological crises confront us, wild unspoiled areas disappear, and traditional modes of appreciating nature prove impossible.

But a true paradigm shift requires more. Some Buddhist writers claim that people need to reject anthropocentrism, which is bouyed by human reason, science and technology, and embrace a cosmocentric outlook, which is found not only in Buddhism but also in other religions and philosophies around the world. But this, too, requires more than a mere intellectual reorientation. People need to overcome their entanglement in fixated subjectivity, in the 'small self', which fails to realise how intimately a part of the natural world it is. One *rōshi* writes:

> If you are a mountain climber or someone who enjoys the countryside, or the green forest, you know that the forests are our lungs outside of our bodies. Yet we have been acting in a way that has allowed two million square miles of forest land to be destroyed by acid rain. We are imprisoned in our small selves, thinking only of the comfortable conditions for this small self, while we destroy our large self.[46]

To get beyond the 'small self' and the dangers of anthropocentrism, one needs to see the other, including nature, as oneself. 'We should be able to be the river, we should be able to be the forest, we should be able to be a Soviet citizen. We must do this to understand, and to have hope for the future. This is the non-dualistic way of seeing.'[47] Zen practice and aesthetics are especially well-equipped to promote this epistemological shift and reevaluation of nature. Allowing the myriad things to 'advance and confirm the self', one can, like the environmentalist Aldo Leopold, 'think like a mountain'. At this point one realises what might be called 'being-in-nature', an intimate connection with nature as an equal or, more exactly, *as oneself.*

Ecological cosmocentrism and being-in-nature do not, however, presuppose or lead to a static harmony. Change is part of the overall ecological process, as each order or integration is thrown into chaos and disarray a new order arises. Harmony is not order as opposed to chaos, but the overall balance and fluidity achieved in the ongoing dialectic of order and chaos. In more experiential terms, we cannot have life without death; though we may avoid the taking of life by not eating meat, we kill countless plants when we consume our salads, microorganisms when we breathe, and insects when we walk or drive. In time, this comes full circle, for other creatures devour or at least assimilate into themselves the elements currently constituting our bodies.

This cosmocentrism does not undermine or trivialise reflection on human society and history. In fact, a cosmocentric approach provides a deeper foundation for such reflection. Society and history do not occur in a vacuum or in front of the backdrop of nature. Rather, they are rooted in nature, in a larger ecosystem, in a universal matrix of dependent co-arising. Given that nature and history arise out of and yet never separate from the larger natural world, people can grasp them from a deeper basis by recontextualising them in this field. They also can deepen their sociological, political and historical insights by regarding themselves as citizens not of mere human societies but of 'socio-ecosystems', of a process of social interaction intimately related to and *part of* natural processes. Further, looking toward the future, one can see that without a sustainable accordance with the larger biosphere there may be no societies or history at all.

As a practical system of transformation – rather than a mere theoretical paradigm or approach to *external* institutions, laws, and policies – Zen can provide a pragmatic way of bringing about the profound change in human experiencing necessary for the creation of a compassionate, just, and ecologically-sound system of economics. No mere advocacy of new indicators, policies, or structures is enough. Without the kind of fundamental change in our ways of being, knowing, and acting that Zen (and perhaps other paths) facilitates, approaches to economics and the environment will ultimately fail.

Consideration of 'cosmocentrism' raises the issue of the rights of the non-human part of the world. As a whole, nature has the intrinsic 'right' to unfold free from devastation wrought by human ignorance and greed. Plants and animals have a right to participate in this world in the way they evolved prior to destructive human intervention. Maintaining faith in and reverence for natural patterns and balances, people need to reject practices that radically alter the way of being of plants and animals. This includes such acts as inflicting pain unnecessarily, introducing new or mutated species into the biosphere and disturbing ecosystems in ways that drive species to extinction or force remaining members of endangered species to rely on humans for their continued survival (e.g., the California condor). This ascription of intrinsic value to other species presupposes trust in the overall process of nature as something good and complete in and of itself prior to anthropocentric attempts to change it, control it ('tame' the wilderness), or make it more efficient.

From the standpoint of *śūnyatā*, at the absolute level all things are relational, 'empty' beings with equal intrinsic value: a human is not *essentially* better or more valuable than a chicken, protozoan, or carrot. And insofar as *śūnyatā* allows for difference, a Zen Buddhist recognises the different modes of being of things in the world as events occurring in terms of dependent co-arising. At the relative level where we make practical distinctions and decisions, we do respond to things differently. Although the chicken and the carrot are equal at the absolute level, most Buddhists would find the carrot easier to eat than the chicken, or would go to great lengths to avoid hitting a dog on the road while not worrying about the countless protozoa that perish whenever they drink a glass of water. As stated earlier, Zen advocates a compassionate, nonviolent attitude toward things, which implies consideration of how to avoid the infliction of unnecessary pain and suffering. With this orientation, at the relative level a Zen Buddhist can and does make distinctions about inflicting pain, and hence may opt for vegetarianism, although perhaps not go to Jain lengths and sweep mountain trails while walking.

Again, the perspective here is that while things are equal at the absolute level, at the practical level chickens, protozoa and carrots differ. More specifically, they differ in terms of self-consciousness, which relates directly to the type of suffering beings experience. Given that human beings are more self-conscious than species with less conscious ways of interacting and communicating, our capacity for suffering and for joy is especially pronounced. The capacity for not only feeling physical pain but also worrying about it – that is to say, the capacity for experiencing not only physical but also psychological anguish – distinguishes us from other species.[48] Buddhism recognises this uniqueness of human self-consciousness in making statements about how ignorance and Awakening are primarily a human issue, about how birth as a human is a blessing that must not be wasted, about how all things accord with the dynamism of *śūnyatā* while only humans self-consciously awaken to that fact, and so forth.

In taking account of this difference in suffering, Zen can engage in what might be called a 'calculus of suffering'.[49] Recognising how things suffer differently and how actions *inevitably* cause suffering in other things, and basing themselves in the standpoint of the compassionate aspiration to reduce suffering as much as possible, Zen Buddhists can make distinctions between different species as various options are weighed. Though nothing is intrinsically *better* than anything else and though nothing has more intrinsic *value* at the absolute level, one may opt for the carrot over the chicken because of the level of possible suffering experienced by the latter.

Needless to say, a 'calculus of suffering' would not provide the clarity of its cousins in mathematics; there is no cut-and-dried set of equations giving unambiguous answers to such questions as how many laboratory animals' suffering adds up to the suffering of one human patient. To avoid appearing divorced from any distinctions whatsoever and hence irrelevant to issues arising in day-to-day living, Zen must take account of these factors and acknowledge the role of such practical and compassion-based distinctions at the relative level.

It is interesting to note that Zen could argue even on anthropocentric grounds that other species must be nurtured. Human life and experience derive from complex patterns of processive inter-relationship still largely beyond the ken of human understanding. To maintain human life, the complexity and diversity of dependent co-arising must be preserved. To exterminate other contributing parts of the whole is not only an assertion of ignorant self-attachment but also an infliction of injury to ourselves in that we have eroded the actual or potential groundwork for the sustenance of our life.[50]

At this point in the discussion a devil's advocate might argue that a focus on reducing suffering undermines consideration of how society at times needs to inflict suffering in the form of coercion and punishment, of how social existence inevitably in-volves the exercise of power and violence. Given the nature of *śūnyatā*, a systematic Buddhist formulation of power will diverge from the conception of power found in many other philosophical systems. Joanna Macy states:

> In the patriarchal, hierarchical construction of reality, you have a one-way linear causality. We have been conditioned by that notion since Aristotle, and it has dominated both religion and science. Consequently, power is seen as emanating from the top down. It is essentially power-*over*, and equated with domina-tion, having one's way, pushing things around, being invulner-able to change. Such a notion of power requires defenses, whether of the ego or the nation state.
>
> But in dependent co-arising, causality is not linear; it is re-ciprocal. Power is a two-way street. It is not power over, but power-with, where beings mutually affect and mutually en-hance each other. The old linear notion is essentially that of a zero-sum game: the more you have the less I have. 'You win, I lose.'[51]

Macy goes on to characterise this as similar to synergy, found in ecosystems and neural nets. This relational power is found in the compassionate openness and responsiveness of the archetypal *bodhisattva* as well: 'It is also the power of the *bodhisattva*, of the "boundless" heart which opens in compassion and muditha [*mudi-tā*] to the griefs and joys of others.'[52] This is not a paranoid clinging to power, for it empowers others as well. Macy elaborates the practical ramifications of 'power with' in *Despair and Personal Power in the Nuclear Age*, which offers an approach to moving humanity beyond despair and a fatalistic sense of impotence in the face of the nuclear threat.

From the Buddhist perspective, then, power is a positive factor when contextualised in the above way. But in actual social situations, in realpolitik, is synergistic power possible? Is this the optimal type of power to be exercised by those who are oppressed in a society? Even if such a network of power could be actualised in society, would it be sufficient? Are there not cases in societies when democratically established institutions and the people in them have no other choice than to bring coercive power to bear on certain individuals, groups and organisations? More strongly put, when might coercive power – violence – be unavoidable, necessary and hence acceptable as a necessary evil?

Throughout its history, Buddhism has held up nonviolence (Skt., *ahiṃsā*) as a prime virtue. Explicit rejections of violence and examples of nonviolent behavior abound in Buddhist scriptural literature. In the *Jātaka Tales*, while functioning as a *bodhisattva*-king who renounces the use of violence to defend the state, Buddha declares, 'None shall suffer because of me. Let those who covet kingdoms seize mine, if they will.'[53] In calling for 'right livelihood' as one step of the Noble Eightfold Path, Śākyamuni counsels against involvement in killing. The *Dhammapada* includes the verses:

All beings tremble before danger, all fear death. When a person considers this, the person does not kill or cause to kill.

All beings fear before danger, life is dear to all. When a person considers this, the person does not kill or cause to kill.[54]

In Buddhism, violence is judged in terms of the intention of the actor and seen as deriving from the Three Poisons: ignorance, greed and hatred. And in the Theravāda tradition, 'Non-injury (*ahiṃsā*) has also its positive counterpart. It demands not only abstention from injury but also the practice of loving-kindness, *mettā*, to all.'[55] The Theravāda path attempts to cultivate a non-violent way of being, largely in terms of the four 'sublime abodes': loving kindness, compassion, sympathetic joy and equanimity.

The violence rejected by Buddhism takes a variety of forms, not simply the use of physical force against another. In arguing that the 'keynote of Buddhist economics . . . is simplicity and non-violence',[56] Schumacher points out, 'The optimal pattern of consumption, producing a high degree of human satisfaction by means of a relatively low rate of consumption, allows people to live without great pressure and strain and to fulfill the primary injunction of Buddhist teaching: "Cease to do evil; try to do good."'[57] Elaborating on this, he writes that resources need to be used sparingly, for reckless exploitation of non-renewable resources on a global scale increases the likelihood of violent conflict (not to mention the threat to long-term sustainability), and from the Buddhist perspective, reckless use of resources or the devastation of ecosystems, even when wars are not thereby caused, is itself an act of violence. People hence must take a 'reverent and non-violent attitude'[58] toward not only other living things, but the inorganic part of the world as well.

Various Zen Buddhists have advocated rejection of violence. Thich Nhat Hanh considers violence unacceptable and regards the claim that violence is acceptable as deriving from a lack of insight or awareness. He writes, 'Non-violence has another name: awareness. We should be aware of what we are, of who we are, and of what we are doing.'[59] Nonviolence and peace originate in the way of being of humanity, not simply in external actions or structures. 'It is not by going out for a demonstration against nuclear missiles that we can bring about peace. It is with our capacity of smiling, breathing and being peace that we can make peace.'[60] Certain Japanese *rōshis* explicitly advocate the way of nonviolence. Yamada Mumon states, 'In the long eons of human history with various vicissitudes . . . the principle of not killing other human beings is the great victor.'[61] Joshu Sasaki Rōshi claims that true peace is based on 'no-conflict *samādhi*' (*mujō-zanmai*), realised when the distinction between self and other has dissolved and the unity of subject and object is realised in a 'total embrace' of the other; at this point one can truly *be* peace and *work for* peace. Though 'no-conflict *samadhi*' eradicates the root of suffering and war and constitutes a necessary condition for peace (and though interpersonal conflict ceases for the Zen Buddhist when subject and object are undifferentiated), is this a *sufficient* response to the wars and violence that already exist?

Further, although *ahiṃsā* is an important Buddhist virtue, in actual practice there is no commonly exhibited Buddhist stance concerning war and the use of force. In Thailand, Kittivuddho

Bhikkhu responded to a question about whether it is demeritorious to kill Communists by arguing that it is not, given that it does not constitute the murder of a person, 'because whoever destroys the nation, the religion, the monarchy, such bestial types (*man*) are not complete persons. Thus, we must intend not to kill people but to kill the Devil (Mara); this is the duty of all Thai'.[62] Moreover, as mentioned earlier in this work, Shaku Sōen reportedly backed the Japanese war effort against Russia in 1904 after calling for 'arbitration instead of war' at the World Congress of Religions a decade earlier, and Zen temples prepared soldiers for war – and imperialist aggression – during World War II. Yet despite these examples of 'militant Buddhism', one also finds many Buddhists actively expressing their commitment to nonviolence, such as Vietnamese monks actively protesting the Vietnam War in the early 1960s and Zen, Nichiren and other Buddhists presently engaged in peace work. In wrestling with this diversity, Zen Buddhists can critically deepen their position on nonviolence and peace by listening to such advocates of nonviolence as the Society of Friends and such critics of it as Reinhold Niebuhr.

What stand can Zen take concerning violence? If committed to overcoming entanglement in egocentricity and to promoting awareness of *śūnyatā*, Zen Buddhists need to actualise power as synergistically as possible, to advocate basing social, political and economic activities on cooperation, mutuality, dialogue and openness rather than competition, domination, coercion and defensiveness. This approach brings Zen to a stance of nonviolence. From the Zen perspective, one can argue that violence – the infliction of physical or mental harm to another – causes immediate pain and suffering, triggers further violence, and in the ensuing vicious cycle causes continued suffering and indulges egocentricity with its us-them orientation and, at times, accompanying self-aggrandisement and hatred. While arguing this, however, Zen needs to discern violence in all forms, including sanctioned and institutionalised violence on the one hand and the often more visible violence that occurs in response to certain structures or people in society.

Though synergistic power and nonviolence stand as the ideal template for living daily lives and considering social measures, Zen should discern situations when coercive 'power-over' may prove unavoidable, when minimal necessary force may be called for. These extreme situations arise when innocent human lives are immediately in danger because of violent action being committed by another person or other people.[63]

Gandhi's view of nonviolence and cowardice provides a valuable input here. Aware of the complexity of actual social circumstances and the actions taken in response, Gandhi refrained from drawing a hard-and-fast line between violence (*hiṃsā*) and nonviolence (*ahiṃsā*). He conceptualised various nonviolent approaches along a spectrum,[64] and realised the hardship (violence of a sort) his nonviolent actions could cause. Further, he contended that there is one response worse than violence: cowardice. At one point he stated,

> I do believe where there is only a choice between cowardice and violence I would advise violence. Thus when my eldest son asked me what he should have done, had he been present when I was almost fatally assaulted in 1908, whether he should have run away and seen me killed or whether he should have used his physical force which he could and wanted to use, and defended me, I told him that it was his duty to defend me even by using violence.[65]

While allowing for unavoidable use of physical force in attempts to save an innocent life immediately in danger, Zen should reject violence. This rejection pertains to physical and psychological abuse, the death penalty, violent protest, warfare and the construction and stockpiling of weapons. Zen Buddhists can work in the creative tension between a stance of nonviolence and the existing brutality in the world, making realistic, sustained efforts at personal and social transformation.

In conjunction with issues raised earlier, the ideas sketched in this and the previous chapter can serve as a starting point for sustained consideration of Zen and society. As indicated by the discussion in this book, Zen practice and its philosophical orientation provide resources for a unique approach to the human 'self', relations between people, and social issues. In large part due to the overwhelming emphasis on *satori*, however, Zen Buddhists have not formulated systematic approaches to ethical issues in society, even though, as argued in this work, such formulation could contribute to the solution of certain issues and could deepen Zen practice, especially for lay Zen Buddhists. As part of a larger discourse currently taking place, this work has offered an overview of Zen and ethics, a highlighting of the issues contained in this topic, and initial suggestions for directions in which the tradition might advance as it begins to construct self-critical systems of social ethics.

Notes

FOREWORD BY MASAO ABE

1. The entire Fourfold Great Vows reads:

> However innumerable sentient beings are,
> I vow to save them;
> However inexhaustible the binding passions are,
> I vow to extinguish them;
> However immeasurable the Dharma-teachings are,
> I vow to learn them;
> However unsurpassable the Buddha-Way is,
> I vow to attain it.

2. A lay study/practice group started by Hisamatsu Shin'ichi (1889–1980) and some of his students at Kyoto University.
3. The foremost Zen reformer of contemporary Japan and founder of the F.A.S. Society.

INTRODUCTION

1. D. T. Suzuki, 'Ethics and Zen Buddhism', in R. N. Anshen (ed.), *Moral Principles of Action* (London: Harper & Brothers, 1952) p. 607.
2. D. T. Suzuki, *Essays in Zen Buddhism*, First Series (London: Rider and Company, 1980) p. 27. Quoted by A. D. Brear, 'The nature and status of moral behavior in Zen Buddhist tradition', *Philosophy East and West*, 24 (October 1974) 432.
3. M. Weber, *The Religion of India: The Sociology of Hinduism and Buddhism*, tr. and ed. by H. H. Gerth and D. Martindale (Glencoe, IL: The Free Press, 1958) p. 213.
4. Although the literal meaning of 'metaphysical' is perhaps inappropriate for the Buddhist world-view, the term is used guardedly throughout this book in the sense of 'concerning the nature of reality'. Usage of 'ontological' has been avoided, for the term may connote substantial, independent essences or a transcendent Being from which beings derive.
5. 'Fixation' is a rendering of the Japanese term *kotei*, which literally means 'set up an individual'. It refers to the psychological positioning of oneself as a subject over and against objects and as an enduring entity with set boundaries. The term does not carry any Freudian connotation of a focus of attention and energy on a specific object or on a specific psycho-sexual stage of development.

145

6. *Webster's New Collegiate Dictionary* (1981), s.v. 'ethic'. As a doctrine or system of good conduct, 'morality' often encompasses social norms and mores, unlike 'ethics' in a strict sense, which, as indicated in the definition, designates not only a system of moral conduct but also a rational discipline that wrestles with the formulation of ethical principles and with meta-ethical issues. Accordingly, this work primarily uses the term 'ethics' and avoids using 'morality', even though the two terms are virtually synonymous in common usage.

7. Some Western thought trickled into Japan through earlier Jesuit missionary efforts during the 'Christian century' (roughly 1549 to 1638) and restricted Dutch trade with Japan during the Tokugawa period (1600–1867) when the shoguns enforced a 'closed country' (*sakoku*; literally, 'chained country') policy. Much of this learning was suppressed until Japan opened up more to the outside world in the mid-nineteenth century.

8. G. K. Piovesana, *Recent Japanese Philosophical Thought, 1862–1962: A Survey* (Tokyo: Enderle Bookstore, 1968) p. 11.

9. The first character of this compound, *shū*, means essence, purport, or sect, as in *Jōdō-shinshū* (the True Pure Land Sect). Accordingly, *shūkyō* literally means 'teaching of the essence' or 'sect teaching'.

10. E. Norbeck, 'Religion and Society in Modern Japan: Continuity and Change', *Rice University Studies*, 56 (Winter 1970) 120.

11. Between father and son, ruler and subject, elder brother and younger brother, husband and wife, and friend and friend.

12. Christianity is omitted here because of its small following in Japan.

13. The 'Basket of Discourses', which constitutes one of the three 'baskets' in the Pali canon.

14. Though the Eightfold Path in large part functions developmentally, the eight 'components' are mutually supportive and often practiced simultaneously, so some Buddhists avoid using such sequential terms as 'steps' and 'stages'.

15. The Pali term, *sīla* (Skt., *śīla*), indicates morality in the sense of self-control brought about by observing precepts and other guidelines for Buddhist practice.

16. In contrast, many Zen Buddhists have regarded ethical behaviour as primarily a *result* or expression of Awakening.

17. Found in the *Sutta Piṭaka*.

18. The 'Basket of Discipline'.

19. E. Sarkisyanz, *Buddhist Backgrounds of the Burmese Revolution* (The Hague: Martinus Nijhoff, 1965) pp. 40–41.

20. W. L. King, *In the Hope of Nibbana: An Essay on Theravada Buddhist Ethics* (LaSalle, Illinois: Open Court Publishing Company, 1964) p. 160.

21. The passive nuance of this term led Winston King to characterise *upekkhā* as part of the 'ethic of Nibbana' rather than the ethic of this world (the 'ethic of Kamma'), as 'that quality which still retains some direct semblance of the ethical and yet in a considerable measure transcends it in the Nibbana-ward direction.' *Nibbana*, p. 162.

22. The 'Path of the Teaching' or 'Path of Truth'.

23. *The Dhammapada*, tr. by S. Radhakrishnan (Madras: Oxford University Press, 1966) p. 120.
24. Ibid., p. 180.
25. K. Jones, *The Social Face of Buddhism: An Approach to Political and Social Activism* (London: Wisdom Publications, 1989) p. 238.
26. D. Lardner Carmody, *Women & World Religions* (Nashville: Abingdon, 1981) p. 49. Given the cultural contexts in which Buddhism developed, the positive views of women and resultant gains at the time of Śākyamuni gradually crumbled. Carmody writes, 'By the time of the canonical literature (second century B.C.E.), however, this positive view of women began to abate and one notes the beginning of a fateful theme that women are dangerous temptations. The likely source of this theme was the pressure of male celibacy' (p. 49). According to Diana Y. Paul, in many Buddhist texts 'the sacred is represented as masculine while the profane or imperfect is represented as feminine, [and here] we have a polarisation that suggests both internal psychological conflicts and external social barriers between the sexes' (*Women in Buddhism: Images of the Feminine in Mahayana Tradition* (Berkeley: Asian Humanities Press, 1979) p. xiv). Concerning Mahayana literature she writes, 'From a feminist perspective, one perceives a destructive, complex set of images preventing women from fulfillment within the Buddhist religion' (p. xiv).
27. T. W. Rhys-Davids, *Pali-English Dictionary* (1959), s.v. *'nibbāna'*; as quoted in G. Rupp, 'The relationship between nirvāṇa and saṃsāra: An essay on the evolution of Buddhist ethics', *Philosophy East and West* 31 (January 1971) 58.
28. T. Ling, *Buddha, Marx, and God: Some Aspects of Religion in the Modern World* (New York: St. Martin's Press, 1966) p. 57.
29. G. S. P. Misra, *Development of Buddhist Ethics* (New Delhi: Munshiram Manoharlal Publishers Pvt. Ltd., 1984) p. 111.
30. R. A. F. Thurman, 'The Edicts of Ashoka', in F. Eppsteiner (ed.), *The Path of Compassion: Writings on Socially Engaged Buddhism*, 2nd edn (Berkeley: Parallax Press, 1988) pp. 111–19.
31. W. L. King, 'Buddhist Self-World Theory and Buddhist Ethics', *The Eastern Buddhist* 22 (Autumn 1989) 26.
32. Sarkisyanz, *Buddhist Backgrounds*, p. 24.
33. D. E. Smith, *Religion and Politics in Burma* (Princeton: Princeton University Press, 1965) pp. 92–99.
34. G. Rupp, 'The relationship between nirvāṇa and saṃsāra: An essay on the evolution of Buddhist Ethics', *Philosophy East and West* 21 (January 1971) 64.
35. Jones, *The Social Face of Buddhism*, p. 235.
36. J. Macy, *Dharma and Development: Religion as a Resource in the Sarvodaya Self-Help Movement*, 2nd edn (West Hartford: Kumarian Press, 1985) p. 13.
37. Winston King states, '. . . *Theravada Buddhism must make up its mind in which world it expects to live and strive* before it can give a clear answer to its ethical problems. For there are two worlds here with their respective

values and ways [:] . . . the world of absolute transcendent value
(Nibbana) and the world of relative mundane concerns (Kamma).'
Nibbana, p. 270.

38. King sketches how, in the standard Theravāda formulation of *kamma*,
    good or meritorious acts are thought of as resulting in 'hedonistic' – to
    use King's term – consequences, that is, nonmoral goods such as
    health, wealth, power or fame.

39. At times the actual attitude of the *arhat* and Theravāda ethics in
    general have been obscured by those who from the Mahāyāna per-
    spective claim that

    > the Arhat rests satisfied with achieving his own private salvation; he
    > is not actively interested in the welfare of others. The ideal of the
    > Arhat smacks of selfishness; there is even a lurking fear that
    > the world would take hold of him if he tarried here too long. The
    > Bodhisattva makes the salvation of all his own good.

    T. R. V. Murti, *The Central Philosophy of Buddhism: A Study of the
    Mādhyamika System* (London: George Allen & Unwin, 1980) p. 263.

40. R. A. F. Thurman, 'Guidelines for Buddhist Social Activism Based on
    Nagarjuna's *Jewel Garland of Royal Counsels'*, *The Eastern Buddhist* (New
    Series) 16 (Spring 1983) 19–51.

41. Jones, *The Social Face of Buddhism,* pp. 260–61.

42. Often discriminated against in the areas of employment and marriage,
    the *burakumin* are descendents of Japanese who were engaged in
    occupations traditionally considered impure.

CHAPTER 1: THE ZEN PATH

1. The somewhat ahistorical approach taken in this chapter does not
   attempt to account for each of the concrete forms of Zen in specific
   times and places, for it aims at providing a general backdrop for later
   examination of specifics.

2. Seng-t'san [Sengcan], 'On Believing in Mind (Shinjin-no-Mei)', in
   D. T. Suzuki, *Manual of Zen Buddhism* (New York: Grove Press, 1960)
   p. 78.

3. Also referred to by Zen writers as the thinking self, the particular self,
   the small self, the ego, or the ego-self.

4. F. H. Cook, 'Dogen's View of Authentic Selfhood and Its Socio-ethical
   Implications', in W. R. LaFleur (ed.), *Dōgen Studies,* Studies in East
   Asian Buddhism, no. 2 (Honolulu: University of Hawaii Press, 1985)
   p. 134.

5. For a detailed discussion of this process, see R. J. DeMartino, 'The
   Human Situation and Zen Buddhism', in N. Katz (ed.), *Buddhist and
   Western Psychology* (Boulder, CO: Prajna Press, 1983) pp. 167–95.

6. Seng-t'san, 'On Believing in Mind', p. 77.

7. Joko Beck Sensei, 'Beginning Zen Practice', *The Ten Directions* (June
   1983) 13. Reprinted in C. J. Beck *Everyday Zen: Love and Work,* ed. by
   Steve Smith (San Francisco: Harper & Row, Publishers, 1989).

8. In certain ways, despite Zen claims of universality, this 'human situation' may describe the plight of men more than that of women, or certain classes, cultures, or races more than others. As Carol Gilligan points out in *In A Different Voice*, female identity is more relational than atomistic, for it is grounded much more in a social matrix than in the barricaded subjectivity described here. Further, the actual situation of many women is a *lack* of any sense of independent selfhood. Subjectivity may assume a diffuse, unintegrated and unempowered form rather than a crystallised and assertive form. To avoid an androcentric ring to Zen descriptions of the 'human' situation, this difference needs to be acknowledged and explored further. Yet insofar as women do experience reality as something apart from themselves, do at times get entangled in concepts about reality, do confront the death of themselves as finite beings, and do experience pain in the midst of inevitable change, Zen *does* speak to women's basic existential situation. Further, some women have noted how Zen practice provides them with a focused awareness and inner strength and in this way facilitates balanced integration of those who may feel diffuse and fosters an awareness that is neither fractured nor entrenched in self-fixation.

9. Even without engaging in Zen practice, many people have experienced what it is like to slip out of fixated subjectivity, to bridge the gap between subject and object. An analogous experience is that of playing a musical piece without thinking about each note, worrying about mistakes, or wondering what one's audience is thinking; there is no distance between oneself and the music, and one may describe this as 'the music playing through me'. Another example is the psychological expansion that arises when one becomes engrossed in a sunset or a symphony; after the fact one might say that it was as if 'the whole universe was filled' with the crimson sky or the flowing notes and there was no sense of a self 'here' experiencing the sunset or the music 'out there'.

10. C. J. Beck, *Everday Zen: Love and Work*, ed. by Steve Smith (San Francisco: Harper & Row, Publishers, 1989) p. 19.

11. Such as the *Rinzairoku* (Ch., *Linji-lu*), *Mumonkan* (Ch., *Wumen-guan*), or *Hekiganroku* (Ch., *Biyan-lu*).

12. The Japanese word for attention, *chūi*, consists of two characters, 'pour' and 'mind'.

13. This is reflected in the oft-cited exclamation by the lay Chan practitioner, Bo-zhang (J., Hōkoji):

How wondrously strange, how miraculous this is!
I draw water, I chop wood.

14. In Japan, *kōan* practice is found primarily in Rinzai Zen, although *kōans* are sometimes used in a less-structured manner in the other main strand, Sōtō Zen, which generally focuses on the practice of 'just sitting' (*shikantaza*).

15. D. T. Suzuki, *An Introduction to Zen Buddhism* (New York: Grove Press, 1964) p. 106.

16. Ibid., p. 108.
17. Ibid., p. 109.
18. DeMartino, 'Human Situation', p. 187.
19. Hakuin, 'Appendix' to *Orategama*, tr. by Heinrich Dumoulin, *A History of Zen Buddhism* (Boston: Beacon Press, 1969) p. 259.
20. *Satori* can be written with either of two Sino-Japanese characters: 悟 (made from the sub-characters 'mind' and 'I'), which in ordinary usage means to realise or notice, and 覚, meaning to awaken or remember.
21. Hakuin, 'Appendix', p. 259.
22. In Rinzai Zen 'abrupt' (J., *ton*) refers to a negation or discontinuity in a psychological and existential sense rather than to mere temporal suddenness.
23. In some ways this distinction between abrupt and gradual awakening is false, for ultimately Zen encompasses both facets in that practice usually consists of a gradual transformative process highlighted by certain abrupt shifts ('small' *satori* experiences) or perhaps one decisive shift in experience.
24. Cook, 'Dogen's View of Authentic Selfhood', p. 138.
25. In John Hick's language, this is a transformation of human existence from 'self-centredness' to 'Reality-centredness'. See *God Has Many Names* (Philadelphia: Westminster Press, 1982) p. 9.
26. This view of the 'self' is not limited to Zen. 'From the overall Buddhist perspective, it [the self] is an interdependent, self-organizing process shaped by the flow of experience and the choices that condition this flow. Possessed of no "I" apart from what it feels, sees, thinks, does, the self does not *have* experience, it *is* its experience.' J. Rogers Macy, 'Dependent Co-Arising: The Distinctiveness of Buddhist Ethics', *Journal of Religious Ethics*, 7 (Spring 1979) 42.
27. K. Nishida, *'Bashoteki ronri to shūkyōteki sekaikan'* (The Logic of Place and the Religious World View), *Nishida Kitarō zenshū* (The Collected Writings of Nishida Kitarō), 2nd edn, vol. 11 (Tokyo: Iwanami Shoten, 1965) pp. 424–25.
28. This is a key expression in the *Vajracchedika* (Diamond Sūtra).
29. The following overview of this concept will serve as a foundation for later discussion of its ethical ramifications.
30. R. Robinson and W. L. Johnson, *The Buddhist Religion: A Historical Introduction*, 3rd edn (Belmont, CA: Wadsworth Publishing Company, 1982) pp. 36–37.
31. *Abhidhamma* (Skt., *Abhidharma*) refers to the scholastic strand of Buddhism that engaged primarily in analysis of the various constituents (*dharmas*) that make up reality, with a special focus on how they combine in such a way as to constitute what people mistakenly take to be an independent, enduring 'self'.
32. Tr. by H. V. Guenther, *Philosophy and Psychology in the Abhidharma* (Delhi: Motilal Banarsidass, 1957) pp. 69–70.
33. R. E. A. Johansson, *The Dynamic Psychology of Early Buddhism* (Oxford: Curzon Press, 1979) p. 197.

34. W. Rahula, *What the Buddha Taught* (New York: Grove Press, Inc., 1959) p. 42.
35. P. de Silva, *An Introduction to Buddhist Psychology* (New York: Harper & Row Publishers, Inc., 1979) p. 9.
36. K. N. Jayatilleke, *Early Buddhist Theory of Knowledge* (London: George Allen & Unwin Ltd., 1963) p. 467.
37. R. E. A. Johansson, *The Psychology of Nirvana* (Garden City, NY: Anchor Books, 1970) p. 131.
38. Johansson, *Dynamic Psychology*, p. 29.
39. T. Izutsu, *Toward a Philosophy of Zen Buddhism* (Boulder: Prajna Press, 1982) p. 13.
40. F. J. Streng, *Emptiness: A Study in Religious Meaning* (Nashville: Abingdon Press, 1967) p. 91.
41. In this way Nāgārjuna's formulation of *śūnyatā* gives a new connotation to dependent co-arising (Skt., *pratītya-samatpāda*), which at this point in the development of Buddhist thought becomes roughly synonymous with *śūnyatā*.
42. One way of rephrasing this negation is to say that reality eludes conceptual thought and must be realised in a different experiential mode (*prajñā*), and that theories about reality should be used as tentative, practical constructs rather than as fixed constructs referring to an objective Reality.
43. D. T. Suzuki, *On Indian Mahayana Buddhism* (New York: Harper & Row Publishers, 1968) p. 232.
44. More exactly put, *prajñā* discerns that *true* emptiness is not something standing apart from form, but the *dynamism between* form and emptiness, just as true *nirvāṇa* is a realisation of the dynamism between '*saṃsāra*' and '*nirvāṇa*'. D. T. Suzuki conveys this dynamism in his logic of *sokuhi*, which is sometimes rendered in English as a 'logic of self-identity'. The logic of *sokuhi* indicates that 'to be myself is/not to be myself, whereby I am myself.' (*The Essence of Buddhism*, 2nd edn (Kyoto: Hozokan, 1968) p. 42.) Something is what it is by not being itself, that is, by being constituted by other 'things', which is possible because it is not something with an independent nature impervious to external influences.
45. To some extent, the *Yogācāra* School's psycho-cosmological concept of the 'storehouse consciousness' (Skt., *ālaya-vijñāna*) conveys this wealth of possibilities.
46. Streng, *Emptiness*, p. 82.
47. Ibid., p. 98.
48. In his treatise, *Prajñā is Not Knowledge*, Sengzhao defines *prajñā* as 'sage wisdom'. As Kenneth Ch'en writes, 'Ordinary knowledge has an object of knowledge, whereas sage wisdom has as its object the absolute truth, which cannot be an object of knowledge, since it is empty and without phenomenal qualities. This absolute truth, however, is not isolated from events and things.' *Buddhism in China: A Historical Survey* (Princeton: Princeton University Press, 1973) pp. 87–88.

49. H. Dumoulin, *A History of Zen Buddhism* (Boston: Beacon Press, 1969) pp. 36–37.
50. Though beyond the scope of this book, such claims have triggered lively dialogue with philosophers adhering to epistemologies based on Kantian conceptions of the 'thing in itself' (*Ding an sich*).
51. Z. Shibayama, *On Zazen Wasan* (Kyoto, 1967) p. 29.
52. K. Nishida, 'The Problem of Japanese Culture', in W. T. deBary, D. Keene, and R. Tsunoda (eds), *Sources of Japanese Tradition*, vol. 2 (New York: Columbia University Press, 1958) p. 362.
53. T. Nhat Hanh, *Being Peace* (Berkeley: Parallax Press, 1987) p. 38.
54. D. T. Suzuki, *Mysticism Christian and Buddhist* (New York: Collier Books, 1957) p. 31.
55. Ibid., p. 36.
56. See *An Inquiry Into the Good*, tr. by M. Abe and C. Ives (New Haven: Yale University Press, 1990), p. 6.
57. T. P. Kasulis, *Zen Action/Zen Person* (Honolulu: The University Press of Hawaii, 1976) p. 57.
58. As discussed in greater detail later in this chapter, the *bodhisattva* is the ideal religious figure in Mahāyāna Buddhism, who defers personal liberation from rebirth until all others are liberated and takes vows to assist them.
59. *Buddhist Wisdom Books*, tr. by E. Conze (London: George Allen & Unwin Ltd., 1975) p. 34.
60. *The Threefold Lotus Sutra*, tr. by B. Kato, Y. Tamura and K. Miyasaka (New York: Weatherhill/Kosei, 1984) p. 89.
61. *The Record of Lin-chi*, tr. by R. F. Sasaki (Kyoto: The Institute for Zen Studies, 1975) p. 5. Translation partially adapted here.
62. R. Aitken, *The Mind of Clover* (San Francisco: North Point Press, 1984) p. 173.
63. M. Williams, *A Sanskrit-English Dictionary* (Oxford: The Clarendon Press, 1964) p. 255.
64. T. W. Rhys-Davids and William Stede, *The Pali Text Society's Pali English Dictionary* (London: Luzac and Company Ltd., 1959) p. 540.
65. H. Dayal, *The Bodhisattva Doctrine in Buddhist Sanskrit Literature* (London: Kegan Paul, Trench, Trubner & Co. Ltd., 1932) p. 179.
66. Chagdud Tilka, 'The Power of Peace', in F. Eppsteiner (ed.) *The Path of Compassion: Writings on Socially Engaged Buddhism* (Berkeley: Parallax Press, 1990) p. 94.
67. W. L. King, *In the Hope of Nibbana: An Essay on Theravada Buddhist Ethics* (LaSalle, Illinois: Open Court Publishing Company, 1964), p. 159. It is important to note here that in Buddhist talk of attachment and non-attachment, the object of attachment is seen primarily as the self, not society. Wisdom and compassion increase to the extent people are unattached to themselves (i.e., not entangled in fixated subjectivity and the accompanying 'greed' and 'hatred'). Historically, Buddhists have facilitated *non-attachment to self* by temporary *detachment from society*. Unfortunately, however, many have conflated the two, arriving at a view of non-attachment as primarily a rejection of society rather than a rejection of narrow self-centredness. Again, what one is

called on to be detached from is this narrow self-centredness, the primary cause of most social problems and an obstacle to our opening up to others and engaging in *full, compassionate participation* in society.
68. Ibid., p. 100.
69. Ibid., p. 156.
70. Ibid.
71. Although to some extent the *bodhisattva* stands as a religious ideal in Theravāda Buddhism, it is overshadowed by the *arhat*, does not assume as much of a soteriological role, and usually does not receive a trans-human characterisation.
72. Dayal, *The Bodhisattva Doctrine*, p. 9.
73. Interestingly, Buddhist iconography depicts many *bodhisattvas* in highly androgynous forms.
74. K. Jones, *The Social Face of Buddhism: An Approach to Political and Social Activism* (London: Wisdom Publications, 1989) p. 127.
75. Dayal, *The Bodhisattva Doctrine*, p. 271.
76. Ibid., pp. 275–77.
77. Ibid., pp. 173–74.
78. Ibid., p. 178.
79. Ibid., p. 196.
80. This finds expression when the *śīla* components of right speech, right action, and right livelihood precede the three meditative components of the path.
81. M. Pye, *Skilful Means: A Concept in Mahayana Buddhism* (London: Gerald Duckworth & Co. Ltd., 1978) p. 1.
82. Ibid., p. 248.
83. K. K. Inada, 'Environmental Problematics in the Buddhist Context', *Philosophy East and West*, 37 (April 1987) 144.
84. This point connects with the function of language in Buddhism. Śākyamuni's approach is, without doubt, overwhelmingly practical. After discerning human *duḥkha* and finding a way of resolving it, Śākyamuni worked to convey his insight in such a way that others can resolve *duhkha*, too. With his commitment to assisting others, he criticised speculation that lacks practical, transformative effect. He contended that many of the questions addressed by philosophy are 'unanswerable' and/or irrelevant to realising Awakening and hence 'do not edify', and that attention to those questions can lead the practitioner down fruitless sidetracks. Following his lead, most Buddhists have understood religious language as 'something useful, pedagogical, heuristic, but never something referential or formally philosophic.' (Nathan Katz, *Buddhist Images of Human perfection: The Arahant of the Sutta Pitaka Compared with the Bodhisattva and the Mahasiddha* (Delhi: Motilal Banarsidass, 1982) p. 286.) And because any Buddhist utterance ideally should originate in a concern for the well-being of others and serve as a pragmatic 'skilful means' of leading others to Awakening, compassion functions as the basis of an 'ultimate criterion for religious language' (Ibid., p. 200). As the inseparable companion of compassion, *prajñā* plays a role here as well, especially

in the creation and evaluation of various religious expressions or modes of discourse.
85. T. Nhat Hanh, *Being Peace*, p. 15.
86. Some Zen thinkers have compared compassion to such ethical ideals in the Sermon on the Mount as 'turning the other cheek'. Zen *rōshi* Ōmori Sōgen writes, 'Christ does not differ at all from a great Zen monk.' *'Rinzai no Zen'* (Rinzai's Zen), in T. Maruyama (ed.), *Gendai no Zen* (Contemporary Zen) (Tokyo: Kawade Shobō Shinsha, 1976) p. 21.

CHAPTER 2: ETHICAL DIMENSIONS OF ZEN PRACTICE AND PHILOSOPHY

1. This raises interesting questions about how one should select a *rōshi*. If one lacks *prajñā* at the outset of practice, how can one discern whom might be a qualified teacher as opposed to a sham?
2. The stance that ethical engagement should begin only after a *satori* experience has been termed 'Manyana Buddhism', from the Spanish word *mañana*, tomorrow. K. Jones, *The Social Face of Buddhism: An Approach to Political and Social Activism* (London: Wisdom Publications, 1989) p. 201.
3. In recent years many Japanese have published works on the benefits of Zen practice for daily living.
4. Silence is observed, with the exception of chanting and time spent with the *rōshi* during interviews.
5. D. T. Suzuki, *An Introduction to Zen Buddhism* (New York: Grove Press, 1964) p. 131.
6. The *rokudō* account of transmigration sets forth six types of incarnations: denizens of hell, hungry spirits, animals, demons, humans and heavenly beings. This theory of transmigration was widely believed in medieval Japan and provided many of the themes in Noh Drama. See W. R. LaFleur, *The Karma of Words: Buddhism and the Literary Arts in Medieval Japan* (Berkeley: University of California Press, 1983).
7. The *zendō* is the meditation hall, which is the hub of Zen life.
8. Joshu Sasaki Rōshi of the Mt. Baldy Zen Center in California asks this of students in his style of *kōan* practice.
9. Strictly speaking, *samu* is not limited to physical labour. Keeping records, handling correspondence and meeting with others about monastery or centre business all constitute *samu*.
10. See Chapter 3 for further discussion of monastic codes.
11. D. T. Suzuki, 'Ethics and Zen Buddhism', in R. N. Anshen (ed.), *Moral Principles of Action: Man's Ethical Imperative* (New York: Harper & Brothers, 1952) p. 614.
12. Ibid.
13. This brief list does not exhaust the fruits of Zen practice. Morioka Kaneyoshi offers a long list of benefits accruing from Zen practice in daily life. He includes such things as concentration, joy, enjoyment of work, vigor, appreciation of others, kindness, good health, and loss of feelings of inferiority. *Seikatsu Zen: kurashi no naka ni ikiru Zen* (Daily-

Life Zen: Zen that Lives in Living) (Osaka: Sōgensha, 1967) pp. 5–6.
14. R. Aitken, *The Mind of Clover: Essays in Zen Buddhist Ethics* (San Francisco: North Point Press, 1984) pp. ix–x. As laid out the Introduction, the Theravāda variation of this scheme advances the following as the last five precepts: 6. not eating after midday, 7. not experiencing such worldly amusements as song or dance, 8. not using perfumes and ointments, 9. not sleeping on wide, luxurious beds and 10. not handling or possessing gold or silver.
15. Ibid., p. 3.
16. The type of Rinzai Zen practice in which the monk or nun works with and 'passes' approximately 1700 *kōans* one by one, deepening *satori* and clarifying its various facets.
17. Abe Masao writes, 'In "dependent co-origination", "Emptiness" and "suchness", everything is realised as reciprocal and reversible. There is nothing one-sided or unidirectional. Accordingly, the Buddhist notion of "dependent co-origination" as the ultimate is completely free from any teleological character.' *Zen and Western Thought*, ed. by W. R. Lafleur (London: The Macmillan Press Ltd., and Honolulu: The University Press of Hawaii, 1985) p. 247.
18. Painted by Guoan Shiyuan (J., Kakuan Shien; Song Dynasty), these pictures express the various 'stages' of Zen practice.
19. For this reason many looked askance at Beat Zen in the early 1960s.
20. As mentioned earlier, the main ethical significance of Zen lies in its transformative effect on practitioners, not simply in external responses to extreme situations, although a viable social ethic must consider both.
21. D. T. Suzuki, *The Essence of Buddhism*, 2nd edn (Kyoto: Hozokan, 1968) pp. 10–11.
22. Irrationality, intuitive insight, authoritativeness, affirmation, sense of the beyond, impersonal tone, feeling of exaltation and momentariness.
23. D. T. Suzuki, 'Satori, or Enlightenment', in W. Barrett (ed.), *Zen Buddhism: Selected Writings of D. T. Suzuki* (Garden City, NY: Doubleday Anchor Books, 1956) p. 105.
24. M. Abe, 'Kenotic God and Dynamic Sunyata', in J. B. Cobb, Jr. and C. Ives (eds), *The Emptying God: A Buddhist-Jewish-Christian Conversation* (Maryknoll, NY: Orbis Books, 1990) p. 32.
25. Buddhism claims that one does affect all people and things, no matter how removed spatially, though to different degrees and in different ways, some of which are too subtle to detect.
26. The discrepancy between this sense of *prajñā* as set forth by Abe and other Zen Buddhists and the sense of *prajñā* set forth by Nāgārjuna can in part be attributed to the intervening 'positive' inputs from Kegon Buddhism and Taoism.
27. D. T. Suzuki, *The Essence of Buddhism* (Kyoto: Hozokan, 1968) p. 11.
28. Abe and other Zen figures argue that it is only by overcoming distinctions or discrimination and arriving at non-distinction or non-discrimination that one can truly enter into the world, see things as they are and begin to make distinctions again, but now on a very

different basis. As the Zen saying goes, first mountains are mountains and waters are waters (objectifying discrimination), then the mountains are not mountains and the waters are not waters (non-discrimination as the self merges with surroundings no longer objectified as 'out there'), and then finally the mountains are truly mountains and the waters are truly waters (the discrimination of non-discrimination, non-thinking thinking (*hishiryō*), i.e., the reconstruction of thinking on a deeper basis, allowing for practical yet 'emptied' discrimination).

29. In some cases actual reflection is lacking, either when actions emerge reflexively from unconscious acceptance of socialised values or more or less spontaneously from an intuitive knowledge of what is good and evil or of what action is best in a particular situation.

30. M. Abe, 'God, Emptiness, and Ethics' (unpublished) p. 5.

31. H. Kim, *Dōgen Kigen - Mystical Realist* (Tucson: The University of Arizona Press, 1980) p. 290.

32. *The Platform Sutra of the Sixth Patriarch*, tr. by P. B. Yompolsky (New York: Columbia University Press, 1967) pp. 146–47; as quoted in A. D. Brear, 'The nature and status of moral behavior in Zen Buddhist tradition', *Philosophy East and West*, 24 (October 1974) 433.

33. This approach parallels Nāgārjuna's two-truths theory. He distinguishes between practical, conventional truth or knowledge (*saṃvṛti-satya*) and ultimate truth or religious knowledge (*paramārtha-satya*) achieved in the realisation of *śūnyatā*.

34. Kim, *Dōgen Kigen*, p. 290.

35. A. D. Brear, 'The nature and status of moral behavior in Zen Buddhist tradition', *Philosophy East and West* 24 (October 1974) 432.

36. Kim, *Dōgen Kigen*, p. 289.

37. *In principle* Buddhist ethics do diverge from the Confucian emphasis on hierarchy, obedience to authority, subordination of women, propriety and set patterns of interaction in terms of the Five Relationships.

38. C. W. Fu, 'Morality and Beyond: The Neo-Confucian Encounter with Mahayana Buddhism', *Philosophy East and West* 23 (July 1973) 392.

39. As sketched earlier, *prajñā* is acquired to some extent even by practitioners who have not undergone a thorough *satori* experience, and in this regard Zen practice from the start may function to transform one's view of good and evil, to liberate one from moralism and self-righteousness.

CHAPTER 3: ETHICAL AND POLITICAL STANCES IN JAPANESE ZEN HISTORY

1. In the broad sense of reflection on monastic rules, precepts, good and evil, and society.

2. The two characters in 'Eisai' can also be read 'Yōsai'.

3. T. Akamatsu, '*Chūseibukkyō-no-seiritsu*' (The Establishment of Medieval Buddhism), in T. Akamatsu (ed.), *Nihon-bukkyōshi* (History

of Japanese Buddhism), vol, II, *Chūsei-hen* (Medieval Volume) (Kyoto: Hozokan, 1981) p. 50.

4. The *'bodhisattva* precepts' are set forth in such sutras as the *Brahmajāla-sūtra* and include the ten major precepts discussed in Chapter 2 and forty-eight other precepts. Dōgen's formulation involved sixteen precepts.
5. M. Collcutt, *Five Mountains: The Rinzai Zen Monastic Institution in Medieval Japan* (Cambridge, MA: Harvard University Press, 1981) p. 37.
6. According to a Buddhist pseudo-history, Buddhism would unfold through three periods following the death of the historical Buddha, the last of which would involve little practice and no realisation. Many Buddhists in the Kamakura period felt that this last stage was upon them.
7. H. Dumoulin, *Zen Buddhism: A History, Volume 2, Japan,* tr. by J. W. Heisig and P. Knitter (New York: Macmillan Publishing Company, 1990) p. 16.
8. Akamatsu, *Nihon-bukkyō-shi,* p. 50.
9. After the capital was moved from Heijō (Nara) to Heian (Kyoto) in the late eighth century, Enryakuji wielded great religious and political power, partly due to the large number of warrior-monks (*sōhei*) living on the mountain. Although older Nara monasteries initially opposed it, the power of Enryakuji was not thwarted until Oda Nobunaga attacked and destroyed the monastery in 1571.
10. Although used as a blanket term for Zen as a whole, this name primarily denoted the form of Zen taught by Dainichi Nōnin (n.d.) around Kyoto in the late twelfth century. 'Nōnin was 'an uncompromising opponent of any accommodation between Zen and Japanese Tendai scholasticism. His defiance was an invitation to hostilities which Enryakuji supporters could not allow to go unchallenged.' Collcutt, *Five Mountains,* p. 39.
11. Martin Collcutt writes, 'All Eisai's later writings stand on a double foundation – Zen and the precepts. The two are inseparable in his thought. This conviction derived from the *Chan-yuan Code* and his general experience in Chinese monasteries.' *Five Mountains,* p. 147.
12. While in China, Eisai encountered this set of regulations ('pure regulations', *qinggui*), based on the teachings of Baizhang, who reportedly took as his guiding maxim, 'A day without work is a day without eating.' Eisai interpreted the *Chanyuan quinggui* around 1200 in his *Shukke taikō* (1200 (Yanagida Seizan's date for it) or 1195 (Collcutt)).
13. *Kōzen-gokoku-ron,* in H. Ichikawa, Y. Iriya and S. Yanagida (eds), *Chūsei-zenka-no-shisō* (The Thought of Medieval Zen Figures), *Nihonshisō-taikei* (The Outlines of Japanese Thought), vol. 16 (Tokyo: Iwanami Shoten, 1982) p. 11.
14. Ibid., p. 41.
15. H. Kim, *Dōgen Kigen: Mystical Realist,* 2nd edn. (Tucson: University of Arizona Press, 1987) p. 210.
16. Ibid., p. 213.
17. Dumoulin, *Zen Buddhism,* p. 92.
18. Collcutt, *Five Mountains,* p. 148.

19. Ibid.
20. Ibid.
21. Kim, *Dōgen Kigen*, p. 173.
22. Ibid., p. 176.
23. This 'song' is the verse from the *Dhammapada* quoted on page 6.
24. M. Takahashi, *The Essence of Dōgen*, tr. by Y. Nobuoka (Boston: Kegan Paul International, 1983) p. 24.
25. Ibid., p. 25.
26. Ibid.
27. Dumoulin, *Zen Buddhism*, p. 61.
28. Ibid., p. 121.
29. See Robert Aitken's *The Mind of Clover* and Francis Cook's essay, 'Dōgen's View of Authentic Selfhood and Its Socio-ethical Implications' (in W. R. LaFleur (ed.), *Dōgen Studies*).
30. This system was formulated in the seventh and eighth centuries and served as the administrative blueprint for Japan until the Tokugawa period, when it was replaced by systems based on Neo-Confucianism.
31. Like many of his peers, Eisai was quite eclectic in his teaching, blending elements of Tendai Buddhism into his teaching.
32. Enryakuji was a major economic and political power until Oda Nobunaga destroyed the monastery in the 16th century.
33. Collcutt, *Five Mountains*, p. 38. Interesting to note here is that major patrons like 'Hōjō Masako, Minamoto Yoriie, Minamoto Sanetomo, Kujō Michie and Emperors Takakura, Go-Saga and Kameyama displayed no more than a passive interest in Zen practice.' *Five Mountains*, p. 56.
34. Ibid., p. 51.
35. Ibid. Unfortunately, this text is no longer extant.
36. Quoted by Dumoulin, *Zen Buddhism*, p. 78.
37. Collcutt, *Five Mountains*, p. 67.
38. D. T. Suzuki, *Zen and Japanese Culture* (Princeton: Princeton University Press, 1973) p. 66. It is interesting to note here that during this crisis Zen monasteries throughout Japan offered prayers and ceremonies to protect the country (Collcutt, *Five Mountains*, p. 71).
39. Collcutt, *Five Mountains*, p. 26.
40. Ibid., p. 67.
41. Ibid., p. 71.
42. Ibid., pp. 152–65.
43. Dumoulin, *Zen Buddhism*, p. 152.
44. Collcutt, *Five Mountains*, p. 108.
45. Dumoulin, *Zen Buddhism*, p. 153.
46. Ibid., p. 273.
47. Suzuki, *Zen and Japanese Culture*, p. 46.
48. Ibid., p. 55.
49. Dumoulin, *Zen Buddhism*, p. 173.
50. Ibid., p. 261.
51. Ibid., pp. 261–62.
52. Ibid., p. 176.
53. Collcutt, *Five Mountains*, p. 241.

54. Ibid., p. 262.
55. The Muromachi period gained its name from the area of Kyoto in which the Ashikaga government constructed its administrative buildings.
56. Dumoulin, *Zen Buddhism*, pp. 231–36.
57. Ibid., p. 195.
58. Ibid., p. 196.
59. Ibid., pp. 273–74.
60. Ibid., p. 279.
61. Ibid., p. 281.
62. Ibid., p. 282.
63. D. Victoria, 'Japanese Corporate Zen', *Bulletin of Concerned Asian Scholars*, 12 (1980) 63.
64. It was in the midst of this flourishing Confucian reflection that that Confucian scholar Yamaga Sokō (1622–1685) wrote his treatise on the 'way of the warrior' (*bushidō*), where he works Zen and Confucian elements into an exposition of the warrior ethos.
65. Dumoulin, *Zen Buddhism*, p. 343.
66. Ibid., p. 213.
67. Ibid., p. 214.
68. Ibid., p. 344.
69. Ibid., p. 386.
70. Ibid., p. 327.
71. Ibid., p. 408.
72. Several facets of this are explained in more detail in the next chapter in the context of Ichikawa Hakugen's critique of historical Zen.
73. Victoria, 'Japanese Corporate Zen', p. 64.
74. H. Ichi Kawa, *Zen to gendai shisō* (Zen and Contemporary Thought) (Tokyo: Tokuma Shoten, 1967) p. 173; as quoted in Victoria, 'Corporate Zen', p. 68.
75. Victoria, 'Japanese Corporate Zen', pp. 61–62.
76. Traditional scholarship has characterised Tokugawa Zen as being in a state of religious and artistic malaise, thus necessitating Hakuin's reforms. This view has been questioned recently as many scholars turn to the Tokugawa period with more of a positive attitude, arguing that it was a flourishing time for religion, the arts, and economic life in Japanese society as opposed to the former view that this was a stagnant period characterised by a loss of 'high' Buddhism and by popularisation in the arts.

CHAPTER 4: RECENT CRITIQUES AND DEVELOPMENTS

1. Nishida Kitarō (1870–1945) was a student of Zen and renowned philosopher at Kyoto University who founded the Kyoto School of philosophy (*Kyōto-gakuha*), which gives Mahāyāna Buddhism a modern philosophical expression in dialogue with Western thought. In addition to Nishida, the leading thinkers in the Kyoto School have been Watsuji Tetsurō (1889–1960), Tanabe Hajime (1885–1962),

Nishitani Keiji (1900–1990), Takeuchi Yoshinori (1913–), Abe Masao (1915–) and Ueda Shizuteru (1926–).

2. For an account of the early period of Hisamatsu's life, see 'Memories of My Academic Life', tr. by Christopher Ives, *The Eastern Buddhist* (New Series) 18 (Spring 1985) 8–27.

3. For a sketch of Hisamatsu's later life and work, see M. Abe, 'Hisamatsu Shin'ichi, 1889–1980', *The Eastern Buddhist* (New Series) 14 (Spring 1981) 142–47.

4. S. Hisamatsu, 'Ultimate Crisis and Resurrection, Part I: Sin and Death', tr. by G. Tokiwa, *The Eastern Buddhist* (New Series) 8 (May 1975) 64.

5. S. Hisamatsu, '*Jinrui no chikai*' (The Vow of Humankind), *Hisamatsu Shin'ichi chosakushū* (The Collected Writings of Hisamatsu Shin'ichi), vol. 3: *Kaku to sōzō* (Awakening and Creation), ed. by S. Higashi and S. Ueda (Tokyo: Risōsha, 1977) p. 232.

6. S. Hisamatsu, '*Dōjō no atarashii kihonsen to shite no FAS*' (F.A.S. as a New Foundation for the Place of the Way), *Hisamatsu Shin'ichi chosakushū*, vol. 3, p. 464. Emphasis added.

7. S. Hisamatsu, '*Atarashiki sekai no bukkyōteki kōsō*' (A Buddhist Conception of a New World), *Hisamatsu Shin'ichi chosakushū*, vol. 3, p. 72.

8. Hisamatsu would not argue that the passage of *kōans* in *hashigo* Zen is merely quantitative; the relative qualitative shifts cannot be denied. But, if no absolute shift occurs, the person will remain in a gradual, 'quantitative' process, and will fail to realise true Awakening.

9. Hisamatsu, '*Jinrui no chikai*', p. 247.

10. Higashi Sen'ichirō asserts that the functioning of the Fundamental *Kōan* has two aspects: 'Right now, if nothing you do is of any avail', the aspect of absolute negation, and 'what will you do?' the aspect of absolute affirmation. Although the *Kōan* is expressed by two phrases arranged sequentially, 'in an immediately present koan, a koan functioning here and now, these two parts must be a simultaneous event. Herein lies the life and perfection of the Fundamental Koan' ('The Funadamental Koan', tr. by C. Ives, *FAS Society Newsletter* (Fall 1979) 3).

11. Hisamatsu's view of the Great Doubt Block will be discussed in greater detail later in this chapter.

12. Indicating human existence thoroughly grounded in a realisation of *śūnyatā*, the 'Formless Self' is also referred to by Hisamatsu at various stages of his career as 'Oriental Nothingness', 'Absolute Subjectivity', and the 'True Self'.

13. Traditional Zen holds up Great Faith (*daishinkon*), Great Resolution (*daifunshi*) and a Great Doubting Spirit (*daigijō*) as the three requisites for authentic practice.

14. S. Hisamatsu, 'On the *Record of Rinzai*: Part One', tr. by G. Tokiwa and C. Ives, *The Eastern Buddhist* (New Series) 14 (Spring 1981) 8.

15. Ibid.

16. S. Hisamatsu, 'Ordinary Mind', tr. by G. Tokiwa and H. Curtis, *The Eastern Buddhist* (New Series) 12 (May 1979) 8.

17. Ibid., p. 11.
18. In Zen parlance often used by Hisamatsu, Zen practitioners must engage in *kūfu*, the creation and testing of new methods of study, practice and praxis.
19. *Bendō*, a term central to Dogen's system, indicates the practice and realisation of Awakening.
20. M. Abe, 'Hisamatsu Shin'ichi, 1889–1980', *The Eastern Buddhist* (New Series) 14 (Spring 1981) 143. The letters, F, A and S, also constitute the acronym in the name of the organisation started by Hisamatsu and his students: the F.A.S. Society.
21. S. Hisamatsu, 'Ultimate Crisis and Resurrection', p. 16.
22. Ibid., p. 20.
23. Ibid.
24. Ibid.
25. Ibid.
26. Ibid., p. 23.
27. Ibid.
28. Here one needs to ask how 'value and anti-value' underlie 'rationality and irrationality'. Hisamatsu does not fully spell this out, either.
29. S. Hisamatsu, 'Ultimate Crisis and Resurrection, Part II: Redemption', tr. by G. Tokiwa, *The Eastern Buddhist* (New Series) 8 (October 1975) 45. Translation adapted slightly here.
30. Hisamatsu, 'Ultimate Crisis and Resurrection, Part I', p. 24.
31. S. Hisamatsu and C. G. Jung, 'Unconsciousness and No Mind', *Psychologia* 3 (1960) 87.
32. Hisamatsu, *'Dōjō no atarashii kihonsen to shite no FAS'*, p. 516.
33. Hisamatsu draws here from Buddhist understandings of Original Awakening (J., *hongaku*), a concept central to Dōgen's wrestling with the relationship between practice and attainment while a young Tendai monk on Mt. Hiei outside Kyoto.
34. See p. 30.
35. Hisamatsu, *'Atarashiki seikai no bukkyōteki kōsō'*, p. 154.
36. Ibid., p. 152.
37. Hisamatsu, *'Jinrui no chikai'*, p. 325.
38. Ibid., p. 326.
39. Ibid. The expression, 'same womb', appears in Hisamatsu's 'Vow of Humankind' (see p. 82) and can be rendered 'brothers and sisters' in English.
40. Ibid., p. 266.
41. S. Hisamatsu, 'For the Postmodernist', *FAS Society Newsletter* 2 (Autumn 1977) 1.
42. S. Hisamatsu and R. Watanabe, *'Posutomodanisuto hōdan'* (Conversation about the Postmodernist), *Budisuto* (Buddhist) 4 (1982) 7.
43. Synonymous with the 'Formless Self', 'True Person' (*shinjin*) appears in such texts as the *Record of Linji*, where Linji (Rinzai) exhorts his disciples to realise the 'one True Person without rank'. This expression has been used in reference to Hisamatsu. For example, the festschrift compiled in his memory is entitled, *Shinjin Hisamatsu Shin'ichi*.

44. Hisamatsu, 'Ordinary Mind', p. 28.
45. S. Hisamatsu, *Nothingness* (Kyoto: Association for Self-Awakening, 1957). p. 16.
46. S. Hisamatsu, 'Postmodernist Manifesto', *FAS Society Newsletter* 1 (Spring 1976) 4.
47. Hisamatsu, 'For the Postmodernist', p. 4.
48. Ibid.
49. Hisamatsu, '*Dōjō no kihonsen to shite no* FAS', p. 487.
50. S. Hisamatsu, 'On Zen Art', *The Eastern Buddhist* (New Series) 1 (November 1966) 31.
51. M. Abe, *Zen and Western Thought*, ed. by W. R. LaFleur (London: The Macmillan Press Ltd., and Hawaii: The University Press of Hawaii, 1985) p. 114.
52. Ibid., p. 191.
53. M. Abe, 'The Problem of Evil in Christianity and Buddhism', in P. O. Ingram and F. J. Streng (eds), *Buddhist-Christian Dialogue: Mutual Renewal and Transformation* (Honolulu: University of Hawaii Press, 1986) p. 146.
54. Ibid., p. 147.
55. M. Abe, 'Kenotic God and Dynamic Sunyata', in J. B. Cobb, Jr. and C. Ives (eds), *The Emptying God: A Buddhist-Jewish-Christian Conversation* (Maryknoll, NY: Orbis Books, 1990) p. 38.
56. Ibid.
57. Ibid., p. 40.
58. Ibid., p. 37.
59. M. Abe, 'The Problem of Evil in Christianity and Buddhism', p. 142.
60. Abe, *Zen and Western Thought*, p. 191.
61. Abe, 'Kenotic God and Dynamic Sunyata', p. 44.
62. Abe, *Zen and Western Thought*, p. 132.
63. Abe, 'Kenotic God and Dynamic Sunyata', p. 37.
64. Abe, 'The Problem of Evil in Christianity and Buddhism', p. 145.
65. Abe, 'Kenotic God and Dynamic Sunyata', p. 37.
66. Abe, 'The Problem of Evil in Christianity and Buddhism', p. 151.
67. Ibid.
68. Ibid., p. 152.
69. Ibid.
70. Ibid.
71. Ibid.
72. Abe, *Zen and Western Thought*, p. 227.
73. Abe, 'The Problem of Evil in Christianity and Buddhism', p. 153.
74. Masao Abe, 'Kenotic God and Dynamic Sunyata', pp. 57–58.
75. Ibid., p. 58.
76. Ibid.
77. Ibid., pp. 59–60.
78. Ibid., p. 60.
79. Ibid.
80. Abe, *Zen and Western Thought*, p. xxii.
81. Abe, 'Kenotic God and dynamic Sunyata', p. 51.
82. Ibid., p. 52.

83. Ibid., p. 53.
84. M. Abe, 'Religious Tolerance and Human Rights – A Buddhist Perspective', in L. Swidler (ed.), *Religious Liberty and Human Rights in Nations and in Religions* (Philadelphia: Ecumenical Press, 1986) p. 202.
85. Abe, *Zen and Western Thought*, p. 256.
86. Abe, 'Religious Tolerance and Human Rights', p. 203.
87. Abe, *Zen and Western Thought*, p. 257.
88. Ibid., p. 252.
89. Ibid., p. 253.
90. H. Ichikawa, *Zen to gendai-shisō* (Tokyo: Tokuma Shoten, 1967) p. 63.
91. Ibid., p. 177.
92. Ibid., pp. 111–12.
93. About this event, historian Hane Mikiso writes, 'He refused to bow toward it because he believed that to do so would be tantamount to recognizing the Emperor as a divinity. He was denounced as a traitor and summarily dismissed from the school. . . . Buddhism, which earlier had suffered at the hands of intolerant Shintoists, had by now recovered, and many of its leaders joined the nationalistic attacks against Christianity.' *Modern Japan: A Historical Survey* (Boulder: Westview Press, 1986) pp. 133–34.
94. H. Ichikawa, *Bukkyōsha no sensō-sekinin* (Tokyo: Shunjūsha, 1970) pp. 7–8.
95. Ibid., p. 150.
96. Ibid., p. 151.
97. R. Tsunoda, W. T. de Bary, and D. Keene (eds), *Sources of Japanese Tradition*, Vol. I (New York: Columbia University Press, 1965) p. 48.
98. Ichikawa, *Bukkyōsha no sensō-senkinin*, p. 151.
99. Ibid.
100. Ibid., p. 153.
101. Though extremely difficult to translate, these aesthetic terms have been rendered 'subtle profundity', 'rustic antiqueness', and 'ancient solitariness'.
102. Ichikawa, *Bukkyōsha no sensō-sekinin*, p. 154.
103. This is the copula meaning 'just as it is' that appears in such Mahayana expressions as 'Form just as it is is Emptiness'.
104. Ichikawa, *Bukkyōsha no sensō-sekinin*, p. 154.
105. Ibid., pp. 167–68.
106. T. Nhat Hanh, *Being Peace* (Berkeley: Parallax Press, 1987) pp. 89–100.
107. Ibid., p. 67.
108. Ibid., p. 65.
109. F. Eppsteiner, 'In the Crucible: The Order of Interbeing', in F. Eppsteiner (ed.), *The Path of Compassion: Writings on Socially Engaged Buddhism*, 2nd edn. (Berkeley: Parallax Press, 1988) p. 154.
110. Needless to say at this point, Buddhism was not totally passive prior to its introduction to Europe and North America. Buddhism manifested various degrees of social concern and involvement throughout its history, whether with Ashoka, socially active members of the Sangha, rebellious Burmese monks during British rule, Sarvodaya workers, or Vietnamese monks during the Vietnam War; in Japan,

such Zen figures as Uchiyama Gudō and Ichikawa Hakugen have
spoken out, and such Buddhist movements as Nipponzan Myōhōji
and Risshō Kōseikai have wrestled with social issues, especially the
threat of nuclear war.

111. Dr. Martin Luther King, Jr. nominated Thich Nhat Hanh for the
Nobel Peace Prize.
112. S. J. Holmes, 'Greyston Family Inn', *Buddhist Peace Fellowship* 11
(Summer 1989) 20.
113. To date, unfortunately, no one has done a comprehensive study of
this topic.
114. Some of these essays were recently compiled in a book entitled, *Not
Mixing Up Buddhism: Essays on Women and Buddhist Practice* (Kawahai
Collective (eds); Fredonia, N.Y.: White Pine Press, 1987).

CHAPTER 5: WISDOM, SUFFERING, AND PRACTICE

1. Various figures in Japanese history have been equated with or likened
to *bodhisattvas*. A historical overview of this would provide an interesting
glimpse into the use and possible abuse of a religious ideal.
2. One other possible position here is to argue that Zen practice and
Awakening do generate a specific ethical stance or way of being and
that those who do not accord with it are not awakened. Some contemporary Zen figures say that Zen Buddhists who have supported
militarism in World War II or engaged in sexual relations with disciples are not awakened, for if they were awakened they would not do
such acts and would naturally do what is 'good' (whatever that might
be).
3. M. Abe, *Zen and Western Thought*, ed. by W. R. LaFleur (London: The
Macmillan Press Ltd., and Honolulu: The University Press of Hawaii,
1985) p. 197.
4. Zen in effect did consider social issues insofar as it supported the
status quo and embraced Confucianism. The tradition needs to ask,
however, whether Zen has *fully* and actively expressed compassion,
and whether alignment with Confucianism as it existed in Japan was
true to the principles of Zen and the larger tradition of which it is part.
5. No *totally* separate spheres of life exist; true *prajñā* realises the inter-
connections between the arenas of human life labelled religious,
social, political, and economic, and thereby militates against compart-
mentalisation.
6. Strictly speaking, although 'religious' ignorance and suffering as a
fundamental human problem give rise to certain types of social suffering, social suffering does not give rise to religious suffering as
defined by Zen, though it may exacerbate it and make its solution
more difficult. In terms of the solution of these two types of suffering,
it is safe to say that the solution of one contributes to the solution of
the other, especially in terms of the effect on social suffering exerted
by a solution of religious suffering.
7. This will be examined later in a discussion of 'enoughness'.

8. This parallels Reinhold Niebuhr's critique of those in the 'Social Gospel' movement in the early twentieth century who thought that most social suffering would end if all people converted to Christianity.
9. As we have seen, certain Zen thinkers, including Hisamatsu, imply that Awakening is the only basis for genuine human existence, ethics and social transformation. This can lead to a type of Zen exclusivism with the attitude that Awakening is the *only* or the most profound form of human religious liberation and that Awakening is the only basis for true socio-historical transformation.

   A Zen Buddhist can either marshall arguments to justify this attitude or acknowledge how other traditions work to reduce suffering in society and history, even when they do this on the basis of what might be 'unawakened' subjectivity. Though entanglement in dualistic subjectivity does give rise to social problems, when coupled with courage, generosity and love, it *can* contribute to solutions to many of those problems. Of course, Zen might argue in response that social problems will continue to crop up if humanity remains entangled in dualistic subjectivity, and yet Zen itself has already assumed this continuation in its claim that countless suffering beings will appear in the future, extending the scope of *bodhisattvas'* activity ad infinitum.

   Further, even if one were to grant for the sake of argument that Zen Awakening is the sole basis for true social change and that all or most people need to awaken, there remains the further issue of whether Zen practice is the *only* way of bringing about Awakening. To be genuinely self-critical, Zen needs to consider how other traditions can and perhaps do bring people to experiences that are analogous to or even identical with Awakening. It is especially important for Zen Buddhists to realise the extent to which people in other traditions are in many ways profoundly free from entanglement in self-fixation, even when their theology may revolve around distinctions between God and humanity, good and evil, or being and non-being.
10. In the end, or at the deepest level, the distinction between the two disappears. This point is emphasised by Sōtō Zen.
11. Here a devil's advocate might also argue that this distinction between the 'awakened' and 'unawakened' is untenable, given the notion that all people are fundamentally awakened. But, despite Original Awakening, some are indeed 'unawakened', unawakened to Original Awakening, or perhaps 'unawakened' to the fact that thinking they are 'unawakened' is ultimately mistaken.
12. Although 'transformation' implies a gradual process of change, the term is used here inclusive of both gradual shifts in human being and, more importantly, abrupt, discontinuous shifts.
13. K. Jones, 'Buddhism and Social Action: An Exploration', in F. Eppsteiner (ed.), *The Path of Compassion: Writings on Socially Engaged Buddhism*, 2nd edn (Berkeley: Parallax Press, 1990), p. 65.
14. T. Nhat Hanh, *Being Peace* (Berkeley: Parallax Press, 1987) p. 45.
15. Nhat Hanh, *Being Peace*, p. 74.
16. Ibid.
17. Both through the transformation of the student and, at the risk of

sounding abstruse, through the societal 'field effects' of the self-emptying and the mindfulness engendered by practice, a phenomenon similar to the 'radiation' of *mettā* and the transference of merit. Although detailed consideration of this falls beyond the scope of this work, these phenomena point to the possibility of types of extrasensory interaction and subtle mental causation, similar to the phenomena Rupert Sheldrake examines in *A New Science of Life: The Hypothesis of Formative Causation*.

18. J. Kornfield, 'The Path of Compassion', in *The Path of Compassion*, p. 26.
19. As Gandhi realised in his form of *karma-yoga* (way of action), the giving of oneself to nonviolent service constitutes a religious practice that both brings one to, and simultaneously expresses, the Ultimate.
20. This type of giving can be construed as *dāna*, the first of the six perfections (*pāramitās*) emphasised in the Mahayana tradition.
21. Nhat Hanh, *Being Peace*, p. 53.
22. Though this book has not focused on Dōgen and Sōtō Zen, discussion of the idea of the unity of practice and attainment, of *zazen* as an expression of Buddha-nature, can shed further light on this point.
23. G. Gutierrez, *A Theology of Liberation: History, Politics and Salvation*, tr. by C. Inda and J. Eagleson (Maryknoll, N.Y.: Orbis Books, 1984) p. 212.
24. M. Fukuoka, *The One-Straw Revolution* (New York: Bantam Books, 1985) pp. 137–38.
25. Nhat Hanh, *Being Peace*, p. 25. The *dharmakaya* (body of *Dharma*) is a technical term in Māhāyana philosophy and it has been equated with *śūnyatā*.
26. S. Hisamatsu, '*Atarashiki sekai no Bukkyōteki kōsō*' (A Buddhist Conception of a New World) *Hisamatsu Shin'ichi Chosakushū* (The Collected Works of Hisamatsu Shin'ichi), vol. 3 (Tokyo: Risōsha, 1976) p. 73.
27. As seen in Chapter 4, Abe contends that compassion must be accompanied by a vow (*praṇidhāna*) and acts (*caryā*).
28. R. Aitken, *The Mind of Clover: Essays in Zen Buddhist Ethics* (San Francisco: North Point Press, 1984) p. 168.
29. Robert Aitken has spoken of it as violating a basic archetype between teacher and student.
30. The *Wumen-guan* includes a *kōan* about Zen teacher Juzhi (J., Gutei) cutting off the finger of his acolyte attendant and thereby triggering *satori* in him.

CHAPTER 6: ZEN FORMULATION OF THE SOCIAL GOOD

1. M. Abe, 'Kenotic God and Dynamic Sunyata', in J. B. Cobb, Jr. and C. Ives (eds) *The Emptying God: A Buddhist-Jewish-Christian Conversation* (Maryknoll, N.Y.: Orbis Books, 1990) p. 51.
2. M. Abe, 'Religious Tolerance and Human Rights – A Buddhist Perspective' in L. Swindler (ed.) *Religious Liberty and Human Rights in Nations and Religions* (Philadelphia: Ecumenical Press, 1986) p. 207.

3. Or between law and the theological virtues of faith, love and charity.
4. M. Abe, 'Free Will in Buddhism with Special Reference to a Buddhist View of the Holocaust' (unpublished), pp. 26–27.
5. D. T. Suzuki, in 'D. T. Suzuki, Oriental Thought, and the West', *The Asahi Journal* 7 (14 March 1965) tr. by R. DeMartino (unpublished), p. 27.
6. R. DeMartino, in 'D. T. Suzuki, Oriental Thought, and the West', p. 19.
7. Ibid., p. 23.
8. Ibid., p. 25.
9. Ibid., p. 30.
10. N. Foster, 'To Enter the Marketplace: The Politics of Prajña', in F. Eppsteiner (ed.), *The Path of Compassion: Writings on Socially Engaged Buddhism* (Berkeley: Parallax Press, 1988) p. 47.
11. Moreover, as will be discussed later, this perspective leads to a notion of justice different from theories that presuppose an independent self.
12. K. Nishida, 'The Problem of Japanese Culture', in W. T. DeBary, D. Keene and R. Tsunoda (eds), *Sources of Japanese Tradition*, vol. II (New York: Columbia University Press, 1958) p. 362.
13. 'Dōgen's *Shōbō-genzō Genjōkōan*', tr. by N. Waddell and M. Abe, *The Eastern Buddhist* (New Series) 5 (October 1972) 133. *Genjōkōan* is one fascicle in *Shōbō-genzō* (Treasury of the Correct-Dharma Eye).
14. R. Aitken, *The Mind of Clover* (San Francisco: North Point Press, 1984) pp. 169–71.
15. T. Nhat Hanh, *Being Peace* (Berkeley: Parallax Press, 1987) p. 62. The Dalai Lama broadens this Buddhist view of responsibility by adding the element of commonality. He states, 'Basically, universal responsibility is feeling for other people's suffering just as we feel our own. It is the realisation that even our enemy is entirely motivated by the quest for happiness. We must recognise that all beings want the same thing we want.' Dalai Lama, 'The Principle of Universal Responsibility', in F. Eppsteiner and D. Maloney (eds), *The Path of Compassion: Contemporary Writings on Engaged Buddhism* (Buffalo: White Pine Press, 1985) p. 14.
16. A radical instance of this 'liberation into action' in recent times was the action of Thich Quang-Duc, who took his life by sacrificial self-immolation in 1963 to protest the carnage in Viet Nam under the Diem regime and thereby conveyed the plight of the Vietnamese to US citizens via the evening news.
17. Tenzing Gyatso, 'Hope for the Future', in *The Path of Compassion*, 2nd edn, p. 5.
18. Such a focus on pain, healing, and wise living points to a connection between Zen and secular therapies. Further examination of the connection between silent sitting as a 'trans-personal' move and therapeutic work on personal issues may lead to a more complete and deeper process of transformation. In this regard, Ken Wilber's schema (in *No Boundary*) of different therapies and religious paths along a continuum offers a starting point for discussion.

19. M. Yamada, *Chūdō o yuku* (To Follow the Middle Way) (Tokyo: Shunjū-sha, 1984) p. 25.
20. M. Abe, 'Religious Tolerance and Human Rights – A Buddhist Perspective', p. 205.
21. Ibid., p. 203.
22. Ibid., p. 205.
23. Dalai Lama, 'Hope for the Future', in *The Path of Compassion: Contemporary Writings on Engaged Buddhism*, p. 10. This statement was omitted in the second edition of *Path of Compassion*.
24. R. C. Neville, 'Units of Change – Units of Value', *Philosophy East and West* 37 (April 1987) 133.
25. Ibid., p. 132.
26. This discussion omits certain native cultures for which the following formulation is less relevant. One must not fail to emphasise the value so-called 'primitive' cultures hold for 'civilised' cultures, especially in light of the ecological devastation that has been caused by the 'civilised' world.
27. This approach to political campaigns might rectify socio-economically unrepresentative composition of legislative bodies, such as the United States Senate, where nearly all of the senators are millionaires.
28. The derivation of 'economics' is the Greek words, *oikos*, house, and *nemein*, to manage.
29. E. F. Schumacher, *Small is Beautiful: Economics as if People Mattered* (New York: Harper & Row Publishers, Inc., 1975) pp. 54–55.
30. E. Sarkisyanz, *Buddhist Backgrounds of the Burmese Revolution* (The Hague: Martinus Nijhoff, 1965) p. 25.
31. Ibid., p. 141.
32. Ibid., p. 171. A Zen approach diverges, however, from the Theravāda idea that everyone's having wealth is valuable in that it affords equal opportunity to acquire merit by giving alms, for such merit considerations do not play a significant role in Zen life.
33. H. Fielding-Hall, *A People at School* (London, 1906) p. 253, as quoted in Sarkisyanz, *Buddhist Backgrounds*, p. 139.
34. D. T. Suzuki, *Outlines of Mahayana Buddhism* (London: Luzac and Company, 1907) p. 188.
35. T. Nhat Hanh, *Being Peace* (Berkeley: Parallax Press, 1987) p. 17.
36. Sarkisyanz, *Buddhist Backgrounds*, p. 58.
37. Ibid., p. 200.
38. W. L. King, *In the Hope of Nibbana: An Essay on Theravada Buddhist Ethics* (LaSalle, Il: Open Court Publishing Company, 1964) pp. 241–42.
39. N. Jacobson, *Buddhism & The Contemporary World: Change and Self-Correction* (Carbondale and Edwardsville, IL: Southern Illinois University Press, 1983) p. 116.
40. King, *Nibbana*, pp. 241–46.
41. S. Sivaraksa, 'Buddhism and Development – Is Small Beautiful?' *Asia Action* 21 (n.d.) 6.
42. For a provocative treatment of economics and sustainability, see H. Daly, *Steady-State Economics: The Economics of Biophysical Equilibrium and Moral Growth* (San Francisco: W. H. Freeman and Company, 1977).

43. H. Kahn, *World Economic Development: 1979 and Beyond* (New York: Morrow Quill Paperbacks, 1979) p. 240.
44. T. Ling, *Buddha, Marx, and God* (New York: St. Martin's Press, 1966) p. 168.
45. Quoted by W. King, *Nibbana*, pp. 239–41.
46. Nhat Hanh, *Being Peace*, p. 68.
47. Ibid., p. 68–69.
48. Of course, certain animals at least appear to experience a type of mental anguish not unlike ours, though in all likelihood to a much lesser extent.
49. The expression coined here is linguistically – though not philosophically – parallel to Peter Berger's notion of a 'calculus of pain'.
50. One myth behind market determinations of value in economics is the idea that prices (ostensibly based on supply and demand) insure that no ecosystem will ever be irreparably damaged and no resource will be depleted beyond maintenance levels. In fact, however, ecosystems can and do collapse before market prices prevent this, and certain species and resources – such as tropical plants providing oxygen, medical cures and much of the gene pool of the planet – can be eradicated before their value to us or to the rest of the world is discerned, and in some cases before they are even discovered.
51. J. Macy 'In Indra's Net: Sarvodaya & Our Mutual Efforts for Peace,' in F. Eppstein (ed.), *The Path of Compassion: Writings on Socially Engaged Buddhism* (Berkeley: Parallax Press, 1988), p. 172.
52. Ibid. Here Macy is using the term *muditā* to refer not only to 'sympathetic joy' or 'joy in the joy of others', but also to openness to the grief and suffering of others.
53. *Mahāsilava-Jātaka*, as quoted in Sarkisyanz, *Buddhist Backgrounds*, p. 42.
54. *The Dhammapada*, tr. by J. Mascaro (New York: Penguin Books, 1983) p. 54. Translation partially adapted.
55. H. Saddhatissa, *Buddhist Ethics: Essence of Buddhism* (New York: George Braziller, 1970) pp. 89–90.
56. E. Schumacher, *Small is Beautiful*, p. 57.
57. Ibid., p. 58.
58. Ibid., p. 60.
59. Thich Nhat Hanh, 'Please Call Me by My True Names', in *The Path of Compassion*, p. 77.
60. Nhat Hanh, *Being Peace*, p. 9.
61. M. Yamada and K. Awakawa, *Zen ga toku jinsei-ron* (The view of life expounded by Zen) (Kyoto: Yūkonsha, 1968) p. 108.
62. Kittivuddho Bhikkhu, *Caturat*, 26 June 1976, p. 31, as quoted in C. F. Keyes, 'Political Crisis and Militant Buddhism in Contemporary Thailand', in B. L. Smith (ed.), *Religion and Legitimation of Power in Thailand, Laos, and Burma* (Chambersburg, PA: Anima Books, 1978) p. 153.
63. As mentioned earlier in this work, although Zen must wrestle with these extreme scenarios, a Zen social ethic would not focus primarily on what the 'right' action might be in certain scenarios in light of a hierarchy of moral values, norms, or principles, but rather focus on

how to create a participatory matrix from which hatred and violence cease to emerge or emerge to a reduced extent.

64. Mild forms of his active nonviolence include negotiations and demonstrations; severe forms include strikes and economic boycotts; and extreme forms include non-cooperation, civil disobedience, fasting and emigration.

65. *The Words of Gandhi*, ed. by R. Attenborough (New York: Newmarket Press, 1982) p. 49.

Bibliography

Abe, Masao, 'Free Will in Buddhism, With Special Reference to a Buddhist View of the Holocaust.' Unpublished.
——, 'God, Emptiness, and Ethics.' Unpublished.
——, 'Hisamatsu Shin'ichi, 1889–1980.' *The Eastern Buddhist* (New Series) 14 (Spring 1981).
——, 'Kenotic God and Dynamic Sunyata', in John B. Cobb, Jr. and Christopher Ives (eds), *The Emptying God: A Buddhist-Jewish-Christian Conversation* (Maryknoll, N.Y.: Orbis Books, 1990).
——, 'The Problem of Evil in Christianity and Buddhism', in Paul O. Ingram and Frederick J. Streng (eds), *Buddhist-Christian Dialogue: Mutual Renewal and Transformation* (Honolulu: University of Hawaii Press, 1986).
——, 'Religious Tolerance and Human Rights — A Buddhist Perspective', in Leonard Swidler (ed.), *Religious Liberty and Human Rights in Nations and in Religions* (Philadelphia: Ecumenical Press, 1986).
——, *Zen and Western Thought*, William R. LaFleur (ed.), (London: The Macmillan Press, Ltd., and Honolulu: The University Press of Hawaii, 1985).
——, and Waddell, Norman (trs), 'Shōbō-genzō Genjōkōan.' *The Eastern Buddhist* (New Series) 5 (October 1972).
Aitken, Robert, *The Mind of Clover: Essays in Zen Buddhist Ethics* (San Francisco: North Point Press, 1984).
Akamatsu, Toshihide, *Nihon-bukkyōshi*, vol. II, *Chūsei-hen* (Kyoto: Hozakan, 1981).
Attenborough, Richard (ed.), *The Words of Gandhi* (New York: Newmarket Press, 1982).
Beck, Charlotte Joko, 'Beginning Zen Practice.' *The Ten Directions* (June 1983).
——, *Everyday Zen: Love and Work*, Steve Smith (ed.) (San Francisco: Harper & Row, Publishers, 1989).
Brear, A. D., 'The nature and status of moral behavior in Zen Buddhist tradition.' *Philosophy East and West*, Vol. XXIV, No. 4 (October 1974).
Carmody, Denise Lardner, *Women & World Religions* (Nashville: Abingdon, 1981).
Ch'en, Kenneth, *Buddhism in China: A Historical Survey* (Princeton: Princeton University Press, 1973).
Collcutt, Martin, *Five Mountains: The Rinzai Zen Monastic Institution in Medieval Japan* (Cambridge, MA: Harvard University Press, 1981).
Conze, Edward (tr.), *Buddhist Wisdom Books* (London: George Allen & Unwin Ltd., 1975).
Cook, Francis H., 'Dōgen's View of Authentic Selfhood and its Socio-ethical Implications', in William R. LaFleur (ed.), *Dōgen Studies*, Studies

in East Asian Buddhism, no. 2 (Honolulu: University of Hawaii Press, 1985).

Dalai Lama, 'Hope for the Future', in Fred Eppsteiner and Dennis Maloney (eds), *The Path of Compassion: Contemporary Writings on Engaged Buddhism* (Buffalo: White Pine Press, 1985).

——, 'The Principle of Universal Responsibility', in Fred Eppsteiner and Dennis Maloney (eds), *The Path of Compassion: Contemporary Writings on Engaged Buddhism* (Buffalo: White Pine Press, 1985).

Daly, Herman, *Steady-State Economics: The Economics of Biophysical Equilibrium and Moral Growth* (San Francisco: W. H. Freeman and Company, 1977).

Dayal, Har, *The Bodhisattva Doctrine in Buddhist Sanskrit Literature* (London: Kegan Paul, Trench, Trubner, & Co., 1932).

DeMartino, Richard (tr.), 'D. T. Suzuki, Oriental Thought, and the West.' Unpublished.

——, 'The Human Situation and Zen Buddhism', in Nathan Katz (ed.), *Buddhist and Western Psychology* (Boulder, CO: Prajna Press, 1983).

de Silva, Pamasiri, *An Introduction to Buddhist Psychology* (New York: Harper & Row Publishers, Inc., 1979).

Dumoulin, Heinrich, *A History of Zen Buddhism* (Boston: Beacon Press, 1969).

——, *Zen Buddhism: A History, Vol. 2, Japan*, tr. by James W. Heisig and Paul Knitter (New York: Macmillan Publishing Company, 1990).

Eppsteiner, Fred, 'In the Crucible: The Tiep Hien Precepts' in Fred Eppsteiner (ed.), *The Path of Compassion: Writings on Socially Engaged Buddhism*, 2nd edn (Berkeley: Parallax Press, 1988).

Foster, Nelson, 'To Enter the Marketplace', in Fred Eppsteiner (ed.), *The Path of Compassion: Writings on Socially Engaged Buddhism*, 2nd edn (Berkeley: Parallax Press, 1988).

Fu, Charles Wei-hsün, 'Morality and Beyond: The Neo-Confucian Confrontation with Mahayana Buddhism.' *Philosophy East and West*, 23 (July 1973).

Fukuoka, Masanobu, *The One-Straw Revolution* (New York: Bantam Books, 1978).

Guenther, Herbert V., *Philosophy and Psychology in the Abhidharma* (Delhi: Motilal Banarsidass, 1957).

Gutierrez, Gustavo, *A Theology of Liberation: History, Politics and Salvation*, tr. by Caridad Inda and John Eagleson (Maryknoll, NY: Orbis Books, 1973).

Hick, John, *God Has Many Names* (Philadelphia: Westminster Press, 1982).

Higashi, Sen'ichirō, 'The Fundamental Kōan', tr. by Christopher Ives, *FAS Society Newsletter* (Fall 1979).

Hisamatsu, Shin'ichi, 'For the Postmodernist', *FAS Society Newsletter* 2 (Autumn 1977).

——, *Hisamatsu Shin'ichi chosakushū*, Vol. 3, *Kaku to sōzō*, Sen'ichirō Higashi and Shizuteru Ueda (eds) (Tokyo: Risōsha, 1976).

——, 'Memories of My Student Life', tr. by Christopher Ives, *The Eastern Buddhist* (New Series) 18 (Spring 1985).

——, *Nothingness* (Kyoto: Association for Self-Awakening, 1957).

——, 'On the *Record of Rinzai*: Part One', tr. by Gishin Tokiwa and Christopher A. Ives, *The Eastern Buddhist* (New Series) 14 (Spring 1981).

——, 'On Zen Art', *The Eastern Buddhist* (New Series) 1 (November 1966).

——, 'Ordinary Mind,' tr. by Gishin Tokiwa and Howard Curtis, *The Eastern Buddhist* (New Series) 12 (May 1979).

——, 'Postmodernist Manifesto', *FAS Society Newsletter* 1 (Spring 1976).

——, 'Ultimate Crisis and Resurrection, Part I: Sin and Death,' tr. by Gishin Tokiwa, *The Eastern Buddhist* (New Series) 8 (May 1975).

——, 'Ultimate Crisis and Resurrection, Part II: Redemption,' tr. by Gishin Tokiwa, *The Eastern Buddhist* (New Series) 8 (October 1975).

——, and Jung, C. G., 'Unconsciousness and No Mind', *Psychologia* 3 (1960).

——, and Watanabe, Ryoji, 'Posutomodanisuto hōdan', *Budisuto*, 4 (1982).

Holmes, Sandra Jishu, 'Greyston Family Inn', *Buddhist Peace Fellowship*, 11 (Summer 1989).

Ichikawa, Hakugen, *Bukkyōsha no sensō-sekinin* (Tokyo: Shunjūsha, 1970).

——, Iriya, Yoshitaka, and Yanagida, Seizan (eds), *Chūsei-zenka-no-shisō, Nihonshisō-taikei*, vol. 16 (Tokyo: Iwaanami Shoten, 1982).

——, *Zen to gendai shisō* (Tokyo: Tokuma Shoten, 1967).

Inada, Kenneth, 'Environmental Problematics in the Buddhist Context', *Philosophy East and West*, 37 (Spring 1987).

Izutsu, Toshihiko, *Toward a Philosophy of Zen Buddhism* (Boulder, CO: Prajna Press, 1982).

Jacobson, Nolan, *Buddhism and the Contemporary World: Change and Self-Correction* (Carbondale and Edwardsville, IL: Southern Illinois University Press, 1983).

Jayatilleke, K. N., *Early Buddhist Theory of Knowledge* (London: George Allen & Unwin Ltd., 1963).

Johansson, Rune E. A., *The Dynamic Psychology of Early Buddhism* (Oxford: Curzon Press, 1979).

——, *The Psychology of Nirvana* (Garden City, NY: Anchor Books, 1970).

Jones, Ken, 'Buddhism and Social Action: An Exploration', in Fred Eppsteiner (ed.), *The Path of Compassion: Writings on Socially Engaged Buddhism*, 2nd edn (Berkeley: Parallax Press, 1988).

——, *The Social Face of Buddhism: An Approach to Political and Social Activism* (London: Wisdom Publications, 1989).

Kahn, Herman, *World Economic Development: 1979 and Beyond* (New York: Morrow Quill Paperbacks, 1979).

Kaneyoshi, Morioka, *Seitaksu Zen: kurashi no naka ni ikiru Zen* (Osaka: Sōgensha, 1967).

Kasulis, Thomas P., *Zen Action/Zen Person* (Honolulu: The University Press of Hawaii, 1981).

Katō, Bunnō, Tamura, Yoshirō, and Miyasaka, Kojirō (trs), *The Threefold Lotus Sutra* (New York: Weatherhill/Kosei, 1984).

Katz, Nathan, *Buddhist Images of Perfection: The Arahant of the Sutta Pitaka Compared with the Bodhisattva and the Mahasiddha* (Delhi: Motilal Banarsidass, 1982).

Kawahai Collective (eds), *Not Mixing Up Buddhism: Essays on Women and Buddhist Practice* (Fredonia NY: White Pine Press, 1987).

Keyes, Charles F., 'Political Crisis and Militant Buddhism in Contemporary Thailand' in Bardwell L. Smith (ed.), *Religion and Legitimation of Power in Thailand, Laos, and Burma* (Chambersburg, PA: Anima Books, 1978).

Kim, Hee-Jin, *Dōgen Kigen: Mystical Realist* (Tucson: The University of Arizona Press, 1980).

King, Winston L., *In the Hope of Nibbana: An Essay of Theravada Buddhist Ethics* (LaSalle Illinois: Open Court, 1964).

——, 'Buddhist Self-World Theory and Buddhist Ethics', *The Eastern Buddhist*, 22 (Autumn 1989).

Kornfield, Jack, 'The Path of Compassion: Thoughts on Spiritual Practice and Social Action', in Fred Eppsteiner (ed.), *The Path of Compassion: Writings on Socially Engaged Buddhism*, 2nd edn (Berkeley: Parallax Press, 1988).

LaFleur, William R., *The Karma of Words: Buddhism and the Literary Arts in Medieval Japan* (Berkeley: University of California Press, 1983).

Ling, Trevor, *Buddha, Marx, and God: Some Aspects of Religion in the Modern World* (New York: St. Martin's Press, 1966).

Macy, Joanna, 'Dependent Co-Arising: The Distinctiveness of Buddhist Ethics', *Journal of Religious Ethics*, 7 (Spring 1979).

——, *Dharma and Development, Religion as Resource in the Sarvodaya Self-Help Movement*, 2nd edn (West Hartford: Kumarian Press, 1985).

——, 'In Indra's Net: Sarvodaya & Our Mutual Efforts for Peace', in Fred Eppsteiner (ed.), *The Path of Compassion: Writings on Socially Engaged Buddhism*, 2nd edn (Berkeley: Parallax Press, 1988).

Maruyama, Teruo (ed.), *Gendai no Zen* (Tokyo: Kawade Shobō Shinsha, 1976).

Mascaro, Juan (tr.), *The Dhammapada* (New York: Penguin Books, 1983).

Mikiso, Hane, *Modern Japan: A Historical Survey* (Boulder: Westview Press, 1986).

Misra, G. S. P., *Development of Buddhist Ethics* (New Delhi: Munshiram Manoharlal Publishers Pvt. Ltd., 1984).

Murti, T. R. V., *The Central Philosophy of Buddhism: A Study of the Mādhyamika System* (London: George Allen & Unwin, 1980).

Neville, Robert C., 'Units of Change – Units of Value.' *Philosophy East and West* 37 (April 1987).

Nhat Hanh, Thich, *Being Peace* (Berkeley: Parallax Press, 1987).

——, 'Please Call Me by My True Names', in Fred Eppsteiner (ed.), *The Path of Compassion: Writings on Socially Engaged Buddhism*, 2nd edn (Berkeley: Parallax Press, 1988).

Nishida, Kitarō, *An Inquiry Into the Good*, tr. by Masao Abe and Christopher Ives (New Haven: Yale University Press, 1990).

——, *Nishida Kitarō zenshū*, 2nd edn, Vol. XI (Tokyo: Iwanami Shoten, 1965).

——, 'The Problem of Japanese Culture' in Wm. Theodore deBary, Donald Keene, and Ryusaku Tsunoda (eds), *Sources of Japanese Tradition*, vol. II. (New York: Columbia University Press, 1958).

Norbeck, Edward, 'Religion and Society in Modern Japan: Continuity and Change', *Rice University Studies*, 56 (Winter 1970).

Paul, Diana Y., *Women in Buddhism: Images of the Feminine in Mahayana Tradition* (Berkeley: Asian Humanities Press, 1979).

Piovesana, Gino K., *Recent Japanese Philosophical Thought, 1862–1962: A Survey* (Tokyo: Enderle Bookstore, 1968).

Pye, Michael, *Skilful Means: A Concept in Mahayana Buddhism* (London: Gerald Duckworth & Co. Ltd., 1978).

Radhakrishnan, S. (tr.), *The Dhammapada* (Madras: Oxford University Press, 1966).

Rahula, Walpola, *What the Buddha Taught* (New York: Grove Press, Inc., 1959).

Rhys-Davids, T. W., and Stede, William (eds), *Pali-English Dictionary* (London: Luzac & Co., 1959).

Robinson, Richard, and Johnson, Willard L., *The Buddhist Religion: A Historical Introduction*, 3rd edn (Belmont, CA: Wadsworth Publishing Company, 1982).

Rupp, George, 'The relationship between nirvāṇa and saṃsāra: An essay on the evolution of Buddhist ethics', *Philosophy East and West*, 21 (January 1971).

Saddhatissa, H., *Buddhist Ethics: Essence of Buddhism* (New York: George Braziller, Inc., 1970).

Sarkisyanz, E., *Buddhist Backgrounds of the Burmese Revolution* (The Hague: Martinus Nijhoff, 1965).

Sasaki, Ruth Fuller (tr.), *The Record of Lin-chi* (Kyoto: The Institute for Zen Studies, 1975).

Schumacher, E. F., *Small is Beautiful: Economics as if People Mattered* (New York: Harper & Row, Publishers, Inc., 1975).

Shibayama, Zenkei, *On Zazen Wasan* (Kyoto, 1967).

Sivaraksa, Sulak, 'Buddhism and Development: Is Small Beautiful?' *Asian Action: Newsletter of the Asian Cultural Forum on Development*, 21 (n.d.).

Smith, Donald Eugene, *Religion and Politics in Burma* (Princeton: Princeton University Press, 1965).

Streng, Frederick J., *Emptiness: A Study in Religious Meaning* (Nashville: Abingdon Press, 1967).

Suzuki, Daisetz Teitarō, *Essays in Zen Buddhism*, First Series (London: Rider and Company, 1980).

——, *Essays in Zen Buddhism*, Third Series (London: Rider and Company, 1977).

——, *The Essence of Buddhism*, 2nd edn (Kyoto: Hōzōkan, 1968).

——, 'Ethics and Zen Buddhism', in Ruth N. Anshen (ed.), *Moral Principles of Action* (New York: Harper & Brothers, 1952).

——, *An Introduction to Zen Buddhism* (New York: Grove Press, 1964).

——, *Manual of Zen Buddhism* (New York: Grove Press, 1960).

——, *Mysticism Christian and Buddhist* (New York: Collier Books, 1957).

——, *On Indian Mahayana Buddhism* (New York: Harper & Row Publishers, 1968).

——, *Outlines of Mahayana Buddhism* (London: Luzac and Company, 1907).

——, *Zen and Japanese Culture* (Princeton: Princeton University Press, 1973).

——, *Zen Buddhism: Selected Writings of D.T. Suzuki*, William Barrett (ed.) (Garden City, NY: Doubleday Anchor Books, 1956).

Takahashi, Masanobu, *The Essence of Dogen*, tr. by Yuzuru Nobuoka (Boston: Kegan Paul International, 1983).

Thurman, Robert A. F. 'Edicts of Ashoka', in Fred Eppsteiner (ed.), *The Path of Compassion: Writings on Socially Engaged Buddhism*, 2nd edn (Berkeley: Parallax Press, 1988).

——, 'Guidelines for Buddhist Social Activism Based on Nagarjuna's *Jewel Garland of Royal Counsels*', *The Eastern Buddhist* (New Series) 16 (Spring 1983).

Tilka, Chagdud, 'The Power of Peace', in Fred Eppsteiner (ed.), *The Path of Compassion: Writings on Socially Engaged Buddhism*, 2nd edn (Berkeley: Parallax Press, 1988).

Victoria, Daizen, 'Japanese Corporate Zen', *Bulletin of Concerned Asian Scholars*, 12 (1980).

Weber, Max, *The Religion of India: The Sociology of Hinduism and Buddhism*, tr. by Hans H. Gerth and Don Martindale (eds) (Glencoe, IL: The Free Press, 1958).

Williams, Monier, *A Sanskrit-English Dictionary* (Oxford: The Clarendon Press, 1964).

Yamada, Mumon, *Chūdō o yuku* (Tokyo: Shunjusha, 1984).

——, and Awakawa, Ko'ichi. *Zen ga toku jinsei-ron* (Kyoto: Yūkonsha, 1968).

Yompolsky, Philip B. (tr.), *The Platform Sutra of the Sixth Patriarch* (New York: Columbia University Press, 1967).

Index